MS 1-00

3

Au

Tit:

Acc

D0260860

WHITE ROBE, BLACK ROBE

Charles L. Mee, Jr.

WHITE ROBE, BLACK ROBE

HARRAP LONDON

First published in Great Britain 1973
by GEORGE G. HARRAP & CO. LTD
182-184 High Holborn, London WC1V 7AX

© *Charles L. Mee, Jr* 1972

ISBN 0 245 51857 6

Printed by Clarke, Doble & Brendon Ltd., Plymouth
Made in Great Britain

For Suzi

ACKNOWLEDGMENTS

I MUST ACKNOWLEDGE very special debts to the library staff of the General Theological Seminary in New York and to the staff of the Frederick Lewis Allen room in the New York Public Library for making the greater part of the research for this book a pleasant task; to Professor Jay P. Anglin for invaluable help in developing a bibliography for my research; to Mrs. J. Muriel Vrotsos, who helped tirelessly with the research, ferreting out books, copying source material, and finally, typing the manuscript; and to my wife, Suzi Mee, who listened to me read the book, chapter by chapter, in its rough form and its revised forms, helping each time to clarify passages and very often, indeed, leading me to an idea that had not occurred to me. She shared both the burdens and the inspiration of the book.

—C.L.M.

CONTENTS

PROLOGUE

IN 1513 Giovanni de' Medici, son of Lorenzo de' Medici of
Florence, was elected pope of the Roman Catholic Church,
and he took the name of Leo X. He was a pleasure-loving man
who entertained poets and painters and dramatists at his papal
court and, in order to complete St. Peter's Cathedral, that great
monument to the church united and triumphant, proclaimed the
sale of indulgences in Germany. In 1517, on a clear, crisp day,
Martin Luther tacked his ninety-five theses to the door of the
Wittenberg church. In 1521 Luther was summoned to the Diet
of Worms and his teachings were condemned—and in that same
year Pope Leo X died, pleased in the knowledge that he had
satisfactorily settled "that monkish squabble."

That is the story of this book. It is a story that has been told
many times before and, like the myth of Oedipus or of Prome-
theus, seems to have an ineluctable hold on our unconscious.
According to one biographer of Luther, more than 600 books,
monographs, and articles are published every year about that tantalizing rebel. (At the same time—such is the fate of historical
losers—no biographer has turned his hand to Leo since 1908.)
Each time the story is told it changes, to be sure. The religious
historians who had the first crack at it naturally saw it as a
revolution in the church, brought about by a villain (or a hero),
or as a theological great leap forward (or a lamentable heresy).
Leibnitz saw Luther as the hero of conscience, and Federick the
Great viewed him as a champion of German nationalism. The

11

nineteenth-century historians seem—at least to me—to have been
preoccupied with a sense of moral fitness about the whole encounter. William Roscoe, in his biography of Leo, sniffed at the
question of Vatican mistresses and explained them away as "after
all, not to be especially remarked in the time in which these men
lived." And Luther's barnyard imagery is similarly explained away
by his partisans. Manners and appearances need to be kept up, and
both these men, after all, have heroic proportions to them.

In our own century the social historians have been over the
story to see it as a struggle between one emerging class and
another, corrected by the economic historians who have provided
us with the new capitalism and a gradual depression in the
fifteenth century, corrected yet again by historians who perceive
here the warring of proto-nations. Recently Erik Erikson has
analyzed Luther as a psychological case history. In most of these
works we see how inevitable the Reformation was, because of the
economic forces, or the general sociopolitical background of the
era, or the forceful temperament of our hero, or whatever. Luther is seen to have been destined to prevail; destiny works fa-
mously well in hindsight.

It should not be surprising that in this book, given my own
times, I see the story of Leo and Luther as a confrontation between the classic, the archetypal establishmentarian and the archetypal revolutionary. But I would not wish to burden the story
with just one more interpretation. While my bias is to see arche-
types of some contemporary interest in the story, I have tried to
keep closely to the characters of the two men and see the story as
they did: a destiny worked out moment by moment, with no
certain future. In my defense, and in defense of others who have
not entirely succeeded in writing the story in this way, I must
acknowledge it is not easy, for Luther very early develops a
powerful, purposeful character that will not be denied.

I have relied heavily, and gratefully, on the work of Luther
scholars in writing this book. If I were to make any claim on
historiography with the book, it would be that I have restored
Leo X to what I believe is his rightful, though astonishingly

neglected, place in the story. (Even Erik Erikson, in his otherwise superb psychological study of Luther, in which he sees Luther's principal conflict as revolving about his father, gives us no glimpse of the pope—*il papa*.) I am surprised to be the first to bring Leo back into his crucial role in this historical era and hope I shall not be the last. For revolutionaries are made at least as much as they are born, and every protagonist has an antagonist who helps to shape his destiny and that of the world they share. If we do not understand that, we do not understand revolutionary movements.

WHITE ROBE, BLACK ROBE

I

GIOVANNI'S CHILDHOOD

EARLY in December of 1475, the wife of Lorenzo de' Medici awakened to report that she had dreamed she had given birth in the Florentine cathedral to a large but docile lion. In our own day, perhaps, no woman would have the temerity to admit to such a dream for fear of what her family would make of it. But at that time it was a mighty dream—one to be conjured up at midday if one were not so fortunate as to have conceived it while asleep.

Shortly thereafter her second son was born. As was the custom among Italian families, the second son was destined for a career in the Roman Catholic Church, and the portent before his birth was doubly fortunate. It signaled eminence, of course; it signaled that a veritable king was to be sent out into the jungle of church politics. But the lion is the ancient symbol of Florence, too, and thus the mother's fortuitous dream signified that her son's illustrious destiny was to be linked to that of his native city. Here was a son fit for the Medici dynasty. Here was a son to ensure Medici rule of both church and state. Here was a son to devour the world. It never seemed to occur to the Medicis that the world might one day devour him.

For such a son there can never be too many good omens and portents and auspices, and so the boy was named Giovanni. The name, like the dream, was a double invocation of august tradition, for San Giovanni was the patron saint of Florence, and the boy's great-great-grandfather was Giovanni di Bicci de' Medici.

17

Born in 1360, Giovanni di Bicci was the first notable member of young Giovanni's family. He was a rotund country squire who concealed under a good-humored simplicity a vast resource of quiet shrewdness. He avoided political entanglements and, all but unnoticed, amassed a fortune in commerce and managed to become banker to the pope and his court in Rome. Henceforth, 90 percent of Medici wealth would come from banking, half their banking profits and most of their working capital from Rome. There was never any doubt in the Medici family that Christ's representative on earth was a person of particular importance.

By 1427 Giovanni di Bicci was listed in the tax records as the wealthiest man in his quarter of Florence. He left only one visible trace in passing through his life in Florence: He commissioned the architect Filippo Brunelleschi, then at work on the dome of the Florentine cathedral, to design a sacristy for the Church of San Lorenzo. But it was a pious act, not an ostentatious one, for Giovanni no doubt did it in hopes that God, or at least the pope, would then forgive him for usury. Before he died he left his family this advice: "Never hold an opinion contrary to the will of the people, even if this same people should prefer something that is perfectly useless. Do not speak with the air of giving counsel, but prefer rather to discuss matters gently and benevolently. . . . Be as inconspicuous as possible."

The Medicis all display a genius for ignoring the advice of their fathers. When Giovanni di Bicci died in 1429, his son Cosimo became head of the family. With Cosimo, the Medicis rose from studied obscurity to brilliant prominence with a sure and stunning rapidity. Supremely cunning, cautious, and possessed of an iron will, Cosimo was very conspicuous indeed. He ensured, first of all, that he had firm control of the tumultuous Florentine government. He achieved the control not without struggle and not without an occasional setback (at one time he was exiled by a rival faction). But control the nominal republic he did. He served only three two-month terms as the gonfalonier, the highest political office in Florence. Choosing to remain behind the scenes, he was a boss whose finely wrought political machine managed to "elect"

Medicean governments beginning in 1434 until the death of his grandson Lorenzo in 1492.

To this domination of Florentine political life, Cosimo added a domination of its cultural life. In 1459 he adopted a young Florentine scholar named Marsilio Ficino and charged him with translating all the works of Plato into Latin. The task took eighteen years to complete, but by the time it was done Plato had been established as the patron philosopher of Florence. The Florentine men of letters attempted to harmonize the ideas of the pagan Greek with the teachings of Christ, and the heady philosophical-religious mishmash they created served to inspire many of the finest artistic works of the Renaissance—and to cut the Florentines off from the thoughts and feelings of Christians elsewhere in Europe.

As patron of the arts, Cosimo particularly distinguished himself with his commissions to architects. He pressed Brunelleschi to redesign the whole of San Lorenzo. He built a smaller church, La Badia, on the hills above Florence near the little town of Fiesole, and he commissioned Michelozzo Michelozzi to build a palace for the Medicis in Florence. In the design of his own home, the Medici caution showed. Originally Cosimo asked Brunelleschi to submit a design for the palace. But when he saw Brunelleschi's sketches, he decided they were too grand, and he asked Michelozzo to draw up a less ostentatious plan.

When Cosimo died in 1464 at the age of seventy-five he was the richest man in Florence—at least four times wealthier than any other Florentine. His fellow townsmen loved nothing more than they loved excellence; and so, for his superiority as a builder, for his talents for accumulating a fortune, for his genius as a political manipulator—and for his becoming modesty—he was called Pater Patriae.

The destiny of the Medici dynasty was now in the hands of Piero de' Medici, a capable enough man who might well have achieved something memorable had he lived more than the five years left to him after Cosimo's death. Before he died he did secure one important advantage for the family. For his elder son,

Lorenzo, he chose the first "foreign" bride ever taken by a Medici, Clarice Orsini of a noble Roman family. With that marriage the Medicis joined the Italian aristocracy. A red-headed girl of no great wit or beauty or grace, she was not a prize catch. But her energetic husband was fond of her, and the Medici's calm climb upward continued to draw an enduring strength from a tranquil household.

Many Florentines during the Renaissance were addressed, as a matter of courtesy, as "your magnificence." Yet to only one man has the courtesy title been atttached through the centuries as though it belonged exclusively to him. Lorenzo the Magnificent, Giovanni's father, was a man of robust charm, an imaginative patron of the arts who inspired and influenced Renaissance painting and sculpture profoundly. A natural diplomatist, a connoisseur of ancient gems and cameos, a zestful gentleman-farmer, a poet of some accomplishment, his talents and enthusiasms were so all-encompassing that he stands as a quintessential "the Renaissance Man."

It was to this tradition, to the foremost family of the most dynamic city of the Renaissance, that Giovanni de' Medici was born. This scion of this most privileged family, this bright new hope of a burgeoning dynasty, was a surpassingly ugly child. He was weak; he was sickly; he was hopelessly nearsighted. Marked from the moment of his birth to be pope, he was handled from the first with the fretful attentiveness and something of the cool fastidiousness with which a banker regards his convertible debentures.

"I have three sons," Lorenzo is alleged to have said. "One is good, one is shrewd, and one is a fool." The remark is no doubt apocryphal, but its burden is nonetheless true. Giuliano, the youngest, was the good boy. "Giuliano laughs and thinks of nothing else," Lorenzo's eldest son, Piero, informs his father in a letter from one of the country estates where the family summered. The youngest son was good and happy and taken for granted by his family. Destined for no great role in the dynasty, he was permitted to amuse himself, and amuse himself was all he ever did.

20

Piero, the eldest, was the fool. An arrogant and vain little boy, the child was father to the man. He had an unusually good memory and listened to his father's literary friends reciting their poetry. He attended especially to the humorous verse of Matteo Franco and would recite Franco's verses to household guests— perhaps to their pleasure, most certainly to their applause. In the letters to his father we see him wheedling Lorenzo to deliver him a pony at a summer estate and precociously offering his father bits of unsolicited advice in a time of trouble: "Strong and brave men are not good at subterfuges but shine in open warfare. Thus we confide in you, as we well know that besides your goodness and valor you bear in mind the heritage left to us by our ancestors. . . ." At the time Piero wrote this little lecture on his ancestors to his father he was eight years old.

Giovanni, the shrewd, was a quiet little boy who was learning to read and write by the age of three and a half. He seems never to have had a childhood. While we read in family letters of children riding horses and shouting with glee after their mother returned from a trip, and although Giovanni's sister Lucrezia "sews, sings, and reads" and Contessina "fills the house with her noise," and Giuliano seems "red and fresh as a rose, smooth, clear, and bright as a mirror," Giovanni "also looks well, not much color, but healthy and natural."

He was carefully schooled to have a grave demeanor, to remember his station and his intended vocation. He was a docile little boy who detested unpleasantness and harshness of any kind. He moved in his own splendid home among artists and philosophers and diplomats who treated him with careful deference. Among the tapestries and silks and brocades, among the antique sculptures and fine new bronze medallions, in the private chapel which Benozzo Gozzoli had decorated with a gold-leafed mural of the three Magi—a splendid processional outing with elegantly costumed attendants, but not an especially religious occasion in Gozzoli's rendering of it—Giovanni grew up with rigidly controlled deportment, affable but distant, gentle but not warm, an ideal little man of the court.

Lorenzo was often absent from his family. Preoccupied with business and politics in Florence, he would dispatch his wife, Clarice, and the children to one of the estates. Caffagiolo, near the village of that name in the Apennines, had been Cosimo's favorite retreat. He liked it, he said, because all the country he could see from his windows was his own. Of the other estates, Lorenzo preferred Careggi and Fiesole. At Careggi he had enlarged the gardens, planting everything, whether for ornament or provisions, that painstaking research could find suited to the climate. Careggi was used, too, as a hunting lodge, and it was from watching the men hunt there that Giovanni developed his remarkable passion —one might say obsession—for the hunt.

Fiesole, with its commanding view of Florence in the valley below, became the resort of Lorenzo's literary friends, to many of whom Lorenzo gave homes in the surrounding countryside. There Giovanni heard of the ancient poets and philosophers, and especially of Plato, from Marsilio Ficino, from the poet Angelo Poliziano, and from the flamboyant young scholar Pico della Mirandola, who had set himself the task of bringing all that man had ever known into a single supreme system of thought. When Giovanni was eleven years old, Pico went to Rome and offered to debate 900 separate propositions with anyone in the world. When the pope pronounced seven of the propositions heretical and six of them "dangerous," Pico fled to France. Lorenzo arranged to have him returned safely to Florence, where he provided the young man with a villa, and Pico was happy to remain silent. But, then, like most of Lorenzo's friends, Pico had no profound religious convictions. He was interested in esthetics more than any deeply felt theology, and if politics prevented a display of his intellectual prowess over these 900 propositions, he was content to turn to some Hebrew studies for the time being. Later, the German Johann Reuchlin would take up the Hebrew studies Pico began and pursue them with such diligence as finally to provoke a serious confrontation with the church. Heresy was everywhere about the young Giovanni, but no one took it seriously; it was all a matter of acceptable, polite discourse. Strange fellows, the Germans, who seemed to pursue academic *divertissements* with a dark purposiveness, as though they deeply cared about them.

It was this group of men, and a few others like them, who formed what came to be known as the Platonic Academy. Their select society was "superior perhaps," Voltaire would later say, "to that of the boasted sages of Greece." These were the men from whom Giovanni took his schooling. Interestingly enough, his tutelage provoked the one argument between Lorenzo and his wife that has been recorded. Poliziano taught Giovanni Latin through studies of the ancient Roman poets. And, Poliziano wrote to Lorenzo, Giovanni was progressing well. But "his mothar has taken it upon herself to change his course of reading to the Psalter, a thing I did not approve of." Poliziano had been raised in the school that maintained the reading of church writings would spoil one's literary style. The difference led to a domestic uproar, and soon Clarice was writing Lorenzo, ". . . nor do I like that Messer Angelo should threaten that he would remain in the house in spite of me. You remember I told you, that if it was your *will* he should stay, I was perfectly contented; and although I have suffered infinite abuse from him, yet if it be with your assent, I am satisfied. But I do not believe it to be so."

Lorenzo resolved the matter by having Poliziano move to another of his villas. Yet, however much his mother made him read the Psalter, Giovanni's religious education can only be judged to have developed in him a genial indifference to matters of religion. Whenever he later encountered people with strong religious feelings, he would find himself bewildered.

Giovanni's schoolbooks were illuminated manuscripts. And there can be no doubt that his arithmetic lesson was, for him, an opportunity to daydream over the brightly painted battle scenes that crowded the margins of the pages and to gaze affectionately at the cheerful reds and rich blues in the costumes of the two merchants trading wool for cloth (How many bags of wool does it take to make one bolt of cloth?). Just as learning was an eye-pleasing, sensuous pastime, so was religion less a matter of holy days than it was a profusion of feast days.

23

For San Giovanni's Day the shops were festooned in silk and gold cloth, and the city might be treated to the sight of a hundred gold gilt towers carved with figures of horsemen and dancing girls. Giants walked about on stilts. There were plays and pantomimes and songs. According to one Florentine reminiscence of a festival, "As you make your way along the streets, the houses are all hung with tapestries, and the chairs and benches covered with taffeta. Everywhere you see girls and young women dressed in silk and bedizened with jewels, precious stones and pearls. . . . The whole city, that day, is given over to revelry and feasting, with so many fifes and music, songs, dances and other festivities and merry-making, that this earth seems like a paradise."

Florence was a magnificently worldly city, the center of international banking and of the famous Italian textile trade. Its streets abounded with prosperous little pharmacies, candlemakers' shops, goldsmiths' shops, open-air markets, with tanners and woodworkers and moneylenders. And Giovanni's father drew the bustle of business and pleasure about himself and doubtless seemed to the boy to incorporate the full spirit of the city within his own singular being. Lorenzo wrote songs and plays for the festivals, and moved constantly among the princes and ambassadors from afar. He was both the exalted great man and the boon companion. And for all of his vast concerns, he took enormous delight in his children. If one were to believe Machiavelli, his high spirits were too expansive; for as Machiavelli recalled, with slight distaste for the indecorousness of the aristocracy, "he would forget the dignity of his office in romping with his children, for he would oftentimes indulge in any idle or childish amusement they might put him to." It should have been a happy childhood for Giovanni, and no doubt would have been had he not been excluded from so much of the fun by the injunction to behave, even as a very small child, like a better priest than any he could see about him. But he placed himself in his father's care. He never rebelled; he behaved well.

In April, 1478, when Giovanni was barely two and a half years old, a rivalry between the Medicis and another Florentine banking family, the Pazzis, erupted into awful violence. The politics behind the event are involved and unclear. Pope Sixtus IV, acting as the acquisitive temporal leader Renaissance popes so characteristically were, was frustrated by Lorenzo from taking over a piece of territory near Florence for one of his family. In turn, Lorenzo suffered at the hands of the pope. Intrigue followed intrigue until the ambitious Pazzis replaced the Medicis as banker to the pope. Still more retaliatory measures by Lorenzo led the Pazzis to lose patience. With the connivance of Sixtus, the Pazzi faction plotted to assassinate Lorenzo and his brother, Giuliano, the only sons of Piero.

In the cathedral in Florence on a Sunday morning, April 26, 1478, at the moment the priest raised the consecrated Host and the bells rang to mark the most sacred moment of the mass, the conspirators fell on Lorenzo and Giuliano with their daggers. Lorenzo fought his way to safety. His brother was less fortunate and fell in front of the altar, stabbed to death with twenty-nine dagger blows.

The city rose up, and supporters of the Pazzis discovered, too late, that few would come to their defense. The Florentines, with their fond memories of Cosimo and their fierce affection for Lorenzo, set on the Pazzis, and the carnage went on until 270 conspirators were killed, exiled, or ruined. Chagrined that the plot had failed, Sixtus feigned outrage that an archbishop had not been spared in the bloodbath. Lorenzo was excommunicated, and Florence went to war with Rome.

Lorenzo's children were sent to the country, joined by an illegitimate son of Lorenzo's brother, Giuliano (an attractive young man-about-town, Giuliano had not married, and this boy was his only child). His name was Giulio, and we know little of him as a child except that he was Giovanni's close companion—whether because of mutual affection or parental decree we do not know. He, too, was chosen for a career in the church, and he stayed close by Giovanni's side. In 1523 he became the second Medici pope, Clement VII.

War with Sixtus and his allies dragged on until 1480, when an invasion of the peninsula by the Turks forced the disputants to lay down their arms without significant advantage to either side and turn to meet the threat from the Turks. Lorenzo emerged from all this turmoil with the conviction that it was essential for the Medicis to have some control over the temporal ambitions of the Vatican. His plans for Giovanni, having begun as a desire to enhance Medici prestige, now turned to an urgent, almost frenzied drive to have a Medici cardinal as a measure of self-defense. The machinations of Sixtus had cost him a brother, nearly bankrupted him, and came close to destroying Florence. Lorenzo watched now as the pope first attacked Ferrara and then Venice in his quest for territory to bestow on members of his family. Lorenzo stayed aloof from these wars, putting pressure first here, then there, to keep Italy in treacherous balance; and he served whenever he could as go-between to negotiate peace. At some time in this murky trading of threats and counterthreats, favors and forgiveness, Lorenzo managed to wrest a promise from Sixtus to take Giovanni into the church. The boy was admitted to holy orders and received the tonsure in 1482, at the age of seven, and as Lorenzo recorded in his diary, "from thenceforth [he] was called Messire Giovanni."

Louis XI of France bestowed on Messire Giovanni the abbey of Fonte Dolce. "On the eighth day of June [1483]," Lorenzo notes, "Jacopino, a courier, arrived with advices from the King of France, that he had conferred upon Messire Giovanni the archbishopric of Aix, in Provence. . . . On the twentieth, we received news from Lionetto, *that the archbishop was not dead!*" It was an inconvenience, to be sure—no one had heard from the old fellow for quite a while—but there were other benefices to be given to the Medici boy. Sixtus duly presented him with the rich abbey of Passignano, and in short order Giovanni collected the abbacy of Monte Cassino, of San Giusto and San Clement at Volterra, of San Stefano of Bologna, of Chiaravalle at Milan; he was prior of Montevarchi and precentor of San Antonio in Florence. He gathered in another sixteen offices before the princes and prelates exhausted their paroxysm of casting bread on the waters.

26

In August, 1484, Pope Sixtus died, and he was succeeded to the tiara by Giovanni Battista Cibò, who took the name Innocent VIII. In November Lorenzo dispatched Piero to Rome to convey the compliments of the Medicis to the new pope. Piero was then fourteen years old, and Lorenzo composed a letter of instruction for his son to master on his way to the Vatican: "After having recommended me to his holiness, you will inform him that your affection for your brother induces you to speak a word in his favor. You can here mention that I have educated him for the priesthood, and shall closely attend to his learning and his manners, so that he may not disgrace his profession; that in this respect I repose all my hopes on his holiness; who, having already given us proofs of his kindness and affection, will add to our obligations by any promotion which he may think proper to bestow on him; endeavoring by these and similar expressions to recommend your brother to his favor as much as lies in your power."

Innocent was in a vexing situation. As a condition of electing him pope, the College of Cardinals had made him promise that he would elevate no one under the age of thirty to cardinal and that he would create no new cardinals at all until the college's numbers were reduced in the course of nature to twenty-four. To Lorenzo's entreaty, Innocent returned the Reply Courteous. But Lorenzo had not begun to use all his resources. Before Innocent had joined the church, he had had several children. The eldest, Francesco Cibò, as Lorenzo pointed out, seemed a perfect match for Lorenzo's daughter Maddalena. The Medicis were a good family, and their relationship through Lorenzo's wife to the Orsinis would be helpful to a pope who had suffered from the hostility of that noble Roman family. Lorenzo pressed the arrangement and in 1487 the two were married.

Early in 1488 Innocent wrote Lorenzo that he thought he might create some new cardinals, and he enclosed a list of candidates, asking which of them Lorenzo would favor. The pope's letter provoked a flurry of correspondence from Lorenzo not only to the pope himself but also to as many members of the College of Cardinals as he thought could help the campaign for

Giovanni. Cardinal Ascanio Sforza, a brother of Lodovico Sforza of Milan, and Roderigo Borgia, vice-chancellor at the Vatican, gave Lorenzo essential aid, and the return to them, and others, can be guessed from one of Lorenzo's letters: ". . . the trouble which, as you inform me, Monsig. Ascanio takes every day in my behalf, merits other returns than words." There is no accounting of what the purple cost Lorenzo; there is no doubt he had no care of the cost.

In October, 1488, Lorenzo received the news that Giovanni had been created a cardinal. He was thirteen years old, the youngest cardinal in the history of the church. The pope, feeling still some embarrassment at what he had done, insisted that Giovanni not assume the hat itself for another three years and that, in the meantime, his new rank be kept secret. Lorenzo wrote his envoy in Rome, "Thanks be to God"—more as a matter of form than as an expression of gratitude where it was due—and, after thanking his agents in Rome, he added, "I know not whether his holiness may be displeased with the demonstrations of joy and festivity which have taken place in Florence on this occasion. . . . I did all in my power to prevent them, although I could not wholly succeed. . . . If what I have done is improper, I can only say that it was impossible for me to prevent it, and that I greatly wish for instructions how to conduct myself in future, as to what kind of life and manners M. Giovanni ought to observe, and what his dress and attendants ought to be. . . ."

Innocent cannot have been amused by this final bit of presumption on Lorenzo's part. He had insisted on secrecy for three years, and the Florentines were dancing in the streets the day the news reached Lorenzo. He had said Giovanni must not assume the insignia of his office, and Lorenzo wanted to know, now that the fact was no longer secret, "what his dress and attendants ought to be. . . ." Given an advantage, Lorenzo never failed to exploit it. Innocent responded with restraint that the thirteen-year-old cardinal might profitably spend the next three years studying theology.

Giovanni was packed off to the academy at Pisa, where he

learned little theology but a good deal of civil and pontifical law. His cousin Giulio accompanied him to Pisa, as did Bernardo Dovizi da Bibbiena. Five years Giovanni's senior, Bernardo had been sent to study in Florence at the age of nine, and his family connections provided him with an introduction to the Medicis. He was a tireless student and acquired a stylish facility in Latin composition so that, by the age of seventeen, he was serving as one of Lorenzo's private secretaries. When Giovanni was sent to Pisa, Bernardo was sent with him to handle his finances—for even at that early age it was evident that Giovanni had no sense of money. The clever, urbane financial manager and the pleasure-loving spendthrift would remain close companions all their lives.

Giovanni's mother died in the same year that he was named a cardinal. Although she had seemed too plain and dull for the brilliant Medici court, and although her husband was reputed to have been an energetic philanderer, Lorenzo apparently loved her after his own fashion and was deeply saddened by her death. He had provided well for his dynasty: Piero was married to Alfonsina, the daughter of Roberto Orsini, count of Tagliacozzo and Albi, and Lorenzo fortified the Medicis' place in Florence by marrying Lucretia to a Salviati and Contessina to a Ridolfi. Giuliano remained to be disposed of by his brothers depending on what advantages they might attain later. All that remained for Lorenzo before he died was to see Giovanni formally take on the role of cardinal; only then would he feel entirely secure.

Letters, representations of all sorts, intrigue at the Vatican—nothing availed. Ultimately, Innocent granted the favor, according to the time schedule he had originally proposed. On March 8, 1492, in an inconspicuous ceremony of which Giovanni di Bicci would have approved, and at the church Cosimo had built, La Badia near Fiesole, Messire Giovanni was given the pallium, or mantle; the bireta, as the scarlet cap is called; the galerus, the broadbrimmed hat with its long tassels; and the sapphire ring emblematic of the church's celestial foundation. After the mass, after a procession to the church of the Annunziata, after prayers at the cathedral, Giovanni was escorted to the Medici palace and to his father, who lay sick, dying of the gout, waiting to see the new cardinal.

Three days later, after too brief a time of enjoyment for Lorenzo, the cardinal set out for Rome with his retinue, including, of course, Giulio and Bernardo Dovizi. Lorenzo sent his son off with a letter of advice that has about it the echo of Polonius, and it has within it the elements of the cardinal's character that worried the father still. It is a letter of varying moods. The opening, formal paragraph sounds as though Lorenzo felt obliged to say something fatherly, anything fatherly, and so resorted to such platitudes as, "I would therefore suggest to you . . . that you ought to be grateful to God. . . ." But, then, remembering that platitudes have never been useful to him, he ends the paragraph with a slight rebuke: "It would indeed be highly disgraceful, and as contrary to your duty as to my hopes, if, at a time when others display a greater share of reason and adopt a better mode of life, you should forget the precepts of your youth, and forsake the path in which you have hitherto trodden." It sounds almost as if Giovanni had recently gone out with the boys.

In the second paragraph Lorenzo continues his stern advice: "Endeavor therefore to alleviate the burden of your early dignity by the regularity of your life [Giovanni habitually stayed up late at night and slept late in the morning] and by your perseverance in those studies which are suitable to your profession [that is, study a bit more theology]." Then Lorenzo searches for something on which he might compliment Giovanni: "It gave me great satisfaction to learn, that, in the course of the past year, you had frequently, of your own accord, gone to communion and confession." Giovanni was no monk, to be sure, but his heart was in the right place.

Then in the third paragraph comes a flash of Lorenzo's old energy as he takes on one of his favorite targets, the corruption of the church. Few reformers had as jaded a view of Rome as Lorenzo: "I well know, that as you are now to reside at Rome, that sink of all iniquity, the difficulty of conducting yourself by these admonitions will be increased. The influence of example is itself prevalent; but you will probably meet with those who will particularly endeavor to corrupt and incite you to vice; because, as you may yourself perceive, your early attainment to so great a dignity is not observed without envy . . . there is at present little virtue among your brethren of the college. I acknowledge indeed that several of them are good and learned men . . . and whom I would recommend to you as patterns of your conduct. . . . Avoid, however, as you would Scylla or Charybdis, the imputation of hypocrisy [do not, as Machiavelli would later say, necessarily avoid hypocrisy, but avoid the imputation of it]; guard yourself against all ostentation, either in your conduct or your discourse [as the Medicis had always done]; effect not austerity, nor even appear too serious. This advice you will, I hope, in time understand and practise better than I can express it." These rules were by now so much in the bones of the Medicis—the behavior of a prince in a republic, the absolute rule by charm—that Lorenzo knew he could not hope, in his short letter, to tell Giovanni what he should know himself.

"You are not unacquainted," Lorenzo goes on, "with the great importance of the character which you have to sustain, for you well know that all the Christian world would prosper if the cardinals were what they ought to be; because in such a case there would always be a good pope, upon which the tranquillity of Christendom so materially depends. Endeavor then to render yourself such, that if all the rest resembled you, we might expect this universal blessing. To give you particular directions as to your behavior and conversation would be a matter of no small difficulty. I shall therefore only recommend, that in your intercourse with the cardinals and other men of rank, your language be unassuming and respectful, guiding yourself, however, by your own reason, and not submitting to be impelled by the passions of others, who, actuated by improper motives, may pervert the use of their reason."

Next Lorenzo phrases as delicately as he might Giovanni's duties toward his family: "You are now devoted to God and the church; on which account you ought to aim at being a good ecclesiastic, and to show that you prefer the honor and state of the church and of the apostolic see to every other consideration. Nor, while you keep this in view, will it be difficult for you to favor your family and your native place. On the contrary, you should be the link to bind this city closer to the church, and our family with the city; and although it be impossible to foresee what accidents may happen, yet I doubt not but this may be done with equal advantage to all; observing, however, that you are always to prefer the interests of the church." Yet, Lorenzo might have repeated, "this may be done with equal advantage to all."

Finally, Lorenzo concludes with the advice that sounds most like Polonius: "You are not only the youngest cardinal in the college, but the youngest person that ever was raised to that rank; and you ought therefore to be the most vigilant and unassuming, not giving others occasion to wait for you, either in the chapel, the consistory, or upon deputations. You will soon get sufficient insight into the matters of your brethren. With those of less respectable character converse not with too much intimacy; not merely on account of the circumstance itself, but for the sake of public opinion. Converse on general topics with all [the advice of a diplomat]. On public occasions let your equipage and dress be rather below than above mediocrity. A handsome house and a well-ordered family will be preferable to a great retinue and a splendid residence [remember that Cosimo rejected Brunelleschi's design]. Endeavor to live with regularity [this advice again—so much does Lorenzo fear for Giovanni's eccentric habits and late rising in the morning], and gradually bring your expenses within those bounds which in a new establishment cannot perhaps be expected. Silk and jewels are not suitable for persons in your station. Your taste will be better shown in the acquisition of a few elegant remains of antiquity, or in the collecting of handsome books, and by your attendants being learned and well-bred than numerous. Invite others to your house oftener than you receive invitations. Practise neither too frequently. Let your own food be plain, and take sufficient exercise, for those who wear your habit are soon liable, without great caution, to contract infirmities. . . . Be attentive to your conduct, and confide in others too little rather than too much. There is one rule which I would recommend to your attention in preference to all others: Rise early in the morning."

By now Giovanni must have been heartily tired of this painstaking advice. Lorenzo had certainly begun to repeat himself. The father is tired, his hand cramped no doubt from holding the pen, it is time to lie down—and the letter trails off with an afterthought: ". . . it will be most becoming for you at present to refer the matters in debate to the judgment of his holiness. . . . Be cautious, however, that you trouble him not too often. . . . This you must observe, lest you should give him offense, remembering also at times to converse with him on more agreeable topics; and if you should be obliged to request some kindness from him, let it be done with that modesty and humility which are so pleasing to his disposition. Farewell."

One month later, on April 8, 1492, Lorenzo died, and the cardinal was on his own. No young man had been better trained to negotiate the intricate politics of the church, no young man might be expected to have a broader, more sophisticated view of the world. He knew politics and business and international diplomacy. He was at ease with the new revolutions in the arts and sciences. He knew letters, he knew civil and pontifical law. Added to all this was an upbringing that had instilled in all the Medicis a rare sensitivity to recognize danger and turn it to advantage—indeed, to turn tragedy into exalted expectations, as Lorenzo had turned the death of a brother and an unwelcome war into the creation of a cardinal. He was accustomed to privilege and always expected to come out on top. He had been schooled, excellently well schooled, to know a threat in a dangerous world, to recognize even the subtlest signal of peril, and to know how to manage it. This was, after all, the genius of his remarkably successful family. Unfortunately, he knew very little of theology, but theology was a matter to be left to scholars and monks to thrash out.

II

MARTIN'S CHILDHOOD

MARTIN LUTHER was born without portent on November 10, 1483. His mother was Margarete, nee Ziegler. His father was Hans Lytter, or Luder, or Lüder, or Ludher—the eldest of a peasant family to whom mastery of letters was not an urgent concern. Hans, or Big Hans as he was called, had three brothers: Little Hans, Veit, and Heinz. By the custom of ultimogeniture, the family farm was passed on to the youngest brother, Heinz, and the other brothers left to find their livelihoods elsewhere—all except Little Hans, who stayed on working for Heinz. Little Hans was a notorious drunk and, like most of the Luthers, a man with a violent temper. Between 1499 and 1513 he acquired eleven convictions for offenses significant enough to come before the courts. Nothing else is known of Martin Luther's heritage. His father rarely talked of the past.

Born on the eve of St. Martin's Day, the boy was routinely named for the patron saint of feasting and reformed drunkards. When he was seven months old, his family moved from Eisleben, where Hans had failed to prosper as a miner, to Mansfeld. Like Little Hans, Big Hans had an awesome temper, and it is said that he killed a shepherd in some minor dispute before the family arrived in Mansfeld. In Mansfeld Martin grew up among eight brothers and sisters, while the ambitious and determined Hans worked his way up out of the copper mines until he was able to buy shares in two smelting works. Martin grew up in a struggling, frugal family, its pleasures sacrificed to Hans' rapacious drive to get rich. Fearful of his violent past, or embarrassed by his peasant past, Hans kept an anxious eye on the future. Ultimately he became part owner of six mines, and when Martin was eight years old, Hans proudly took his hard-won place as a representative to the town council. "The more you cleanse yourself," Martin enigmatically said when he was a youngster, "the dirtier you get."

The Luther home was built in the "wattle and dab" style of architecture. Its mud walls were whitewashed. Out back were cow barns, pig sties, hen roosts, and wood bins—the source of much of Martin's literary imagery. The family's general living room was a dingy kitchen, and it is probable that the whole family slept together in one room, perhaps on straw beds on the floor. Such accommodations should not suggest real poverty; they were typical enough for the family of a successful mine manager. The close quarters were painful to Martin, however. They left him no room to escape from a father whom he feared at least as much as he loved. And when his father directed his rage against Martin, Martin could do nothing but absorb it and store it up, for back talk was out of the question.

Martin loved his mother. She probably disappointed him, because she was a dutiful wife and declined to step between the frightened boy and his tempestuous father. But it must have been from her that Martin learned to unburden himself of his fears and passions—at first in fantasy, later in song, and at last in the greatest deluge of back talk any papa might imagine. Martin's mother believed in elves and gnomes and witches and devils. They worked big evils and played little pranks, stealing eggs and butter. His mother so suffered at the hands of one witch that she felt she ought to treat her with great deference and propitiate her, for she caused such agony to her children that they screamed as if they were at death's door. "Many regions," the mature Martin Luther would say, "are inhabited by devils. Prussia is full of them, and Lapland of witches. In my native country on the top of a high mountain called the Pubelsberg is a lake into which if a stone be thrown a tempest will arise over the whole region because the waters are the abode of captive demons." If sometimes the tempests could not be kept at bay, if sometimes the demons got you in spite of your incantations, at least a hostile world could be explained a little bit, and that was a comfort.

His mother taught him to sing, and once Martin's voice was set free, so was his spirit. True, he lost his voice for a time, and his spirit was never set free from a stomach that knotted up in such cramps that he couldn't move. But his voice gave vent to his feelings: He sang the Sanctus and the Benedictus and the Confiteor, and he especially loved the Magnificat. He might have sung nothing but psalms and hymns of praise. But not even Martin's mother was entirely predictable. "My mother caned me for stealing a nut until the blood came, such strict discipline drove me to a monastery although she meant it well." Such strict discipline or many such bewilderingly severe thrashings for trivial transgressions drove Martin to a monastery and to a vow of strictest silence, to be kept until he found his own voice, until he sang not the songs of others but talked back in his own words, with his own understanding, and drowned out all objections with the sheer tremendous torrent of his own resounding voice.

Like Giovanni de' Medici, Martin was the second son in his family, and he was made the vessel of his father's grandest ambitions. In Germany at that time, new capitalists emerged to wrest power from the old feudal lords, independent towns challenged old political orders, and the German princes themselves had to negotiate their places in a more complex and competitive world of shifting alliances. Hans knew little of the world of diplomacy, but he did understand that a lawyer could become rich and respected —perhaps even a burgomaster. So his son was marked out for the legal profession, and he was resolutely sent to school at the age of four.

Martin received the education not of a future burgomaster (and for that reason to be respected by his teachers) but of a sinner. Hell was not roiling with wretched souls because men lived virtuous lives but because men lied and stole and did not honor their fathers and mothers and even, perhaps, wished their fathers and mothers would die and go to hell. Fortunately, there was a cure: fear. If a child could be made sufficiently fearful of a harsh, an inexplicably harsh, God who needed to explain His divine actions to no man, the child might behave. One might never be certain that God in all His mysterious ways was satisfied. After all, not even a child knows as well as God what secret, evil thoughts a boy might harbor without even being aware of them. But fear of fire and brimstone, fear of God's wrath, fear of the loss of God's love—that and an occasional thrashing were as much as one might expect a teacher to give a child. The children would have to pray for themselves and love God so that He wouldn't punish them. That was up to them.

Young Martin lived with a more acute sense of fear and a conscience more tortured by contradictions than perhaps most of his schoolmates. How should a boy honor a father who was unjustly wrathful, who might even be a murderer and himself destined for hell? How was he to grow up in his father's image and yet take care not to relax his self-control for fear his own temper would become the demon that possessed his father and his uncle? How could he honor his father when he feared him, when his father made Martin hate him? Was not Martin's refusal to grow up in his father's image a sin against the Commandments, indeed a mortal sin for which he could not escape hell? What if fear itself was a sin—fear of your father and of God? Was it right to fear a God who loved you and expected love in return—and your only feeling was an awesome, irresistible fear that drove out all other emotions? Can your very existence be a sin? It is, to be sure, impossible to know what bedeviled young Martin. But he grew up with a self-consuming conscience, so tortured in body and spirit, so astonishingly compulsive about dredging out the most insignificant little matters in confession that some very crucial dilemma must have faced him from earliest childhood. Such an extremely scrupulous conscience would not develop from a small worry. Martin was worried that he was on his way to hell, the destination of the irretrievably bad. It may have been this conflict over love and horror of his father—a very real and supremely important conflict that a sensitive boy might well be expected to feel deeply—that turned Martin into a profoundly troubled theologian by the age of five. It was not simply a wrathful father who made Martin the youngster he was but the fact that somehow, inexplicably, his father's wrath made Martin damned.

It should surprise no one that Martin was judged to be a bright boy and a poor student. Education and Latin were synonymous. He learned to write by copying Latin texts. He learned the rudiments of language from Latin. When the children sang, they sang parts of the Latin liturgy for the mass. It was all a matter of drill and repetition, and the boys were often given a good beating—not for misbehavior, but simply to speed the learning process along. There were no amenities, no kindly tutors watching encouragingly and proudly over their charges—no one like Giovanni's mentor Poliziano, then Italy's most admired poet. The teachers were young and inexperienced or half-educated, or otherwise unemployable, and they treated the children like so much cattle to be prodded and whipped and taught discipline and got rid of as soon as possible. There were no illuminated manuscripts in Martin's school. (He might have been fortunate enough to see an occasional rough, no doubt gloomy woodcut. There were manuals about, such as one *On the Art of Dying*, decorated with lurid woodcuts.) There were three grades, or levels, of achievement in Latin in Martin's primary school. In eight years Martin never got past the second grade. School, religion, and home life were all one to Martin. The Latin examination, he said, "was like a trial for murder."

In the spring of 1497, at the age of thirteen, Martin was sent to the town of Magdeburg to continue his studies. Magdeburg at this time was one of the richest and busiest towns in Germany. It was the center of trade up and down the Elbe River, the crossroads of many of the chief cities of the Holy Roman Empire. Surrounded by ramparts and casements and bastions and dominated by the great citadel of the Wartburg, the huge stone fortress set forbiddingly in the middle of the river, the city was a melange of bales of goods and cannonry along castellated wharves, of seamen and merchants and monks. Martin apparently attended the choir school and, like almost all boys at the time, sang for his supper. One must not think of poor Tom Tucker; begging for alms was roughly comparable to summer jobs for students today. The crumb-seekers, as they were called, had rugged competition from pilgrims and begging monks and the Magdeburg poor, but there is no reason to assume they did not go about their begging with a light heart.

It is all the more remarkable, therefore, that Martin was so impressed by the sight of Prince William of Anhalt-Zerbst, who had turned mendicant Franciscan by choice. "I saw with my own eyes," Martin later recalled, "a Prince of Anhalt . . . who went in a friar's cowl on the highways to beg bread, and carried a sack like a donkey, so heavy that he bent under it, but his companion walked by him without a burden . . . he had so fasted, watched, and mortified his flesh that he looked like a death's head, mere skin and bones; indeed he soon after died, for he could not long bear such a severe life. In short, whoever looked at him had to gasp for pity and must needs be ashamed for his own worldly position."

The worldly Magdeburg apparently hadn't quite the effect on Martin that his father had in mind. He was snatched abruptly away from Magdeburg and sent instead to the school of Saint George the dragon-killer at nearby Eisenach. In Eisenach, a small town nestled near rugged mountain ranges, Martin's schoolwork improved, and he had his first pleasant and relaxed years. Eisenach was his mother's hometown, and it was supposed that his relatives there would keep an eye on Martin. But either they rebuffed him or, as seems more likely, he avoided them.

In the course of his crumb seeking he chanced upon a family of Italian descent named Cotta. The woman of the house, Ursula Cotta, was much taken with the boy for his singing and, no doubt, because Martin presented himself as pitifully cast out by his relatives. He came to live with the Cottas and got on well with the entire family—including the father, I hasten to add—and flourished under the warm, motherly interest of Ursula Cotta. In exchange for this hospitality, Martin took charge of a young boy of the family, seeing him to school and attending him during school hours. He was in some measure in the position of one of the junior tutors in the Medici household. The Cottas were by no means so rich and distinguished a family as the Medicis, but they were well-to-do patricians who had books in their home and glass panes in their windows and real furniture, not built-in planks for tables and benches. They were a devout family to whom religion was a source of comfort and hope, not anxiety. Their religious feelings did not instantly reform Martin's own thoughts, but they must at least have intrigued him and given him some notion that religion might be something other than frightening. The Cottas were not irreligious, they were not lax in their morals, but they lived according to their consciences, and they were good and kind.

Through the Cottas, who were wealthy enough to have founded a small Franciscan monastery near the Wartburg, Martin met some cordial men of the church. He also met and grew very fond of the compassionate and friendly vicar of St. Mary's, Johann Braun. When he celebrated his first mass, Martin would invite the vicar to attend and ask him to tell the Cottas of his ordination. But he could not quite bring himself to presume to invite the Cottas directly.

Martin graduated among the top students in his class at Eisenach. He had done so well that his father felt justified in stretching his resources even further and sending him off to the old and famous university at Erfurt. With a degree in law from Erfurt Martin would assuredly bring esteem to the family and security for Hans' old age. So, at seventeen, the same age at which Giovanni de' Medici set off for Rome, Martin Luther, future burgomaster, was sent to Erfurt—without a letter of advice and very possibly with an angry injunction to behave himself.

III

THE CARDINAL'S
COLLEGE EDUCATION

THE Cardinal de' Medici's brutal education in church politics began with cinematic appropriateness in a rainstorm. He arrived drenched in Rome on March 22, 1492, and dried out that night in the monastery of Santa Maria del Popolo, where Martin Luther would stay when he visited Rome eighteen years later. The following day he slogged through rain and mud to pay his respects to Pope Innocent. He was received well. His attendants were permitted to kiss the feet of the pope. The cardinals crowded around him. He paid particular marks of respect to his relative, Cardinal Orsini, and his two principal supporters for the red hat, Cardinal Ascanio Sforza and the vice-chancellor Rodrigo Borgia.

The College of Cardinals was composed, like Europe itself, of constantly shifting factions and alliances. The families of the old Roman barons, the Orsinis and Colonnas, maneuvered to maintain control of the roads and lands around Rome and to hold the power of the pope in check. Neapolitans, fearful that an ancient French claim to Naples might one day be pressed, labored to keep French influence out of the college and so were suspicious of the three Della Roveres in their midst who seemed to have strong ties to that foreign country. Milan and Venice and Florence connived to keep the two great powers of Naples and the pope from joining forces against them. Or perhaps Venice and Milan would join with the pope against Naples. Or the pope might join with his traditional baronial enemies, the Orsinis, to diminish the in-

fluence of the Sforzas in Milan. Orsinis, Caraffas, Cibòs, Picco-
lominis, Borgias all jostled, allied, realigned themselves, bargained,
bribed, and murdered on behalf of that most sacred of all Italian
institutions, the family.

Nothing was fixed, nothing settled. Lorenzo's enemy Sixtus IV
brought Giovanni into the church, and in the College of Cardinals the Cardinal de' Medici joined Raffaelle Riario, who had
played a major role in the Pazzi conspiracy against the Medici.
The cardinal entered Rome a member of the Borgia faction, and
the three Della Roveres watched him closely to see how he might
be brought into their camp. And the pope presided over all,
amidst the mud flats and marshes and slums of Rome, in white
taffetas and shoes of crimson velvet trimmed with ermine, the
vicar of Christ on earth and the center of European intrigue.

Politics and religion, those two most dangerous dinner-table
topics, were all that Rome had. There were no weavers, no farmers, no businesses of any kind to speak of. There was no middle
class; there were no prosperous little craft shops—only a mob of
unruly parasites living off the souvenir trade. The population
numbered 40,000, and every year 50,000 pilgrims came to sleep in
the inns, drink at the taverns, and make the rounds of some of the
280 ramshackle churches. The ancient Roman walls had crum-
bled; the Roman Forum was a cattle market; Nero's palace on the
Palatine Hill was abandoned to gardens and vines; the Forum of
Trajan was covered with trash.

In order to raise Holy Mother the church out of this sprawling,
pestiferous slum, Pope John XXII had decreed as early as 1318
that the holder of any benefice in the church must pay the pope
the first year's income derived from the monastery or bishopric or
whatever had been granted. Combined with the income the pope
received from the papal states—after Naples, the largest domain
in Italy—this wealth began to raise Rome out of the mud. Pope
Nicholas V advised his successors from his deathbed in 1455 that
the faith of men needed to be inspired and strengthened by
"majestic buildings, imperishable memorials, and witnesses seemingly planted by the Hand of God." God's majesty being, of

course, infinite, there was no end of inspiring to be done and no end of the money needed to do it.

When Cardinal de' Medici arrived in Rome, the city still presented a disconsolate aspect. St. Peter's Cathedral was an uninspiring hulk, and the fines imposed for dumping garbage in the streets had not yet had much effect. But the Piazza Navona had been paved to make a marketplace, and new bridges spanned the Tiber. More and more domes replaced the medieval towers of the skyline. New palaces had been built by the Cardinals Borgia, Giuliano and Domenico della Rovere, and Nardini. Cardinal Sforza lovingly described Vice-Chancellor Rodrigo Borgia's palace as "splendidly decorated; the walls of the great entrance halls were heavy with tapestries depicting various historical scenes. A small drawing room led off this, which was also decorated with fine tapestries; the carpets on the floor harmonized with the furnishings which included a sumptuous bed upholstered in red satin with a canopy over it, and a chest on which was laid out a vast and beautiful collection of gold and silver plate. Beyond this there were two more rooms, one heavy with fine satin, carpeted, and with another canopied bed covered with Alexandrine velvet; the other even more ornate with a couch covered in cloth of gold. . . ." Such splendor required more and more money, of course. Cardinals' offices were sold, wars of conquest were launched, monopolies sought over alum mines, and one of the Vatican's concerns had of necessity to be sacrificed to the other. Politics, not religion, became the all-consuming passion of the popes. It had to be so—for the greater glory of the church, for the inspiration of Catholics everywhere.

On July 25, 1492, Pope Innocent died. He had been a lackluster pope, and there were not even the customary rumors of poison to lend a *frisson* to his passing. The College of Cardinals assembled in conclave on August 6, while the Roman mobs abandoned themselves to the rioting that always erupted after the death of a pope. The terrified cardinal-chamberlain Riario imposed a rigid rule on the city and managed to keep murders to a mere 220 during the interregnum.

There were twenty-seven cardinals in the college in 1492, and twenty-three entered the conclave that autumn, the four others being too distant from Rome to return in time for the election. Cardinal Sforza led one faction. Milan, home of the Sforzas, had long feared the powerful southern kingdom of Naples, and Cardinal Sforza was able to count on the patronage of King Charles VIII of France, who was still anxious to press France's claim to the right of sovereignty over Naples. Cardinal Giuliano della Rovere stood in opposition to Sforza, and Della Rovere had 200,000 ducats deposited in a Rome bank by King Ferrante of Naples to help his candidacy. On the sidelines stood Rodrigo Borgia with his own following. Neither Sforza nor Della Rovere could win the two-thirds majority necessary, and Sforza suddenly abandoned his own candidacy and threw his support to Borgia. In the streets in Rome four mules laden with silver were said to have been noticed going from Borgia's palace to Sforza's. The divided college abruptly agreed on its new candidate, and at dawn on August 11, Borgia was elected pope. Only a single dissenting vote was recorded, that of Della Rovere. When the cardinals lowered their canopies in obeisance to him, Borgia, a dignified sixty-one-year-old Spaniard, cried out with the pleasure of a boy, "We are Pope and Vicar of Christ!" Cardinal de' Medici allegedly whispered to Cardinal Cibò, "Now we are in the jaws of a ravening wolf, and if we do not flee he will devour us."

The coronation ceremonies were held on the steps in front of St. Peter's and they surpassed in splendor any pageant the Romans had ever before seen. Foreign ambassadors, cardinals with their richly turned out retinues, squadrons of cavalry, the curial officials all attended the new pope in sumptuous array. Then, in a procession from St. Peter's to the Church of the Lateran, Alexander passed under triumphal arches that proclaimed him conqueror and God—"*Alexandro invictissimo, Alexandro magnificentissimo*"—and the crowds roared their approval. It was all overwhelming for the new pope; he fainted twice during the celebrations.

Much has been written of the Borgias, nearly all of it nasty: about the Borgias' secret formula for poison, about the murders at

44

their hands, about Alexander's incestuous relationship with his daughter Lucrezia. In the epic morality play of history, Alexander VI and Cesare Borgia are the great princes of evil. The catalog of their crimes is a prodigious listing of almost all the delicious and repulsive vices known to man. A very few men of history stand out as unmitigated scoundrels and evildoers. In any list of supreme bad men, the Borgias rank near the top. It was Cesare Borgia who was, for Machiavelli, the most perfect example of "the Prince."

How much this reputation is deserved is questionable. Alexander had a disturbingly large number of illegitimate children—at least nine that we know of—and he gave the world a tremendous show of nepotism. Cesare was a brutal administrator, and a number of men were killed at his order. And Alexander certainly had a gargantuan sexual appetite. Yet, beyond these, few charges can be convincingly proved. To be sure, the Borgias distinguished themselves by excelling in those vices in which other men of their time merely dabbled. Nonetheless, it took a concerted effort to turn even highly accomplished Renaissance immorality into a vision of the devil incarnate.

The Borgias would not have enjoyed such transcendent ill-fame had not their real vices been so gleefully broadcast and augmented and affectionately improved upon by Alexander's rival Giuliano della Rovere. Given the appearance of bribery at the conclave that elected Alexander, given the nepotism in which Alexander indulged himself, given the harsh character of Cesare, Della Rovere helped to fashion an icon of evil. The Borgias were Spanish, and, especially in the time of the Spanish Inquisition, it took little effort to arouse a suspicion that the Borgias were possessed of an innate viciousness. Della Rovere was joined by Humanist writers whose sensibilities were genuinely offended by the crude and arrogant display of power Alexander put on, for the Humanists had been dreaming for a century that they were witnessing the rebirth not of Imperial Rome but of Republican Rome. Della Rovere was joined, too, by the Roman barons, notably the Orsinis, who were determined, as always, to keep the power of the pope from threatening their own control of Rome and the surrounding countryside. Ultimately Della Rovere was joined by Cardinal de' Medici and his followers. The disreputable Alexander was elevated to the role of Antichrist, and all Europe relished the lurid gossip. In terms of political expediency, the campaign worked for Della Rovere. The Borgias were kept from establishing as pervasive a control over Italy as they would have liked, and Della Rovere was elected pope in 1503. But, in broader terms, the admitted vices of Alexander, combined with the war on his reputation, ripped aside the façade of pieties and exposed the papacy and the College of Cardinals, too, as a den of carnal, scheming thieves and murderers, men interested in perpetuating their names and families by giving kingdoms and cardinal's hats to their bastard sons, men who would wear the triple crown of the vicar of Christ only to have the majesty of God sanctify their pride and avarice and gluttony and lust. Alexander and his enemies cast themselves with abandon into an orgy of real and rumored vice so stupendous and so exhausting that the Catholic Church has never recovered from it. In discrediting one pope, the princes of the church discredited the papacy. After this, after the Borgia infamy was attached to Saint Peter's chair, no pope could go unchallenged in his claim to be the final arbiter in matters of faith and morals. With excruciatingly fine poetic justice, Cardinal de' Medici, one of the men who helped make a bad man into a monster, would live to experience the vengeance taken on the church for having dragged the vicar of Christ so low.

In Alexander VI, the Florentine historian Francesco Guicciardini wrote, "were united a singular degree of prudence and sagacity, a sound understanding, a wonderful power of persuasion, and an incredible perseverance, vigilance, and dexterity, in whatever he undertook." Alexander was a worthy enemy—but enemy he assuredly was. "But these good qualities," Guicciardini continues, marshaling his resources as he goes, "were more than counterbalanced by his vices. In his manners he was most shameless; wholly divested of sincerity, of decency, and of truth; without fidelity, without religion; in his avarice, immoderate; in his ambition, insatiable; in his cruelty more than barbarous; with a most ardent desire of exalting his numerous children, by whatever means it might be accomplished; some of whom (that depraved instruments might not be wanting for depraved purposes) were not less detestable than their father." It is fit that a Florentine should criticize a man for being *immoderate* in his avarice. The charges could be made against most of the princes of the church—all but immoderation, which was the worst charge a Florentine might lodge in that day when the balance and grace of ancient Greece and Rome provided an esthetic morality against which no transgression could be pardoned.

In retrospect, the Italian cardinals found that Borgia had been immoral and ambitious all his life. But, for some reason, they had not noticed those traits until it suited them to discredit the new pope. As a Spaniard, Borgia had naturally acquired an array of Spanish benefices. Surprisingly, he had also been granted some essential benefices in Italy and several fortresses and a group of villages and the abbey of Fossanova around Rome, which gave him a powerful hold on the routes going in and out of the city. With these strategic strongholds and his office as vice-chancellor, he was the richest and most powerful cardinal in the college. Guicciardini assigned him the attributes of vigilance and dexterity; Alexander must have possessed the qualities to a remarkable degree to have been given such benefices and offices by previous popes who were themselves intent on building their own dynasties.

By virtue of having such riches, Borgia was in a superb position to be elected pope—for smaller riches must be traded for greater ones, and it was the custom for newly elected popes to divest themselves of their old benefices when they assumed the tiara. This, partisans of Borgia hasten to point out, is not bribery but simply tradition. Thus, to keep the jealous Roman barons content, Alexander divided up among the Cardinals Orsini, Colonna, and Savelli the abbey of Subiaco, the castles of Soriano and Civita Castellana, including twenty towns, the bishoprics of Cartagena, Majorca, and Porto, and some smaller plums. To Sforza he gave the new palace that Sforza had so enviously admired, the town of

Nepi, and some other favors including the office of vice-chancellor. To Riario he gave the huge palace that Sforza vacated and the office of cardinal-chamberlain. He scattered other tidbits and baubles among the others, and it was said that only five cardinals emerged empty-handed. One of them, of course, was Della Rovere.

Having lavished these gifts on his erstwhile colleagues, Alexander announced that Juan Borgia Lanzol was to be made a cardinal and Cesare Borgia was to be made archbishop of Valencia and a cardinal, and it was learned that matches with the Italian aristocracy were being arranged for three other offspring. Before the Borgias were finished, two of Alexander's sons were dukes of Gandía, one prince of Squillace, one duke of Camerino, and his daughter Lucrezia was married off in political consummations first to a Sforza, then to Alfonso d'Aragona, and finally to Alfonso d'Este. The ambassador from Ferrara noted "ten papacies would not be sufficient to satisfy this swarm of relatives."

Cardinal de' Medici looked about himself in Rome—at the ravenous swarm of Borgias, at the implacable hostility of Della Rovere toward the pope—and he discreetly packed up and moved back to Florence to place himself at a safe distance from Rome's warring factions. From the security of Florence the cardinal commenced to play the time-honored Medici game of dealing cordially with all factions simultaneously. In this period of his life, the cardinal would develop a fine sense of amiable vacillation and good-humored procrastination that would become his political style for the rest of his life. Playing both sides against the middle, he plied a sinuous course through the treacherous politics of his time, promising here, demurring there, refusing no one, and always intent upon advancing his family. With his approval, Cardinal della Rovere arranged the sale of Francesco Cibò's castles to Virginio Orsini. Commanding, as they did, several of the routes into Rome, the castles were crucial to the control of the city; and, when Alexander learned of the sale, he was enraged. Yet, while Cardinal de' Medici dealt quietly with Della Rovere, he always assured the pope of his loyalty, and he maintained an alliance with the pope's allies, the Sforzas of Milan. To be sure, he had a secret understanding with the pope's other enemy, King Ferrante of Naples, but this was counterbalanced with other secret understandings with Ferrante's enemy Charles VIII of France. He maintained friendly relationships with everyone, in secret, and supported everyone, in secret, and it does not appear that anyone resented his behavior, for he was the most agreeable young man in Italy, however deucedly vague and difficult to pin down he might be.

During the reign of Alexander, the Medici fortunes would reach their lowest point ever, and it is a measure of the cardinal's subtlety and persistence that he was able to restore the Medici family and raise it to its greatest station. In the end, the cardinal turned out to be the most brilliant politican the Medici family produced. It seems all but inconceivable that, shrewd as he was on behalf of his family, he should have made such a resounding blunder on behalf of the church. Unfortunately, while he was receiving his political education during Alexander's reign, he was also receiving a religious education at the same time from Girolamo Savonarola, an education that would instill in him all the wrong instincts when it came to dealing with religious reformers.

Girolamo Savonarola was born in Ferrara in 1452. A weak and brooding boy of sudden and savage passions, he had fallen in love at the age of nineteen, had been rebuffed, and had been so shattered by the rebuff that he had fled his home to lock himself in a monastery. From the monastery he wrote his father to explain what had moved him to join the Dominicans: "first, the great misery of the world, the iniquities of men, the rapes, adulteries, larcenies, pride, idolatries, and cruel blasphemies which have brought the world so low that there is no longer anyone who does good; hence more than once a day I have sung this verse, weeping: 'Ah, flee the lands of the unfeeling, the shores of the grasping flee!' "

Years later, when Pico della Mirandola heard Savonarola preach, he encouraged Lorenzo to bring the friar to Florence to give him a home from which he could make his sallies against the vices of the church. A man of no profound convictions himself, Pico was intrigued by the passionate friar. Savonarola arrived in Florence in 1489, and his manner in the pulpit was harsh, violent, and terrifying. He roared of God's impending revenge on Florence for its reprobate ways. He foretold deaths and famines and plagues, spoke of invasions and wracking calamities that would befall the unrepentent. And he called up the images of a hell broiling with the screams of tormented sinners. Thousands flocked to his sermons and overflowed the church where he preached. Pico, Ficino, Poliziano, Botticelli—all came to hear, to tremble, and to believe. Sixty years later, Michelangelo would say that he could still hear ringing in his ears that chill, direful voice.

While Savonarola railed against the vices of the church and the vices of the Florentine aristocracy, the politicians in Italy fumbled their way toward making one of his predictions, that of invasion, come true. In the struggle between the pope and other contending forces in Italy, Lodovico Sforza of Milan sensed danger in a surprising new alliance between Alexander and Ferrante of Naples, an alliance formalized by the marriage of Jofre Borgia and Sancia d'Aragona. While the Medicis smiled on all sides, Lodovico worried that he could get no definite commitment of support from Florence. Thus he turned to Charles VIII of France and invited him to enter Italy with the support of Milan and press his claim to Naples.

Charles has been described eloquently by Frederick Baron Corvo: "He was a self-conceited little abortion, this Christian King, of the loosest morals even for a king . . . with a fiery birthflare round his left eye, and twelve toes to his feet hidden in splayed shoes . . . and, like all vain little men, he was anxious to cut a romantic and considerable figure." Whether his splayed shoes in fact hid twelve toes is subject to debate, but there can be no doubt that Charles cut a pathetic figure. Still, he must have felt grand when he passed through Grenoble at the head of 60,000 well-disciplined troops and the finest of artillery. He crossed the Alps toward the end of August, 1494, and was welcomed at

50

Turin by Bianca, widow of the Duke of Savoy, with festivals and a court so heavily bejewelled that Charles promptly borrowed some trinkets and pawned them for an extra 12,000 ducats traveling money. Next he swooped down upon Chieri, where he was welcomed by an assemblage of what was proudly touted as the most beautiful women in Italy who crowned him "Champion of the Honor of Ladies." At Asti, he was feted by Lodovico Sforza and his duchess Beatrice d'Este and provided with a choice selection of courtesans. War in the Renaissance was not always a mere succession of tedious sieges.

By the end of October the French forces had sacked and pillaged several towns and arrived at Sarzana, one of Florence's outlying citadels. By now, since they had vandalized some defenseless towns, their reputation as ferocious warriors had been heralded throughout Italy. The Medicis prepared to deal on all sides. Paolo Orsini was dispatched to garrison Sarzana. The King of Naples was written to prepare him for whatever concessions the Medici might have to make. And Piero de' Medici, thinking to imitate the sort of diplomatic tour de force that his father commonly tossed off between writing carnival songs, rode out to meet the king. Writing to the city fathers that he would gladly risk his own life to save the republic ("I shall either return to the satisfaction of ourselves and the city, or lose my life in the attempt"), he took to horse in proper heroic style. Yet, where Lorenzo had courage and boldness, Piero had only bravado. Monsieur de Rienne, Charles' chamberlain, and Brissonet, his general, met with Piero and first demanded the surrender of Sarzana. Piero consented to that with such alacrity that the French then asked to have Pisa, Leghorn, and Pietrasanta delivered up to the king with the understanding that they would be returned to Florence after Charles had successfully concluded his campaign in Italy. To this demand, too, Piero bowed, and the French were astonished to have the road to Rome and Naples open so easily before them. Mastering their incredulity, they then demanded a forced loan of 200,000 ducats from Piero, and when they got that as well, they

51

asked for nothing else—whether they could think of nothing else they wanted or whether they choked on contempt for Piero we do not know.

Paolo Orsini, making a brave show at Sarzana, must have been flabbergasted. Florence's bargaining position had been thrown away for nothing. Florence might have been the ally of France. Florence might have wrung concessions from the French for safe conduct through its territories. But Piero had given all away and had given up a humiliating tribute of 200,000 ducats besides. When the Florentines heard of the settlement, they sent out another embassy, this time including Fra Girolamo Savonarola, to arrange new terms. But Charles had reached his understanding with Piero de' Medici, an understanding that let his generals know how little prepared Florence was to defend herself, and he treated the second set of ambassadors coldly. Charles did not escape, however, without chastisement from Savonarola: "Know yourself for an instrument in the hands of the Lord, Who has sent you to heal the woes of Italy and to reform the prostrate Church. But if you do not show yourself just and pitiful, if you do not respect Florence and her people, if you forget the work for which the Lord has sent you, then He will choose another in your place, and His wrath engulf you. I speak in the name of the Lord." Charles must have found the speech quaint. His army prepared to march through Florence on its way to Rome.

Piero rode back to Florence with Paolo Orsini and his troops, apparently to fight the war against the Florentines that he could not bring himself to fight against the French. Back in Florence he went with several attendants to the palace of justice, presumably to explain his actions to the leading citizens there. But the magistrates met him at the gates and barred his entrance, offering to admit him by the postern if he would enter alone. He started to leave; then his friends prevailed upon him to try to storm the gate. The gate was slammed, the gathering crowd started up with catcalls, and some stones were thrown. Piero imperiously drew his sword and, irresolute to the end—put it back into its sheath.

Piero and his friends escaped to the Medici palace, barred the entrances, and armed themselves. Then the mettle of the cardinal showed. As his older brother cowered at home, the nineteen-year-old cardinal went into the streets to talk to the people and to rally allies by the cry of *"Palle! Palle!"*—the old war cry alluding to the Medici coat of arms. But the old Medici charm, that intricate magic tapestry woven by several generations, had worn too thin. As Savonarola cried of God's vengeance and mobs restlessly roamed the streets in search of courage and encouragement to attack, Piero and his brother Giuliano dashed from the city and rode off on the road to Bologna. The cardinal held out for only a few more hours before he donned the habit of a Franciscan monk and slipped out of the city at night to join his brothers in exile. The Medici palace was assaulted, its rooms plundered, its collections of manuscripts scattered, and paintings and statues defaced and smashed. A week afterward, Charles VIII entered Florence in triumph and stayed in the Medici palace. What the mobs had left Charles tidily swept up; he picked the palace clean before he left.

First from Bologna, then from more-distant Pitigliano, then from Castello, finally from his exile's refuge in Urbino, the cardinal heard the reports of Savonarola's speeches from the pulpit: "Oh my people, you know that I have never wanted to intervene in matters of state: do you think I would do so now, if I did not see that it was necessary for the health of our souls?" And so the cardinal heard the voice of reform. It was clear, as Savonarola rose from spiritual purger to political dictator of Florence, that his inspiration was sincere. He was no opportunist. He had no family dynasty to advance. He cared not at all for wealth. He was a new sort of political opponent for the cardinal, and new strategies would be required to undermine the base of the preacher's power. One had only to know from whence the power derived. On that mystery the cardinal meditated.

On the dubious assumption that a weak friend is better than a firm enemy, Charles VIII toyed with schemes to have Piero de' Medici reinstated in Florence. Piero, by now ensconced in Venice, received dispatches from the French assuring him of the king's support if he would show himself near Florence. With absolute breathtaking milksoppery, Piero went cap-in-hand to the Venetian Senate to ask their advice. The Venetians cared little for the success of France and took positive delight in the tumult in Florence, and so they advised Piero to wait. Venice, they promised, would support his return when the ideal opportunity presented itself. Piero left reassured, and Venetian spies were directed to watch him day and night to make certain he did not attempt to leave the city. How much the cardinal had to do with all these mistakes is unclear. Piero, the eldest son, was the head of the family, and it would have been in his character to act without the advice of his canny younger brother. Yet, whether the cardinal shared in making all these errors or not, he was no doubt learning a great deal by watching. In the course of the next several years his notions of political competition would expand to encompass all of Europe and his notions of reformers would contract to see only the Savonarola archetype.

Charles careered through Italy, plundering here, parading there. Before he reached Rome one of his raiding parties had the good fortune to capture one of Alexander VI's mistresses. Thus, even before he reached the Vatican, Charles was able to wrest a ransom of 3,000 scudi out of the pope for the safe return of the young lady. With this extra dividend in his pocket, Charles entered Rome in a cheerful display of majesty and was permitted safe passage through the papal states to Naples. Approaching Naples, the king sent two men ahead to the fortress of Monte San Giovanni to demand surrender of the fortress and provisions for the French troops. Sent back without their noses or their ears, Charles' bleeding messengers aroused the king's pique. Several days later the French cannon blasted the fortress and Charles was not finished with it until every soldier there was dead. Moving on to Naples itself, Charles' two-pronged offensive of pomp and ruthlessness won him the kingdom, and the French settled down to dancing and feasting and raping the women. According to the contemporary writer Bernardino Corio, the Italians later found a book that had been in the king's possession: "A book was found in which at different times have been shown many naked women whom the French had raped. The king kept it with him as a souvenir."

Charles' comic-opera war in Italy ended in the autumn of 1495, when he crossed back over the Alps with ragtag Italian forces nipping at his heels. His army was reduced to a fourth of its original strength. The ruling forces he left in Naples proved incapable of holding out for long. And while venereal disease swept the peninsula, the French whined of the *mal de Naples*, while Italians complained bitterly that Charles' army had introduced a new disease, which they called the *mal Francese*. Real people had been slaughtered in this false war; yet, it might still have been considered a passing *divertissement* for Italy had not this invasion by France irretrievably plunged Italy into European politics. In the past—as indeed they would continue to be in the future—Italians were notorious for fighting among themselves. However, while now Milan might fight Naples, or the Colonna the Orsini, or the Borgias the Della Roveres, a new element had been added: the threat of foreign invasion. Now the idle threat of bringing France in to fight an Italian war would not be so lightly taken. Now Italy was to be the battleground for France—and the other looming international power, Spain. The political world would never again be so provincial for Italy, and rivalry even outside the Italian city states must be considered and brought into the calculations about Italian politics; even unrest in so remote a place as Germany would now have an effect on Rome.

Savonarola might have survived had he not been seduced by the sound of his own thrilling voice and come to depend for his very nourishment on the adulation of the crowd. Magnificent actor that he was, he could not resist the temptation to move closer and closer to the center of the stage until he was a one-man show, extending himself farther and farther to excite the crowd to that fine, roaring ecstasy of approval. The church had seen many reformers come and go and had treated them with respect, had admired many of these good men, had elevated some of them to sainthood—as long as they had not established any independent power. But Savonarola's sermons had had to become increasingly extreme to hold the attention of his audience. And as his sermons more daringly attacked the corruption of the church, he found that he had adherents outside Florence. The Sultan of Turkey, an old foe of Christendom, read copies of the sermons that had been published. The Duke of Milan became an ardent disciple, and the Milanese ambassador wrote to the duke that "the friar is now master of the people and can dictate its devotion to Your Lordship."

The report that Savonarola controlled Florence was his death warrant. He was no longer simply a religious zealot; he was now, wittingly or no, a politician, and the Italian princes sought to bring him into their power struggle. Would he join the new Italian league against the French? No, he thought, "the Florentines do not wish to enter the League, fearing that the Duke and the other powers might aim to destroy the popular government and set up a tyrant in Florence." The remark was swiftly reported to Alexander VI. Savonarola may have been giving a private opinion, naïvely supposing it would be taken as such. But as the Florentine government persisted in refusing to join forces against the French, the pope concluded that Savonarola was intentionally dabbling in politics.

In 1497 the friar's monastery was placed under the jurisdiction of a new congregation administered by the pious Cardinal Caraffa. With that, Savonarola was put on notice that his inflammatory sermons were being attended in Rome, though since Caraffa himself favored reform of the church, the rebuke was a gentle one. Savonarola took umbrage, however, and a mild counterattack turned into a violent excoriation of the church as the friar worked himself up into a frenzy during his Lenten sermons that year: "Come here, wretched Church; I gave you, saith the Lord, fair vestments, and you have made idols of them. You have given my vessels to vainglory and my sacraments to simony; in your lechery you are a shameless whore; you are worse than a beast, you are an abominable monster. Once you blushed for your sins, but not now. The priests used to call their sons nephews; now they are not nephews, but sons, sons plain and simple!" The indictment was not obscure: simony, lechery, nepotism. These were Della Rovere's charges against Alexander, and Della Rovere was in France at the moment calling for a general council to investigate Alexander's election and consider reform of the church. In Savonarola's vision of things, he may have been making moral charges; in Rome they sounded like a political platform.

"My sword shall be over your sons, your brothels, your whores, your palaces, and my judgment shall be manifest. . . . Up, up, send out your couriers! Do you think that we only are good, that God has no servants elsewhere? Jesus Christ has many, and there are plenty in Spain, in France, in Germany, who stand listening and lamenting this infirmity. . . ."

Alexander's advisers urged excommunication, but Alexander had no wish to risk defeat in direct confrontation. Nor were all of his options exhausted. The previous year Piero de' Medici had tried to take Florence by storm with troops led by Virginio Orsini. Orsini had abandoned the project before he reached Florence when a more lucrative expedition for his mercenary force presented itself. Piero, as Alexander knew, was available for a raid on Florence. With the pope's concurrence, and with a promise of support from Venice, Piero rode off once again, this time with 1,300 men, to storm his native city. Partisans within the walls were alerted to expect the attack early one April morning, and it was arranged that the Medici supporters would attack together, from within and without. Piero's forces arrived several miles outside Florence on the evening before the appointed day and made camp for the night. On the following day a torrential rainstorm held up their progress to the walls of Florence. Inside the city, their friends rose up—and were packed off to jail. The town gates were secured and the Florentine troops held ready to repel Piero. The drenched Medici forces stood forlornly outside Florence, waiting for a sign to enter, and as night fell they stood there still, hunched over their wet and shivering horses. They debated for four hours whether to ride on the city alone; then, their martial spirit spent in argument, they turned and rode away in the drizzle.

Alexander VI cannot have been disappointed by this dismal maneuver. If Piero had not conquered the town, he had filled it with anxiety. It was not a full-fledged attack; it was a warning. The Florentine government responded to it by closing all the churches in Florence on the pretext of fear of spreading plague, but in fact to deprive Savonarola of his pulpit. The friar gave one more sermon before the churches were closed, and a band of young troublemakers taunted him, fights broke out, and Savonarola was rushed from the church back to the monastery. The Arrabbiati, an anti-Savonarola party that was growing in strength, tried to force through the Florentine assembly a resolution censuring Savonarola as the cause of Florence's unrest. Failing in that, they wrote to Rome to ask for a bull of excommunication. Now, for a divided, tumultuous, violently confused city, Alexander provided a firm statement. The Holy Father pronounced Savonarola a "son of iniquity" and excommunicated him, cut him off root and branch from the Catholic Church, deprived him of the right to administer the sacraments or speak from the pulpit, banished him from the Christian world. Not defeat, not death, but eternal obliteration—that was Savonarola's punishment for being a bad politician. The papal bull of excommunication was drafted for Alexander by Fra Mariano de Gennazzano, an old pet who had been kept by the Medici family for years.

"This excommunication," Savonarola cried, as all the excommunicated would ever cry, "is invalid before God and man." His own party still controlled the government in Florence, and they appealed to the pope to lift the ban. But having set the Florentines one on the other, the pope settled back in silence.

The two parties in Florence fought. Savonarola thrashed spasmodically first one way and then the other. It was a matter of individual conscience, he insisted. Of course, he looked to the Holy See for guidance. But Rome was a monstrous Babylon. Then, in abject fawning, "Holy Father, I kiss the feet of Your Holiness as a child, grieving at having incurred the displeasure of his father. . . . I humbly crave forgiveness. . . ." But forgiveness of whom? Of one who preaches contrary to the scriptures? "He therefore that commands us contrary to charity, which is the fullness of our law, anathema sit!" Let the pope be excommunicated, then! Savonarola writhed in torment. It had long been his rhetorical style in the pulpit to ask himself questions his congregation might be presumed to think of. Now the dialogue turned inward, and Savonarola's two voices answered doubt with greater doubt. The pope was a villain—but what if it was the devil who drove Savonarola to attack the church at its very center? A man could not act contrary to his conscience and the manifest teachings of the church, but what if his visions and his transports and his certainty that he communed with God, what if it was inspired by the Devil? The rage he had usually vented in the pulpit turned in on him and now consumed him. The papal bull of excommunication set Savonarola off alone. And alone with his terrors, he careened back and forth from attack to utter submission. He seemed to beg for someone to stop him. He asked only that his questions be considered—he would accept any answers so long as someone would listen to his doubts and fears. But the pope was resolutely silent.

Tortured beyond endurance, Savonarola called for a general council of bishops to reform the church, and he went so far as to write secretly to the sovereigns of France, England, Spain, and Hungary. A copy of the letter was pirated by Milanese spies and sent on to the pope. To call for a general council was a recognized tactic in Vatican power politics; Della Rovere had been calling for one ever since Alexander's election. Savonarola's correspondence confirmed the pope's apprehensions that Savonarola was in that enemy camp vaguely clustered about Della Rovere. It does not seem to have occurred to Alexander that the friar might be crying in public for someone, anyone, to answer his private doubts. But the pope was saved from responding to this fresh threat: The *coup de grâce* was administered to Savonarola by his most devoted follower, Fra Domenico, a simple monk who was tortured by none of the doubts that ravaged his mentor. Challenged by a monk of the Franciscan order to an ordeal by fire, Fra Domenico promptly accepted. Savonarola was swept up in the fiasco, and although none of the monks entered the flames (each side objected to one technicality or the other until the government put a stop to the spectacle), the humiliation was public and complete. When the monks returned to their monasteries, they left behind a throng of Florentines who had waited in the Piazza Signoria all day to see the ordeal, and the crowd was exasperated.

On the following day people gathered at Savonarola's monastery, San Marco. They spent the afternoon shouting and milling about, the evening setting fires at the doors of the monastery to burn them down, and the night smashing windows and banking the fires higher and higher. They would give Savonarola an ordeal by fire of their own sort. But the signoria intervened and called for Savonarola's arrest, and in the middle of that fiery night the friar walked out into the mob who bore him, with a minimum of finger-twisting and kicking, to the signoria's palace.

Alexander VI wrote the signoria that he was pleased by the way Savonarola had been handled, that the Florentines' request for a 10 percent tax on church property might well be considered now, and that he consented to a civil trial for the monk. Alexander had provided a crucial and well-timed blow at Savonarola with his excommunication; he was content to have the civil authorities accept whatever onus might be attached to finally doing him in. The rack was applied as a matter of course, and Savonarola proved to be exceptionally susceptible to it. Nonetheless, it took ten days and fourteen sessions on the rack to elicit a confession acceptable to the punctilious tribunal. When it was over, Savonarola and Fra Domenico and another disciple were hanged and burned at the stake in the Piazza Signoria to the intense pleasure of the spectators.

Savonarola, driven by his own unknowable furies, had summoned up the demons that pursued many Florentines in that anxious time of plague, domestic turmoil, foreign invasion, and the splintering and cracking of old traditions. He had predicted the utter collapse of the civilization he saw about him, the death of princes, the liberation of the spirit, a new City of God on earth. Unfortunately for the prophet, as his expectations became more apocalyptic, his followers saw nothing that was either as bad or as good as he judged or predicted. And they took their vengeance on the man for rousing such extreme expectations only to leave them disappointed. Something to surpass and redeem all the friar's sermons was called for—a miracle, a sign from God in the ordeal by fire. Failing that, some other extreme was called for—the blood sacrifice, the death of the deceiver. In classic Aristotelian terms (the Humanists should have been more pleased than they were) the flaw was built into the character of Savonarola. He succeeded in arousing hopes of the Apocalypse, and the Apocalypse destroyed him.

Alexander VI, and Cardinal de' Medici, may well have perceived that Savonarola would destroy himself. Alexander said he believed the friar to be motivated not by malice but by a "certain simplemindedness and zeal." Relying on that simplemindedness, he permitted the monk to go to an irredeemable extreme; then he cut the monk off from the church at the proper tactical moment and made his feeling clear to the Florentine government. At the end, he let the civil courts do the church's work. It was a well-tested method for dealing with reformers who got out of hand, and it was a method that would be used again.

That the church needed reform escaped no one. The stories of Alexander's court gave even the ruthless and hedonistic Italian courtiers an uneasy feeling. It was said that Ramiro d'Orco, whom Cesare appointed governor of Cesena, one night called for a flagon of wine, and when the page tripped and spilled some of the wine on Ramiro's feet, the governor took the boy and threw him into the fireplace. Taking hold of a halberd, Ramiro pinned the boy to the burning logs until he was cooked to death. Then the governor called for another flagon of wine. After Ramiro had brought civil order to Cesena, Cesare decided to relax his rule. So he rode into town one evening, and several days later the citizens found Ramiro's body in the snow. His head was perched atop a pike nearby.

On another occasion one Girolamo Marciani published a *Letter to Silvio Savelli* in which Cesare was subjected to a set of insulting epigrams. Marciani had his right hand cut off and his tongue cut out. When someone mentioned it to the pope, Alexander replied, "What can we do? The Duke means well; but he does not know how to bear insults. We often have advised him to follow Our example and to let the mob say what it will: but he answered Us with choler that he intended to give these scribblers a lesson in good manners."

Opponents in Senigallia were invited to dinner and, after dinner, put to the rack and ceremonially strangled in the courtyard. Cesare's brother-in-law was stabbed on the steps of St. Peter's, and when he survived that, Cesare strangled him where he lay recovering in the papal palace. When men died they were presumed poisoned—at the hands of the Borgias. When bodies were found floating in the Tiber, it was assumed Cesare had thrown them there. And when there was some confusion whether Giovanni Borgia was the son of Cesare or Alexander, the gossips said he was Alexander's son—by Alexander's daughter Lucrezia.

The Borgias provided inspiration for gossip of all kinds. Johann Burchard, the pope's master of ceremonies, recorded that on one Sunday evening "Don Cesare Borgia gave supper in his apartment in the apostolic palace, with fifty decent prostitutes or courtesans in attendance, who after the meal danced with the servants and others there, first fully dressed and then naked. Following the supper too, lampstands holding lighted candles were placed on the floor and chestnuts strewn about, which the prostitutes, naked and on their hands and knees, had to pick up as they crawled in and out among the lampstands. The pope, Don Cesare and Donna Lucrezia were all present to watch. Finally prizes were offered—silken doublets, pairs of shoes, hats and other garments—for those men who were most successful with the prostitutes." Indeed, there were enough true stories about the Borgias to keep the gossips in a fever. And whatever was made up—well, it was hard to *dis*prove, after all, and certainly sounded plausible.

During his conflict with Savonarola, in June, 1497, Alexander invested his favorite son, Juan Borgia of Aragon, Duke of Gandia, and captain-general of the church, with the Duchy of Benevento, the cities of Pontecorvo and Terracina, and their surrounding territories. It was on this son that Alexander depended to perpetuate his dynasty, and he lavished favors on the boy, who was at the time just twenty-one years old, so that Don Juan was envied as much by members of his own family as by others. On Wednesday, June 14, Don Juan and Cesare had dinner with their mother, Vanozza Catanei, to celebrate Don Juan's latest advancement.

After dinner, as Burchard recorded in his diary, the two brothers "left with only one or two servants to accompany them. They rode together almost to Cardinal Ascanio's palace . . . and there Don Juan obtained permission to leave his brother on the plea that he wanted to go in pursuit of further pleasure. . . . Don Juan therefore withdrew, dismissing even those few servants that he had, except for one footman and a masked man who had joined the duke during supper, and who had, moreover, visited him almost every day at the Vatican for a month or so beforehand . . . together they rode to the Piazza degli Ebrei. There Don Juan dismissed his one remaining footman . . . the duke left the groom and galloped away with his masked friend seated behind him on the mule to an unknown place, where he was murdered and then thrown into the river . . . to that particular place, next to a conduit, there was a direct way . . . by which horse teams were accustomed to take the sewage and rubbish and dump them in the river."

That is all that is known about the murder of Don Juan. A day passed, and then Alexander become anxious about his son. A wood dealer told some of the pope's servants that he had seen several men, one on a white horse, throw a body into the river. "When the Pope's servants asked him why he had not revealed such a crime to the city governor," Burchard recorded, "his reply was that during his time he had seen a hundred bodies thrown into the river at that point on different nights and he had never thought anything of it." The river was dragged, and Don Juan's body, slashed with nine dagger wounds, one in his throat, was brought up. The pope neither ate nor slept for three days but raged and cried and fainted, only to awake with convulsive, echoing wails that terrified his servants and family.

There was no shortage of suspects. An Orsini had been jailed by the pope and died, possibly of poison; it was a sufficient motive for the Orsinis to retaliate. In the year after Don Juan's death, the rumor went around that Cesare had killed his brother. Others speculated the murderer could have been a cuckolded husband or the father of a girl Don Juan had visited that night. Alexander appointed a commission to investigate the crime, and the inquiry went on for several weeks, when the pope abruptly stopped it. Whether he discovered the murderer and did not want his hand forced to punish him (the suspicion favored by those who wish to blame Cesare for the crime) or he had simply become too sick to wish to know any more remains obscure.

Alexander gloomily interpreted the murder of his son as God's judgment on his own sins, and he appointed a commission of six of the most upstanding cardinals to reform the church, beginning at the top. Alexander apparently took a hand himself in framing the proposals for reform. The reforms called for an end to the sale of church offices, for greater restraint in the dress and gourmandizing of the papal court, for the reading of the Bible to replace masques and dancing girls at dinners, for a limitation on the incomes of the cardinals, for a myriad of housekeeping and administrative changes that would have gone far to make Rome look less like Babylon. But the pope depended on income from the sale of offices to help finance Vatican projects. And the cardinals could hardly be expected to approve of depriving themselves of income. There were so many vested interests to oppose reform in any direction. Then, too, only a general council could properly develop a program of reform for all levels of the church, and a general council was a dangerous element in any time—let alone with Della Rovere ready to turn one to his advantage just then—for the threat they held to the central authority of the pope. Certainly a general council would play havoc with Alexander's dynastic ambitions. The difficulties depressed Alexander; he lost interest and returned to thoughts of strengthening the position of his family.

The Medicis tried once more, in vain once more, to recapture their place in Florence. Charles VIII of France died, and the new king, Louis XII, decided to enter Italy again to impress French rule upon Naples. As Italian rulers aligned themselves in preparation for this new invasion, Cardinal de' Medici found himself without a secure haven and determined to leave Italy altogether. With his cousin Giulio and ten other companions, all of them dressed like mendicant friars, he set out for Venice and from there to Germany and France.

No record of Cardinal de' Medici's impressions of Germany survives, yet a later Italian traveler voiced a typical Latin reaction to "the horror of huge forests, deep marshes and barren plains. Winds and snow whip that unhappy land; the soil is like iron and encrusted with ice. . . . A barbarous people shut themselves up in warm houses and laugh at the Arctic blasts, gaming and drinking far into the night."

Cardinal de' Medici had grown up in a world of bright, illuminated manuscripts, of graceful paintings by Botticelli, of sonnets set to music. When his family commissioned paintings, they showed a peculiar fondness for the theme of the Adoration of the Magi. In Germany wealthy patrons were more likely to commission the Last Judgment. Germany was a harsh country, with a harsh language, populated by a roughly clothed and darkly moody people who produced that master of brooding black-and-white woodcuts, Albrecht Dürer. Cardinal de' Medici may have been offended by the Germans. It is certain that he did not understand them. They would ever call to his mind the image of loud-mouthed, uncouth barbarians.

The cardinal and his retinue passed from Germany to France, where they were instantly arrested. Not until letters of reassurance arrived from Piero de' Medici, then standing by hopefully in the French camp at Milan, were they released. From Marseilles, the company set sail to return to Italy. They fetched up near Genoa and proceeded overland to Savona, where Giuliano della

Rovere had settled. At Savona the three future popes—Giovanni, Guilio, and Della Rovere—settled down to a long dinner and to talk of politics and the church.

Having reassured Della Rovere of his faithful alliance, Cardinal de' Medici soon after hurried to Rome to reaffirm his alliance with Della Rovere's enemy Alexander. While the cardinal ingratiated himself with the pope, Piero de' Medici met Cesare Borgia, then idly in camp with his troops considering what territory he might next assault, and Giuliano de' Medici presented himself at the court of Louis XII. The three brothers persuaded the three most powerful leaders of that time to join forces to restore the Medici to Florence. Cesare approached Florence with 7,000 foot soldiers and 800 horses. Near Barberino he was joined by a contingent from Bologna. He sent envoys ahead to Florence to present his terms for staying the attack and then, unexpectedly, Alexander ordered him to retreat. Louis XII, it appears, had second thoughts about the expedition or had not been informed what a crucial role Cesare was to play in the expedition. Fearing that the restored Medicis would owe too much to the Borgias and that the Borgias would thus be too powerful a force throughout Italy, Louis had told his general to attack Cesare with all his troops if the Borgias refused to accede to his requests to withdraw.

The Medicis stood back once more to watch as Cesare seized Piombino, Urbino, and Camerino, as he negotiated his own personal alliance with Louis XII, as Piero Soderini was elected "gonfalonier for life" in Florence, and as Alexander proposed to the College of Cardinals that Cesare adopt the title of King of Romagna and Umbria. Just as the Borgias seemed on the verge of ruling all, they lost all. On August 18, 1503, Alexander VI died. Both he and Cesare had been ill for several days, and the rumor quickly spread that they had mistakenly taken poison meant for one of their enemies. It was rumored, too, that Cesare had poisoned the pope because they had had a falling out over Cesare's increasing closeness to Louis XII and his independent little wars of conquest. According to this story, Cesare took a small, nonlethal dose of poison to throw suspicion off himself. Burchard recorded in his diary that Cesare sent several "retainers to close all the doors that gave access to the Pope's rooms. One of the men took out a dagger and threatened to cut Cardinal Casanova's throat and to throw him out of the window unless he handed over the keys to all the Pope's treasures. Terrified, the cardinal surrendered the keys, whereupon the others entered the room next to the papal apartment and seized all the silver that they found, together with two coffers containing about a hundred thousand ducats. At four o'clock in the afternoon, they opened the doors and proclaimed that the Pope was dead."

Alexander may well have died of poison, or he may well have died of the fever that afflicted Romans every summer. Whatever caused his death also caused the downfall of Cesare. Bedridden for the critical few days following the pope's death, Cesare was unable to command his partisans, and the enemies of the Borgias rapidly descended on the city. Those who survived of the Orsini and Colonna factions hunted down Borgia partisans and killed them. Della Rovere returned to town, and the cardinals asserted their control of Rome. Divided by many factions, the conclave could not agree on a new pope and so elected the ailing eighty-four-year-old Cardinal Piccolomini, who died in less than a month. That brief interim gave Della Rovere just enough time to employ the device for which he had so castigated Alexander, and so, following several weeks of lavish bribery, Della Rovere was elected pope and took the name Julius II. The new pope kept Cesare befuddled—first by confirming him in his position as captain-general of the church and sending him out on a papal expedition, then by recalling and jailing him, then by sending him to Naples and permitting the Spanish king to jail him. Cesare was broken quickly, and he finally died, in an insignificant battle, in 1507. With him died all the hopes of the Borgia dynasty.

On December 29, 1503, the vagabond pretender to Florentine rule, Piero de' Medici, met his death. Escaping from yet another ill-conceived adventure, Piero and several others had set sail from Gaeta, in the northern reaches of the kingdom of Naples, with four heavy pieces of artillery. The weight of the weapons and the numbers of men trying to escape aboard the ship caused the vessel to founder, and Piero's body fetched up on shore several days later.

In 1504, at the age of twenty-eight, Cardinal de' Medici became head of his family. He had learned much of the politics of the church and of Europe, much of how dynasties are made and lost, much of reformers. Exiled from his native city, his resources from Medici lands and banking interests cut off, impoverished by the misguided attempts at restoration, he and his family were at their nadir. Yet the cardinal had all his hard-earned knowledge, and he had his friend Pope Julius II. Patient, genial, shrewd, the young cardinal pawned his silver plate and invited his friends to dinner.

IV

MARTIN'S VOCATION

IN April, 1501, "Martinus Ludher ex Mansfeld" entered as
a student in the Faculty of the Arts at the University of Erfurt. A walled city of fine buildings set in the midst of fertile
hills, Erfurt had a population of 20,000 souls. Boasting twenty
cloisters, twenty-three churches, thirty-six chapels, and a profusion of religious orders, including the Franciscans, Dominicans,
and Augustinians, the city was known as little Rome. Just two
blocks away from the Augustinian monastery was the student
hostel of St. George (dubbed the beer bag), where Martin took
his room and board while he attended the university. Like the
other students, he wore a gown and rose every day at four o'clock
and attended his first lectures at six in the morning during the
summer, at seven in winter. He passed through initiation ceremonies in which he was dressed to resemble a pig and then
roughly divested of the costume to symbolize that he was leaving
the brutish and ignorant past. With his lute and his good singing
voice, he gathered a circle of friends and settled down to a college existence that a modern student would find rowdier, more
disciplined, and very much the same. His friends nicknamed
him Philosophus, perhaps because he ruminated a great deal and
was given to periodic slumps into deep depression.

In his first year Martin studied the trivium—grammar, logic,
and rhetoric—and he surpassed most of his peers in his accomplishments in these disciplines. He received his bachelor's degree in
a year and a half and went on to study the quadrivium—geome-

try, mathematics, music, and astronomy—for his master's degree. At some point in his second year he happened on a Bible in the university's library, chained, like all books, to its stand. He had time only to glance at it, but he read the First Book of the Kings and was especially taken with the story of Hannah who lamented that she had no children. In the King James version, the chapter reads:

> Then said Elkanah her husband to her, "Hannah, why weepest thou? and why eatest thou not? and why is thy heart grieved? am not I better to thee than ten sons?"
> So Hannah rose up after they had eaten in Shiloh, and after they had drunk. . . . And she was in bitterness of soul, and prayed unto the Lord, and wept sore. And she vowed a vow, and said, "O Lord of hosts, if thou wilt indeed look on the affliction of thine handmaid, and remember me, and not forget thine handmaid, but wilt give unto thine handmaid a man-child, then I will give him unto the Lord all the days of his life."
> The son Samuel was born to Hannah, and she took him to the Lord to be His priest, and Hannah rejoiced and prayed: "[The Lord] raiseth up the poor out of the dust, and lifteth up the beggar from the dunghill, to set them among princes, and to make them inherit the throne of glory: for the pillars of the earth are the Lord's, and he hath set the world upon them. . . . The adversaries of the Lord shall be broken to pieces; out of heaven shall be thunder upon them: the Lord shall judge the ends of the earth; and he shall give strength unto his king, and exalt the horn of his Anointed."

Why this should have appealed so strongly to Martin we can only guess. The passage has some intriguing elements in it, not least the one that shows Hannah appealing to a source of power above her husband. Martin would solve a problem with his father by similarly "going over his head." And the son, dedicated to the Lord, is "set among princes"—a greater aspiration than even Hans had for his son. Martin could not afford a precious Bible, but he went out and bought a book of sermons, and perhaps in his fits of depression he listened anxiously for the thunder.

His course of study for a master's degree brought Martin under the tutelage of the Nominalists, notably Jodocus Trutvetter and Bartholomew Arnoldi of Usingen. The great debate that raged among scholars at the time was whether divine knowledge and human knowledge could be synthesized in a coherent whole as Thomas Aquinas had attempted in his *Summa Theologica*. The Nominalists insisted that abstractions had no reality: Human knowledge was the result of empirical evidence, and facts existed independently of one another, although their relationships might be determined by syllogistic logic. Divine knowledge, on the other hand, was virtually unknowable by men and certainly existed in a realm beyond reason or verification. Thus human and divine knowledge existed in two separate, unrelatable spheres. The Nominalist teachers at Erfurt, inspired by Gabriel Biel of Tübingen and, more remotely, by William of Occam, plied their students with vast quantities of Aristotelian logic applied to Occamist syllogisms, and Martin absorbed a prodigious amount of the stuff. Even so, although some scholars would see in Luther a docile, young Occamist and a mature anti-Occamist, most of the arguments appear to have given him good intellectual exercise and very little spiritual nourishment. Nonetheless, one truly crucial element of Luther's theology might be traced to the Nominalists: the "sovereign liberty" of God. God was free to condemn or save whomever He willed. No man could merit salvation by good works. No man could presume to know God's will. Later Martin would add, if no man can know God's will, then no man can speak with authority of how men may achieve salvation. Rather, each individual must face God alone.

In the midst of all the syllogisms, as Realists fought Nominalists and Trutvetter parsed Occam, Martin behaved like a good student and debated the academic questions with a rigorous brilliance—and all the while, in his bouts of depression, he came closer and closer to facing God alone.

On January 7, 1505, Martinus Ludher, age twenty-one, graduated second in his class of seventeen and was confirmed a master of arts. His father was overjoyed and put together some hard-earned savings to purchase—it was a fond extravagance—the expensive *Codex Juris Civilis*. Martin was sent back to the law school at Erfurt, while his father talked enthusiastically of arranging an advantageous marriage for the promising young lawyer. Henceforth Hans addressed his son by the formal *Sie* rather than the informal *Du* and insisted that the family do the same.

Martin's lecture classes in the law began on May 19, 1505, and he attended the lectures until the latter part of June. Then his life seemed suddenly walled about by death. A friend died. Legend has it that Martin himself fell and stabbed his leg with his own dagger, though the hazily remembered date would seem to assign the incident to a different period. There is some evidence that the plague broke out in the spring and early summer that year in Erfurt and that some students died of it. Event and legend commingle here, and nothing is certain except that a strange, brooding pall was cast over Martin and he sensed the presence of death all around him.

Martin returned to his home for a visit with his family. And what, his father doubtless demanded, was he doing home? Had Hans fled from every small fear that cropped up, he would not have been where he was. Martin had a career to get on with, and Hans was full of thoughts about the proper marriage for his son. There was no thought of discussing the career: The young man's future was well determined—indeed, from Martin's point of view, too well determined. Martin had not yet thought how he might like to spend his life, and here he was committed to a career he had not considered, his father was arranging a marriage to someone whom Martin might not know, certainly on whom Martin would not be asked to pass. If he were to die, what would he like his life to have been—that of a well-married burgomaster? And where would a well-married burgomaster settle down? In Mansfeld? And whom would he marry? The daughter of a town councilman, or the widow of a well-to-do merchant? And what would Martin achieve in his life? Tormented past, chaotic present, and bleak future fused, a life without choice, a life formed and impelled by a harsh father, a life of respectable oblivion, death of a different but no less real order. All is guesswork. But something of these thoughts must have gone through Martin's mind at the time. Whether he had had a genuine religious calling by this time we do not know. There is no evidence of it. Yet a number of unknown, and unknowable, forces were acting upon him, and in the most immediate sense, Martin Luther rebelled against a father who propelled him into a meaningless destiny.

He started back on the road to Erfurt at the end of June, and he wandered. Then, as he reached Stotternheim, a short distance from Erfurt, on July 2, he was caught in a severe thunderstorm. A thunderbolt struck the ground near him. In terror he fell to his knees and prayed to Saint Anne, the patron saint of miners. "Help me, Saint Anne. I want to become a monk."

When he arrived back in Erfurt, he talked with his friends. Had it been a sign from an angry God who summoned him to the monastery? Was the vow to Saint Anne binding? It was essential that Martin believe himself to have been called by God. He wrote later to his father that he had been "called by heavenly terrors, for not freely or desirously did I become a monk . . . but walled around with the terror and pain of sudden death, I vowed a constrained and necessary vow." The circumstances were all that Martin could have hoped for: The vow had been made to his father's own patron saint, and the promise had been made not for trivial reasons but because Martin had heard the thunder of God the Father, to whom all earthly fathers must bow. If Martin needed a higher imperative to place against the demands of his father, the bolt of lightning most certainly provided it. He disobeyed his father only out of the higher duty to obey Saint Anne and God. Martin could not bring himself to defy his earthly father, but he could make an appeal above and beyond him to his Heavenly Father. The incident taught Martin one of the most essential lessons of his life, and on later occasions, when he was walled around with the terror of being crushed or annihilated, he would appeal to a higher imperative. Whether Martin was in truth acting under God's guidance is infinitely beyond our scope here; what matters is that he honestly felt that he was.

Martin's friends were not all persuaded that his vow was a binding one, but Martin was determined it would be so. It is not every day that an event occurs that can be interpreted as a summons from God, and Martin had great need to seize upon this. He sold all his books, keeping his Virgil and Plautus, and had a farewell meal with his friends on July 16, 1505. "Today you see me," he said, already trying out priestly intonations, "and then, never again."

On July 17, Martin presented himself at the gates of the Augustinian monastery as a hopeful novice. He prostrated himself before the altar, and the prior asked, "What do you seek?" "God's grace and your mercy," Martin responded according to form. The prior then had him stand and lectured him on the monastic life—on its deprivations, the labors expected of a novice, the vows of poverty, chastity, and obedience, the very renunciation of the novice's own will—and asked Martin if he could live this way. At the moment, Martin could live no other way. "Yes," came the reply, "with God's help and to the extent that human frailty allows." He was admitted to the probationary novitiate of one year. His head was tonsured, and he put on the rough habit. The choir sang a hymn, and Martin prostrated himself—away from his father's driving ambitions at last and entering, he fervently hoped, a future of peace, he prostrated himself before the altar, his forehead on the cool floor, his eyes closed, his arms stretched out in the form of the cross.

V

THE MATURE MEDICI

AS Martin Luther went into retirement, Pope Julius II, and with him Cardinal Giovanni de' Medici, came out. *Il terribile*, as Cardinal de' Medici's mentor was called, was a tall, rugged, commanding, arrogant man. He was sixty years old when he ascended to the chair of Saint Peter; he had been hungering for it for years, and now he pursued his ambitions with a consuming impatience. "Anything that he has been thinking overnight," the Venetian ambassador Antonio Giustinian wrote home to his government, "has to be carried out immediately the next morning, and he insists on doing everything himself. Everything about him is on a magnificent scale, both his undertakings and his passions. His impetuosity and his temper annoy those who live with him, but he inspires fear rather than hatred, for there is nothing in him that is small or meanly selfish." His first concern, as is natural with any deeply religious man, was for his immortality. So he summoned Michelangelo to Rome to design his tomb. The Florentine sculptor's sketches called for an enormous sepulcher adorned with no less than forty statues celebrating Julius' dominance over the arts and sciences and his sway over prostrate cities, all the while heaven rejoices at the spectacle. The tomb was never finished—Julius had other projects for Michelangelo that interrupted the work—but the artist completed the single figure of Moses. A massive, powerful figure with a fierce stare, there is as much of Julius in him as there is of Moses. When Julius decided that he could no longer live in the rooms

Borgia had inhabited—the Pinturicchio paintings there reminded him unpleasantly of "that circumcized Jew"—he hired Perugino, Lotto, Signorelli, and others to decorate some other rooms for him. Then, in 1508 Raphael arrived in Rome. Julius abruptly fired all the other artists and charged Raphael with painting his *stanzes*. Raphael decorated the walls with such masterpieces as his "School of Athens," and Julius, a sudden enthusiast as always, paid the cheerful, mild-mannered young artist 12,000 ducats for each of the three rooms he decorated. He commissioned Michelangelo to paint the Sistine Chapel. With his famous lament, "It is not my trade," Michelangelo labored for four and a half years before he finished the back-breaking job. Fee paid to the gloomy complainer: a niggardly 3,000 ducats.

With equal quirky abandon, Julius set about his fateful program to rebuild St. Peter's basilica. The eleven-hundred-year-old basilica hovered uncertainly over the tomb of Saint Peter. Siege, earthquake, and neglect had left its fragile walls dizzily leaning six feet out of perpendicular. Its crude timber roof was an offense to the eye. The whole ugly pile threatened to collapse. Julius sorted through restoration plans by Sangallo and Rossellino, cast them aside, and seized on a plan by Bramante, whose floor plan looked rather like a snowflake: an equiarmed Greek cross imposed on a square, with small chapels nestled in the corners, and a great dome crowning the center. Before St. Peter's was completed, more than a dozen architects—notably including Michelangelo and Bernini—would have a hand in shaping its form. But Bramante's design remained the basis for rebuilding St. Peter's, and it took fully a century to remold his Greek cross into the traditional Latin one. Julius laid the cornerstone on April 18, 1506, and sent men scurrying about Italy for the stone to build a church grand enough to rise over the tomb of Saint Peter—and of Julius II. "Today the Pope went to St. Peter's to inspect work," Beltrando de Costabili recorded. "I was there too, the Pope brought Bramante with him, and said smilingly to me, 'Bramante tells me that he has 2,500 men on the job, one might hold a review of such an army.' " Such armies were expensive, of course, and to raise money for St. Peter's, Julius proclaimed a special indulgence in Italy. In laying the cornerstone of Christendom's greatest cathedral, Julius built in a fault that would help to topple the Roman Catholic Church.

He installed some newly found ancient sculptures in the Belvedere Garden. He organized the Swiss Guard and had Michelangelo design the uniforms that the guard still wears today. He reformed the coinage, condemned simony, widened the streets, fattened the royal treasury, and finally, feeling secure, he went to war.

Julius' war policy was simplicity itself. First he subdued some rebellious Italian city-states with the help of the French. Then he drove the French from Italy with the help of the Spanish. And last, but unsuccessfully, he tried to drive the Spanish from Italy. Allying with foes, and turning on friends, he sought to strengthen the papacy and the Della Rovere dynasty.

He was the first pope to ride out of Rome at the head of an army, and on the battlefield he was a holy terror. The leader of the rebellion in Perugia, Gianpaolo Baglione, was so stunned to hear that Julius was at the head of his own cavalry that Baglione laid down his arms and offered Julius some more troops. Then the pope set out over the Apennines to Bologna, crossing flooded rivers and scrambling up rocky ravines on foot. He was up at dawn each day to lead the march. In Bologna Giovanni Bentivoglio heard of Julius' relentless march. Bentivoglio reviewed his troops—and fled the city.

Venice still held two papal cities, Faenza and Rimini, and to recover control of those two Adriatic towns, Julius allied himself with the French in the League of Cambria. "I will make Venice a little fishing village again," he thundered at the Venetian ambassador. When the French subdued Venice and the cities were returned to Julius, the pope announced that "those Frenchmen have taken away my appetite," and he joined with Venice to attack the French and their main ally, Ferrara. Threatening to hang ambassadors or throw them in the river, Julius cursed impatiently at his procrastinating "ninny" generals through the latter part of 1510. Then, on January 2, 1511, he took to the field once again, in snow that was said to be five feet deep, saying, "Let's see who has the bigger testicles, the King of France or I."

He laid siege to the key town of Mirandola, thirty miles west of Ferrara, and went up and down the lines of his troops, cheering them on in their bombardment of the town's walls, helping to place the cannon, and cursing the enemy. On one occasion the little cottage where he was sleeping was struck by an enemy barrage, and two of the pope's cooks were killed. Julius strode forward to a new billet, a little church nearer the town walls. When a break was finally made in the walls and Mirandola surrendered, Julius could not bring himself to wait for the gates to be opened to him. He climbed a ladder and scrambled in through the breach with his sword drawn. The victory over Mirandola had even greater psychological than strategic importance. It was seen now that *il terribile* was deadly serious about driving the French from Italy. Allies joined the pope, and by 1513 Julius had chased the French back north over the Alps.

The calm eye in the midst of this storm belonged to Cardinal Giovanni de' Medici. When he was not accompanying Julius on the battlefield, the cardinal was back in Rome at his *palazzo* near the Pantheon in the heart of the city, gathering artists and writers and political allies around him. His mildness of disposition was constantly remarked upon, as was his scrupulous courtesy, his fastidious abhorrence of bloodshed, and his passion for hunting and hawking. He was a corpulent young man, slow-moving, with delicate white hands, and because of nearsightedness he always held in one hand a gold-rimmed monocle.

Only one event marred the cardinal's contentment, the death of Julius II's nephew Galeotto della Rovere. An engaging young man, Galeotto was the pope's favorite. He was made vice-chancellor of the Holy See when Ascanio Sforza died in 1505, and he was an elegant, popular fellow who had many friends in Roman

78

The Mature Medici

society. His closest friend was the Cardinal de' Medici, and they enjoyed talking about the days when Medici would be pope. He was apparently the only person for whom the Cardinal de' Medici ever had very warm feelings. Nothing more is known of their relationship, but after Galeotto died of a fever, Medici could not bear to hear his name mentioned. Years later, when he was pope, if Galeotto's name was brought up in conversation, Medici would turn his head to hide his tears.

The Cardinal de' Medici lived in Rome with his cousin Giulio de' Medici and Bernardo Dovizi da Bibbiena, who sometimes rebuked the cardinal when the silver plate was once again deposited with the fishmonger for lack of money. But Giovanni knew the value of entertaining friends, and he often observed that favored men need only keep faith in their predestined good fortune. The Medici family motto *Le Temps Revient*, promised, after all, that good fortune would return.

After Piero died, the cardinal abruptly changed the Medici tactics toward Florence. He and his other brother, Giuliano, decided, as Francesco Guicciardini wrote, "that the best way to facilitate their return was not to use force and violence, but to show love and benevolence, benefitting the citizens and never offending them either in public or in private. They never overlooked an opportunity to do a favor to any Florentine citizen, whether he lived in Rome or was just passing through. . . . Soon it became quite clear that the entire house, possessions, resources, and reputation of the Cardinal were at the disposal of any Florentine who cared to use them. The effectiveness of all this was enhanced by the fact that the greedy and self-seeking Cardinal Soderini [also a Florentine] never did anything for any Florentine. By comparison with him, the liberality and generous deeds of the Medici looked even greater than they were."

Even though Florentine law forbade correspondence between a citizen of Florence and the Medici, presently friendships were being avowed openly. As Guicciardini reported, "Many well-to-do young men whose fathers had been hostile to the Medici in '94 [the year they were driven from Florence] now drew close to them when they visited Rome. Indeed, they seemed to become their good friends, either to spite the gonfalonier or because they sought something more, perhaps even a restoration."

Bartolomeo Valori, an Albizzi, a Mortelli, Giovanni di Bardo Corsi, Gino di Neri Capponi, and others whose fathers had played a part in the revolt against the Medici, flocked to Rome to see the cardinal. Increasingly, the cardinal came to be thought of as Florence's ambassador to the Vatican. In 1508 the cardinal determined to test the sentiments of the Florentines, and he announced that a daughter of his brother Piero's was to be married to Filippo Strozzi of Florence. The Florentine government voted immediately to ban the marriage. Piero and all his descendants had been proclaimed rebels, the gonfalonier pointed out, and the government could not tolerate a marriage to a rebel. The marriage was, its opponents insisted, only the first step toward the overthrow of the government. The partisans of the cardinal took up the defense of the proposed marriage, and it was soon clear that the issue was a gentle test whether the Medicis were to be restored to Florence. Discussions and deputations led to bitter arguments in a government tribunal. Young Giovan Battista Ridolfi was accused of leading a band of troublemakers to embarrass the government. Alfonso Strozzi declaimed that the city would not be restored to peace until several leading citizens, including the archbishop, were beheaded. Finally, with an exquisitely Florentine sense of justice, the government declared that the girl was not a rebel, which removed the impediment to marriage, but Filippo was fined 500 gold ducats and banned to Naples for three years. In Rome the cardinal tallied the tribunal's votes and took the rebuff with equanimity. He distributed more favors among the young Florentines and bided his time.

Piero had always attempted to regain Florence with a small force, large hopes, and bravado. When the cardinal's opportunity came in 1512, he would use devastating force, callous realism, and a gentleness of manner. He assembled his army in the service of Julius II, following the warrior pope about the battlefield, dis-

80

playing remarkable calm under fire and a thirst for battle that was carefully modulated to be second only to that of the pope. By 1512 the cardinal had taken the supreme command of the papal troops, and in April, 1512, he led his army against the brash and ferocious twenty-three-year-old nephew of King Louis XII, Gaston de Foix.

Louis charged Gaston with bringing his troops into a definitive engagement with the Italians, and Gaston assembled 800 men at arms, 4,000 archers, and 16,000 infantry for the decisive battle of Ravenna. Under the cardinal and his hesitant Spanish general Don Raymond de Cardona were 1,500 men at arms, 3,000 light horse, and 18,000 foot soldiers. Gaston was the first to attack, storming the walls of Ravenna at a cost of about 1,500 dead. Unable to conquer the city in this one assault, Gaston drew back—only to receive word that the cardinal's troops had descended on Ravenna and raised entrenchments three miles outside the city. Caught in a vise, Gaston determined to storm the entrenchments.

Renaissance warfare, being a matter of siege and surrender, march and countermarch, was rarely a bloody affair. Many a good general could fight a full-scale war without ever losing a man of the rank of captain or above. But on April 11, 1512, when Gaston charged the cardinal's entrenchments, the melee turned to massacre. The Italian troops at first remained in their entrenchments and exchanged two hours' artillery fire with the French. Then another artillery detachment struck the Italians from the flank. Enraged, an Italian general, Fabrizio Colonna, rushed from the entrenchment and, followed by the papal troops, led his men into hand-to-hand combat. The fortunes of the day changed from hour to hour until at last, with 9,000 dead left on the field, the Italians scattered and ran. The victory went to France, but in winning the battle they lost 10,500 dead, including their leader, Gaston de Foix.

While all about him his army fled, the Cardinal de' Medici walked over the battlefield tending the wounded—whether out of a devotion to his spiritual duties or from a sense that men of the church became secure neutrals at the end of a battle we do not know. In any event, the cardinal displayed quintessential composure. He was captured and kept in princely confinement. As a matter of courtesy, his cousin Giulio was permitted to visit him, and the cardinal dispatched Giulio to Rome with a full report on the battle, the loss of De Foix, the disabling of the French army, the quarrels among the new French military leaders, the lack of discipline in their debilitated troops, and his judgment that the French could fight no more. Pope Julius, who had been at the point of fleeing Rome, was overjoyed. Shortly the French received information that 18,000 Swiss were marching toward them. Along the way the Swiss picked up another 12,000 among the Venetians and the resuscitated papal troops. The French gathered their soldiers and limped toward home, taking with them the Cardinal de' Medici.

When the French arrived at the bank of the River Po, the cardinal was suddenly "taken ill." He was carried to a nearby rectory for the night, and there he persuaded the abbot to recruit a band of men to help him escape. The abbot prevailed on a man named Renaldo Zozzi to arm a small party during the night. The next morning some unexpected difficulty kept the cardinal from arriving at the riverbank until almost all the French had already crossed to the other side. Then, riding his mule, he approached the boat being held for him. At that moment Renaldo and his friends rode up to cause a clamor. The cardinal turned and in the confusion rode off with his new friends and escaped through the hills disguised as a soldier.

As he recovered from his ordeal in a villa outside of Mantua, the cardinal must have been amused by reports of Julius' latest ruse in Rome. As part of his campaign against Rome, Louis XII had summoned a council to condemn Julius. The council found Julius "an inveterate simoniac, of infamous and abandoned manners, not fit to discharge the office of a pontiff, as being the author of many wars, and notoriously incorrigible, to the universal scandal of Christianity." They seemed tame enough charges, and councils called for political reasons were common enough. Julius himself had called incessantly for a council to depose Alexander VI. But councils were a troublesome matter. Councils threatened to deny the primacy of the pope and thus limit his power. Renaissance popes rarely understood the conflict as a theological matter; when theology became a central issue for the councils that were to hear Martin Luther, churchmen in Rome would be baffled. In the summoning of them and in the threat they held to papal power, councils had to do with politics.

For a time Julius considered simply declaring the French throne vacant. But then, to avoid a vexing confrontation with Louis XII, the pope summoned his own council, accompanied by 200 of the Swiss Guards, and declared that all decrees of the gathering would take the form of papal bulls—that is, the council could decree nothing without Julius' approval. It was crude, but it solved, however temporarily, the question of whether a council or the pope was the ultimate power in the church by answering that a council was—with the pope's permission. Cardinal de' Medici was learning a great deal from his mentor.

Added to his own instincts for political survival were Julius' lessons of prompt, overwhelming action when action was called for, no half measures, a keen cynicism about councils and democratic notions, and a well-developed callousness in pursuing the main objective.

In the autumn of 1512 the cardinal was at last able to show what he had learned from Julius. In the recent conflict with France, Florence had been disturbingly cordial to Louis XII, having supplied the king with both money and troops. Now, in order to settle his score with Florence, Julius loaned Cordona and his Spanish troops to Cardinal de' Medici. The cardinal's army was made up of 5,000 well-trained and battle-hardened foot soldiers and 200 men at arms. Short on supplies and ammunition, they needed a quick victory. The army camped before the town of Prato, ten miles from Florence, which was defended by about 4,000 hastily assembled soldiers. Having at first insisted that the Florentine gonfalonier be deposed and the Medici restored to rule in Florence, once encamped at Prato the cardinal sent word to the gonfalonier that the Medici would be content to return to the city simply as private citizens. The gonfalonier was given one day to reply to these terms. He hesitated, and on the next day the cardinal's army assaulted Prato. The artillery made a break in the town walls. The soldiers in the town abandoned their defense of the walls. And the cardinal's troops rushed through the breach, slaughtering all who came in their way. The cardinal watched through his gold-rimmed monocle—as he was fond of doing on his hunting parties—from a distance. Estimates vary, but between 2,000 and 5,000 inhabitants of Prato were killed before the riotous carnage came slowly to an end late in the evening two days after it had begun. Every well in town was choked with naked corpses.

"This day," the cardinal wrote to Julius, "at sixteen of the clock, the town was sacked, not without some bloodshed, such as could not be avoided. . . . The capture of Prato, so speedily and cruelly, although it has given me pain, will at least have the good effect of serving as an example and a deterrent to others."

The genial cardinal's example was not lost on Florence. The gonfalonier left town in the middle of the night and did not stop running until he found refuge with the Turks. On the last day of August, 1512, the cardinal entered Florence, welcomed by his friends and fawned on by his enemies. It was left to his modest younger brother Giuliano to establish the terms by which the Medici would return "simply as private citizens." Giuliano agreed to a relatively democratic form of government in which the Medicis played no role. When the cardinal was informed of what his brother had accepted, he assembled some troops. While the Signoria was debating just how to put their new democracy into effect, the government palace was surrounded by 400 Spanish lancers and 1,000 foot soldiers, and the Signoria's discussions came to an abrupt end. Florence's new government was composed of a council of sixty-six citizens, all Medici puppets, and the official head of state was no other than Giuliano de' Medici. Thus Florence was a democracy—with the cardinal's permission.

To make life sweet again in Florence, the cardinal constituted two orders of merit, and the members of these orders presided at holiday festivals and tourneys and triumphs and the other circuses the cardinal put on for the people. As was customary, the cardinal adopted an emblem to serve as the symbol of his reign: a yoke. And then, presumably with a pleasant smile, he had the yoke inscribed with a motto presumptuously recalling Jesus' words: "My yoke is smooth, and my burden light."

On February 4, 1513, *il terribile* summoned the College of Cardinals to his bedside. He was dying, he said, though his doctors did not understand what his illness was. In rebuilding St. Peter's, in bedeviling Michelangelo to finish the Sistine Chapel, in his wars and his political maneuverings he had exhausted himself. With the last of his strength he begged forgiveness of his many sins (although he mentioned none in particular) and demanded that his nephew Francesco Maria della Rovere be given the town of Pesaro in addition to the two he already had. His soul and his dynasty thus secured, he slipped quietly toward death, expiring in his sleep on February 21.

The College of Cardinals assembled once again to select a new pope. It was about this time that the Dutch priest Desiderius Erasmus of Rotterdam, recently a tourist in Italy and now on a visit to his friend Thomas More in England, wrote his *Praise of Folly*. Of the popes, he said:

> . . . if they should endeavor to imitate His life . . . who would purchase that chair with all his substance or defend it, so purchased, with swords, poisons, and all force imaginable? so great a profit would the access of wisdom deprive him of . . . so much wealth, so much honor, so much riches, so many victories, so many offices, so many dispensations, so much tribute, so many pardons; such horses, such mules, such guards, and so many pleasures would it lose them.
>
> . . . scarce any kind of men live more voluptuously or with less trouble; as believing that Christ will be well enough pleased if in their mystical and almost mimical pontificality, ceremonies, titles of holiness and the like, and blessing and cursing, they play

the parts of bishops. To work miracles is old and antiquated, and not in fashion now; to instruct the people, troublesome; to interpret the Scripture, pedantic; to pray, a sign one has little else to do; to shed tears, silly and womanish; to be poor, base; to be vanquished, dishonorable and little becoming him that scarce admits even kings to kiss his slipper; and lastly, to die, uncouth; and to be stretched on a cross, infamous.

VI

DR. MARTIN LUTHER

MARTIN rose from his crucifixion on the stone floor of the monastery to the only year of peace he knew as a young man. His death to the world and his year of purgation were a boon to him. "I was a good monk," he said later, "and kept strictly to my order, so that I could say that if the monastic life could get a man to heaven, I should have entered: all my companions who knew me would bear witness to that."

A monk's novitiate was, in every sense, a gentle but firm brainwashing. Space, time, sight, sound, and, finally, self—all were changed. The world outside slipped away and a new world of silence, broken by tolling bells, shuffling sandals, and voices repeating over and over the same prayers, was gradually persuaded into being. The novitiate's cell was ten feet square. Its high windows let in light and air, but it was too high for the young monk to see out. There was a blanket and a cot covered with straw, a table and chair, and a lamp to study by. The walls were blank.

At two o'clock in the morning the cloister bell tolled, and the monks assembled before the high altar in the church for matins, which lasted for forty-five minutes. These sessions, with the monks singing in choir, appealed greatly to Martin. The first meal came ten hours later, except on fast days, when the monks ate in the early afternoon. Prayers were sung seven times a day. At mealtime there were sermons as the monks ate. There were chores and study. There was a time set aside for all the brothers to gather and confess their violations of monastic rules and to remind others of their unconfessed transgressions. Only subjects of concern to the monastic community were spoken of in these sessions; other matters were confessed privately to the prior.

Rules were precise and intricate: some matters to be confessed in public, some in private; silence in most places; permission to speak in others, but banter nowhere; conversations of any length by permission only, and then in the presence of a superior; meals on some days at noon, on others later, a day or more of fasting on other occasions. For the celebration of the mass, there was a manual by Gabriel Biel to be memorized: A missed word could spoil the mass. And yet it did not spoil the mass, for all that mattered was the intention of the celebrant. But even so, the sacrament was not dependent for its efficacy upon the celebrant. Nonetheless, a priest must not celebrate mass if he suspects—suspects!—he harbors an unconfessed sin. However, if he should recall an unconfessed sin while celebrating the mass, he should continue to the end, confident that the sin will be forgiven afterward. And on and on, the young monk memorizes, observes silence here, sings there, the tolling of the bells marking the seven hours of his new days and leading him from moment to prolonged moment toward eternal peace. The world Martin left behind must have seemed peculiarly unreal by the end of his year-long novitiate.

The young novitiate, age twenty-four, was pronounced ready for his final, binding vows. He was brought before the altar once again and renounced the world. "The Lord divest you of the former man and of all his works," the prior intoned as he removed the novitiate's habit from Martin; and, as he gave his new brother a new habit, "The Lord invest you with the new man." He was ordained first simply a monk, then, selected for the priesthood, he became subdeacon, deacon, and finally priest. Martin's resurrection was not as successful as his death. He invited his father to attend his first mass, and Hans saw to it that Martin was reborn, as he had been first born, into a life of anguish.

The Catholic priest is unique in all creation. On the Catholic altar, so Martin was taught, Christ's sacrifice on Calvary is reenacted. Bread and wine are transubstantiated into the body and blood of Christ; Catholics are permitted to partake of that body and blood, and in this they receive the special grace that the church can provide them. The priest is the mediator between God and man. He alone can perform this sacrifice. In this lies the superiority of church over state: No emperor ever had it in his power to bestow such a gift on mankind. Indeed, not even the angels have this privilege that priests have. It is an awesome power the priest has, and to Martin it was a terrifying one. In the mass the priest confronts God face to face. It is no wonder that Martin, who had not yet been able to face his earthly father, found it excruciatingly difficult to face his heavenly father.

Hans arrived for this marvelous occasion with a company of twenty horsemen and a handsome gift for the monastery. Although Hans had raged against Martin's vocation, when two other sons died of the plague during Martin's novitiate Hans may have been convinced that God was punishing him for his obstinacy, or at least he was convinced he ought to cherish Martin however the boy had disappointed him.

The day began, as always, with the tolling of the bell, the guests crossed the cobblestone courtyard and took their places in church, and the monks entered and chanted a psalm. Father Martin approached the altar, made the sign of the cross, and commenced, "*Introibo ad altare dei. . . .*" Then when he came to the words, "We offer unto Thee, the living, the true, the eternal God," he stopped. "At these words," he said later, "I was utterly stupefied and terror-stricken. . . . Who am I that I should lift up my eyes or raise my hands to the divine Majesty?" Called upon to meditate between an uncertainly merciful God and a certainly wrathful father, Martin faltered, and in that moment many doubts must have crowded into his mind. He forced himself through the remainder of the mass and at the end, badly shaken, he joined his father and the other monks at a celebratory dinner. Seeking still some blessing from his father, and needing reassurance, he said to

Hans, "Dear father, why were you so contrary to my becoming a monk? Perhaps you are not quite satisfied even now. The life is so quiet and godly."

No remark could have been better calculated to anger Hans. "You learned scholar," he said, "have you never read in the Bible that you should honor your father and mother? And now you have left me and your mother to look after ourselves in our old age." As the monks began to argue, Hans turned on Martin and delivered his curse: "God grant that it wasn't a devil's ghost." And with that all of Martin's doubts engulfed him. What if the thunderstorm on the road to Erfurt was an apparition of the devil? "*If* the monastic life could get a man to heaven," Martin said, he would go to heaven. If what he had been taught was true —if bread and wine became the body and blood of Christ, if sins were forgiven in confession, if singing and good works were pleasing to God, if God was just, if Martin could have faith and love God—then he need not worry. But what if none of these was true or possible?

From this moment Martin took nothing for granted. All was subject to doubt and challenge. Now he pushed everything to the limit, until he either destroyed it or found that it withstood his test and supported him. He turned from one source of comfort to another, making extreme demands, exhausting each in turn. If monkery was good, then the anchorites, who fled the corrupt Roman Empire in its declining years to fast in the Egyptian desert, were even better. If fasting till noon found God's favor, Martin would fast for days. If mortification of the flesh reduced man to some elemental spiritual base, Martin would throw off the blanket in his cell and sleep, shivering, on the floor. "After watchings, studies, fastings, prayers and other most severe exercises with which as a monk I afflicted myself almost to death," he later recalled, "yet that doubt was left in the soul, and I thought, 'Who knows whether such things are pleasing to God?'"

If confession was a way to purge the soul and become strong and secure before God, Martin would confess and confess and confess. Martin confessed all he could think of, beginning with his childhood and ending with the moment of his confession. And then he would review his confession and confess that he had made a bad confession the day before. Several hours after he left his confessor, he would think of something he had forgotten and rush back to make an appointment for the following day. What to some would seem purities Martin could break down into several impurities. Where his actions were virtuous, he found impious intentions. Often he confessed daily, and in one session he raked through his sins for fully six hours. A good miner's son, he would dig and dig until he found "pay dirt." He confessed in despair, challenging the sacrament to hold up under his relentless bombardment. He searched for some truth, something he could say, without doubt, that he believed. He needed faith and could not believe. He could not believe until necessity compelled him, until he could no longer ask: "What if?"

With all his efforts to become close to God, Martin only grew farther and farther apart from a Heavenly Father whom he saw as wrathful. "In the monastery," he said, "I did not think about women, or gold, or goods, but my heart trembled, and doubted how God could be gracious to me. Then I fell away from faith, and let myself think nothing less than that I had come under the wrath of God, whom I must reconcile with my good works." On another occasion he speaks of God appearing "horrifyingly angry. . . . There can be no flight, no consolation, neither within nor without, but all is accusation." And again he says, "Then the conscience feels that all the ill fortune which overtakes it is the wrath of God, and it thinks that all the creatures are simply God, and the wrath of God, even if it is just a rustling leaf. . . ."

Martin spoke repeatedly of his gnawing fears to his confessor until one day the infuriated confessor burst out at him: "God is not angry with you. You are angry with God. Don't you know that God commands you to hope?" And did not his confessor know that hope and faith cannot be commanded? Martin persisted in his scruples and his marathon confessions and his anger: His life would be the ultimate test of his religion. It would bring him face to face with God in faith and hope—or else he would take his religion apart piece by piece.

"Is it not against all natural reason," Martin later said, "that God out of His mere whim deserts men, hardens them, damns them, as if He delighted in sins . . . He who is said to be of such mercy and goodness? This appears iniquitous, cruel, and intolerable in God, by which very many have been offended in all ages. And who would not be? I was myself more than once driven to the very abyss of despair so that I wished I had never been created. Love God? I hated Him!"

It was in this final blaspheming frame of mind that Martin first went to Wittenberg, where he found a new father of a gentle, reassuring, and loving manner and a new God who was similarly loving. Wittenberg was a town of only 2,000 inhabitants, a town of brewers, and a "stinking sand dune," according to contemporaries. On one side was the Elbe River, on the other a moat, and through the town, along its two main streets, ran two brooks, or stinking sewers. The whole town was less than a mile long, marked at one end by Martin's new monastery, at the other by the castle that had served for several hundred years as the residence of the dukes and electors of Saxony. Between the castle and Martin's monastery were the marketplace ("a dung hill") and the lecture hall of Wittenberg's new university. Next to the castle was the castle church, which contained an inspiring array of sacred relics, 5,005 of them, including a hair and a drop of milk from the Virgin Mary. The collection was nurtured assiduously —it provided, after all, one of Wittenberg's principal attractions and a source of income from devout pilgrims—and by 1518 there were 17,000 relics invested with indulgences that could reduce a soul's stay in purgatory by 127,799 years and 116 days.

The collection of holy relics and the budding new university, founded in 1502, both were the fond projects of Frederick the Wise, Elector of Saxony, who was determined to raise this inauspicious little town to prominence. His university, he hoped, would rival both Leipzig and Erfurt, which lay in his neighbors' provinces. To this end, he invited the Augustinians and Franciscans to provide the university with some promising new professors. Martin joined the faculty to lecture on the *Nicomachean Ethics* of Aristotle. Johann von Staupitz, the Augustinian vicar-general of the province, took the chair in Biblical theology.

Staupitz was a cultivated, pleasant man in his late fifties when Martin first met him. Of noble family, he had been well educated at the universities of Cologne, Leipzig, and Tübingen. By virtue of his good birth, his vocation, his intellect, and his warmth, he was well suited to be Martin's father, and the young priest adopted Staupitz immediately and kept him as his kindly mentor and comfort all his life. Staupitz was apparently a good listener— the first Martin had found—and he declined to argue. A man of easy, but not glib, convictions, he must have found Martin's passionate brilliance exciting. He drew out the young man's fears, and when Martin became overscrupulous, Staupitz would remark that he himself had stopped trying "to be especially pious; he had lied to God long enough, and without success." That Staupitz could so easily and confidently assume God would not abandon him for being less than perfect lifted a weight from Martin. The young man's intensity was respected and gently assuaged. Staupitz insisted that his young protégé prepare himself for a professorship in Biblical studies, and when Martin complained that the studies were "killing him," Staupitz replied casually, "That's all right, God needs men like you in Heaven, too."

Martin did find his routine of lectures and studies strenuous, however. He wrote to Johann Braun that "the study takes it out of me, especially in philosophy which from the beginning I would gladly have exchanged for Theology, I mean that theology that searches out the nut from the shell, the kernel from the grain, and the marrow from the bones." At about this time he stumbled upon the writings of Saint Augustine, whose complete works had just become available in 1506 in a nine-volume edition. The writings of that protean sinner-saint thrilled Martin completely. Here was a theologian, unlike Aquinas or Occam or the other rigorous syllogistic hair-splitters, who had some understanding of the tortured, contradictory, chaotic nature of an individual man. And in his *Confessions*, Augustine unburdened himself of more vices and failings than Martin had ever dreamed of. Martin's own confessions must have looked like paltry affairs compared to those of the saint. Certainly if such a monstrous sinner as Augustine could find God's favor, there was some hope for Martin. The young priest devoured Augustine's writings and wrote enthuastically in the margins, "Beautiful! Beautiful!"

Martin was not yet formulating his mature theology, but something of Augustine's thoughts must have begun to work in the young man. Augustine believed that faith came to man as a free gift, a "grace," from God. No man could earn this gift by work or prayer, nor could he merit it by virtue of his goodness. God granted it at His discretion, and no man might know His will or reason. But this gift, faith alone, justified man before God.

These thoughts, buried in Augustine and awaiting a kindred spirit to separate "the nut from the shell," would form much of the basis of Martin's theology. Combined with Staupitz's gentle, common-sensical remarks (he had given up trying "to be especially pious; he had lied to God long enough . . .") and his own superbly analytical and logical turn of mind, Martin began to build a new understanding of his religion. He would add many more elements before he was through, of course, and he would reach back into the past to draw on his studies for other elements. But in Wittenberg in 1509 we can see Martin begin to emerge from the confusion of the past and struggle toward a new definition of man's relationship to God. Later he would refer to Staupitz as "father in the evangelium" and speak of "our theology . . . the Bible, St. Augustine and the old Fathers."

Martin took his *baccalaureus Biblicius* at Wittenberg in 1509 and returned to Erfurt to gain the rank of *sententiarius*. As *sententiarius* he lectured at Erfurt on the Sentences of Peter Lombard, who had managed to harmonize the fathers of the church and the Bible just before Aristotle took Europe by storm in the thirteenth century. Lecturing on Lombard reinforced several of

Martin's tendencies: his regard for the Bible and the fathers, and his extreme distaste for Aristotelian scholasticism.

While Martin burrowed his way more and more deeply into his theological studies, Staupitz precipitated a small administrative crisis among the Augustinians. Staupitz argued for a union of all the German Augustinian monasteries. The stricter houses, including Erfurt, resisted a union with their more easygoing brethren. The Erfurt partisans decided to take the dispute directly to Rome, and in 1510 they sent Dr. Johann Nathin, accompanied by Martin, to the Eternal City. It was the longest trip of Martin's life, and it broadened him not at all.

The two brothers traveled overland, passing through France and over the Alps and pausing in Florence, where Martin failed to notice Lorenzo Ghiberti's famous bronze doors or Masaccio's frescoes that revolutionized Western art, or even Michelangelo's statue of David in the town's central piazza. He did credit the Florentines, however, for having excellent orphanages. Martin was a devout tourist, and when he first sighted Rome, he fell to his knees and exclaimed, "Hail, Holy Rome!" The two monks passed through the Porta del Popolo and stayed, as had the young Cardinal de' Medici, at the Augustinian monastery near the church of Santa Maria del Popolo.

Dr. Nathin and Martin went about their business routine automatically, spending a good bit of time in the waiting rooms of minor officials, no doubt. They saw nothing, of course, of the insider's Rome, of the exalted curial officials or the cardinals. They were quintessential outsiders, and once they had finished their errand (though no answer was made to their appeal while they were in Rome, they heard later that their mission was a failure), they plodded around the Eternal City for a month, visiting the sacred tourist sites.

Rome's relics and indulgences were the best the world had to offer. One of the coins paid to Judas for betraying Christ was, by this time, worth 1,400 years' indulgence. There was the portrait of Christ on the cloth that Saint Veronica offered Him on the way to Calvary, and Christ's footprint in a piece of marble. There was half the body of Saint Peter and half of Saint Paul (the other halves were in another church), and Martin made a special point of seeing the arms of Saint Anne. He also toured the seven major churches and took communion at St. Peter's. He was disturbed from time to time by the lack of seriousness—or somberness—of the Italians. He thought his confessor incompetent (it is impossible to know what his confessor thought of Martin), and the Italian priests who were making the rounds of the shrines annoyed him. They could knock off a half dozen masses while Martin made his painstaking way through one. And then some Italian waiting in line to use the altar would badger the German, saying "Keep moving!" (*"Passa! Passa!"*)

Toward the end of his stay he climbed the steps of the Lateran Church on his hands and knees—the same steps, supposedly, that Christ ascended when he was presented to Pilate for judgment—saying a paternoster on each of the twenty-eight steps and, just to go the prescribed ritual one better, kissing each step. Each paternoster, it was said, freed a soul from purgatory, and Martin fleetingly wished his father and mother were dead so that he could give them such a favor. When he reached the top of the steps he stood up and said aloud, "Who knows whether it is true?"

Martin returned to Erfurt to report briefly to his superior, and then he left again for Wittenberg to study for his doctorate in theology, which he received after another year's study and doubt and anxiety, on October 19, 1512. While the Cardinal de' Medici had spent his time maneuvering the length and breadth of European politics, Martin had explored the depths of his own soul.

He was still a young man in turmoil, still ravaged with doubts and tidal rages. But however uncertain of what the divinity might be, he was now doctor of divinity and professor of sacred theology. He was twenty-eight years old, and the course of his life was set. Henceforth, he would lecture twice a week, every week, to his young students. He would lecture for thirty years in this way, until he could lecture no more. Above all, Martin Luther was a scrupulously dutiful professor of theology, who analyzed theological questions with rigorous logic and dogged scholarly care and took some professional pleasure in debating the fine points with his students. He was an artful lecturer, this passionate, beefy young man, and though his students must have found him quirky and pedantic at times, he was a popular young professor. Whatever else he might do with his life, Luther would do between lectures.

VII

POPE LEO X

AFTER the mass of the Holy Spirit on the morning of March 4, 1513, twenty-four cardinals marched in solemn scarlet procession into the Vatican Palace to choose a new pope. Once they entered the conclave, they were not permitted to leave until a pope was chosen. They were each allowed a servant and a secretary, and they slept in cubicles identified by their coats of arms. The doors were locked and guarded, the windows bricked up. At dinner time food entered the airless chamber through a special hatch, and a senior official cut apart each loaf of bread and piece of meat and examined the serving trays to make certain no message passed in or out. Cardinal de' Medici and his entourage arrived two days late for the conclave. Suffering from an anal fistula, he was carried in on a litter accompanied by his physician.

Popes can be elevated to the supreme dignity in one of four ways: by inspiration, compromise, access, or scrutiny. In an election by scrutiny, the cardinals sit down at the conclave table, on which there are pens and paper, and write their own names and the name of a candidate on a slip of paper. Then, with a number of genuflections and other solemn bits of ritual, each one steps up to the altar and places his ballot in a golden chalice. The votes are then counted by the chief cardinal deacon and, providing that there are the same number of votes as cardinals (something never taken for granted), a two-thirds majority elects the new pope. If after several scrutinies there is no clear majority, the cardinals may work a slight variation on the scrutiny—an election by access, in which a cardinal may change his vote after a count has been made, just as in an American political convention, so that a running tally will indicate how vote-switching may produce a two-thirds majority. After each vote, the ballots are burned, making a puff of black smoke above the building if no pope has been chosen on the ballot, a puff of white smoke if a candidate has been elected.

If these means fail, the cardinals may resort to an election by compromise, in which they nominate one of their number to make their decision for them and promise to abide by that decision. Compromise is a risky business. John XXII, appointed to choose a pope by this method, chose himself, causing tremendous consternation among his colleagues.

Finally, the college may resort to inspiration, in which several cardinals call out the name of a candidate as though they had been inspired to speak his name by the Holy Spirit. If enough tough voices can be persuaded to join a faction, it is possible to shout down and intimidate the meeker cardinals. Inspiration was generally held suspect in the college, and the cardinals avoided it.

The first few days of the conclave were given over to elaborate formalities, a lottery for minor administrative posts, and other diversions to allow time for politicking. Then, on March 8, the English Cardinal Bainbridge achieved a measure of fame by becoming one of the few ever to thwart the security precautions of a conclave. On the bottom of a silver platter he scratched with a knife ST. GEORGE (Cardinal Raffaele Riario) OR MEDICI, and bookmakers throughout Italy posted new odds.

Cardinal de' Medici's "conclavist," or floor manager, was Bernardo Dovizi da Bibbiena, and Bernardo showed all his persistence, shrewdness, and capacities for gentle suasion that would mark his later career at the Vatican. By degrees Bernardo wore down the opposition of the Cardinal Soderini, brother of the gonfalonier the Medici had deposed in Florence, and began to attract the younger members of the college under the leadership of Cardinal Alfonso Petrucci to the Medici candidacy. As the time for the first scrutiny approached, it was evident that Medici would be opposed by a faction of older members who closed behind Cardinal Alborese—under the direction of Raffaele Riario. Whether Riario hoped to elect Alborese or to use him as a stalking horse in his own bid for election is not clear.

The first scrutiny took place on March 10, and the two emerging leaders appeared in appropriately unobtrusive places in the ballot count: Cardinal de' Medici had one vote, Riario none. During the day, factions formed, split, and formed again. In one scrutiny the Cardinal Alborese got as many as thirteen votes, but by dinner time it was apparent that he had reached the limit of his strength.

By now the chamber was a foul place of unwashed and over-dressed aristocratic bodies. The vapors from the night torches and the odors from the lavatory were intolerable, and the Cardinal de' Medici's doctor, having performed a minor operation on the cardinal for an abscess, begged to be allowed to leave the room and was refused permission. The conclave had been brought to the moment of decision, and that evening the Cardinals de' Medici and Riario retired to a corner for an hour's secret consultation.

No record of their conversation survives, and we can only guess at what arrangement they made. Riario, nephew of Pope Sixtus IV, had been involved in the plot to murder Cardinal de' Medici's uncle. Riario had been too young then for the Medicis to attach any blame to him, and Giovanni had not yet been born. So, there was no long-standing enmity between them. Indeed, since Riario and Julius II were circuitously related by virtue of both being Sixtus' nephews, and since Medici had helped Julius II, one might imagine that Riario felt somehow indebted to Medici. One might; but, by 1513, Riario had been in the college nearly forty years. He was a formidable old hand at Vatican politics, a tough and unsentimental bargainer, and any debt owing to Medici had long since been paid. Yet Riario got no promises of new territory or income from Medici. Customarily, if one candidate was not willing or able to buy out the other in a deadlocked conclave, a

100

compromise candidate would be found—an innocuous old man who would be expected to die soon—to allow the jostling factions more time to trade and realign. It was in that way that Pius III had been elected to his brief reign in 1503. But in this election, though Medici was only thirty-seven years old, he was himself a compromise candidate: The rumor swept around the hall that the young cardinal was so ill he might not even survive the conclave, and his doctor confirmed the unhappy prognostication. Ill, exhausted, Medici lay on his litter and bargained with Riario, no doubt promising that the Medici faction could be delivered by Bibbiena and others to Riario in the next conclave, a conclave that could not fail to come soon. Either they reached such a bargain, or else Riario gave his forces to Medici out of goodwill. In any case, Riario stepped aside and awaited Medici's death. (Indeed, in a few years he would lose patience and apparently try to hasten Medici's death with poison.)

As the chief cardinal deacon in the conclave, it was Cardinal de' Medici's duty to count the votes at the end of each scrutiny. In the first scrutiny on the following day he counted the votes and discovered that he had been elected pope. According to a diarist present, no change was seen in the countenance of the modest cardinal at this stroke of good fortune. He embraced the other cardinals and, when they asked him what name he would take, he declared himself partial to Leo X if the college thought that suitable. Many hastened to say that they would have chosen the very same name had they been elected, and a window was broken open and Cardinal Alessandro Farnese announced to the crowd, "*Papam habemus Reverendissimum Dominum Joannem de' Medicis, Diaconum Cardinalem Sanctae Mariae in Domenica; qui vocator Leo Decimus.*" With his choice of name Leo neatly combined a recollection of his mother's dream, of the symbol of his native Florence, and of Pope Leo the Great who by dint of diplomacy kept the Huns from overrunning Rome.

Pope Leo X was placed in the glittering pontifical throne and a grateful college followed him out of the fetid conclave to St. Peter's; the crowds cheered, cannon discharged, the clergy sang

101

"Te Deum Laudamus," and the cardinals took deep breaths of fresh air. The full, mature figure of the young pope emerged before the Roman people—a massive body that was impressive on horseback, though, because of short, thin legs that gave him a crablike gait, ludicrous on the ground. His head was enormous, his face pudgy and red, his nearsighted eyes bulging. His delicate, white, well-manicured hands were his only good feature, and he was very proud of them. He would often sit gazing at his hands, posing his fingers gracefully this way and that, admiring them. He was a gentle, awkward, endearing, and slightly pathetic young man, and no one seemed to notice that this mild-mannered, gentle young pope had taken the name of the fierce king of the jungle.

Since Leo had only been a deacon before his elevation to the papacy, it was necessary to have him ordained into the priesthood. His ordination took place on March 15, and on March 17 he was consecrated bishop. On March 19 he was formally crowned and enthroned as pope. That morning, accompanied inevitably by the full complement of cardinals and other august ecclesiastics, Leo was escorted to St. Peter's. There a platform had been erected with columns and an imitation marble cornice over an altar. The master of ceremonies, Paris de Grassis, greeted him before the altar, holding a candle in one hand and a bunch of tow in the other, and performed the ritual that was, on this occasion, marvelously ironic. Putting the candle to the tow, which went up with a gratifying whoosh, De Grassis intoned to the unabashedly worldly young pope, *"Pater sanctae, sic transit gloria mundi."* While the spiritless dignitaries stood around the piazza, a corps of deacons and subdeacons led the pope through his first celebration of the mass. After the mass, Leo was taken to the steps of the church, where two cardinals hefted the huge tiara, encrusted with precious stones and garish baubles, onto his head. The pope conferred his blessing on the gathering and returned to the papal palace.

The coronation was a mean ceremony by Leo's standards; there had not been sufficient time to prepare the elaborate celebration he wanted. So he postponed the Sacro Processo, the procession to the ancient Church of San Giovanni in Laterno, which had been the first church of Christendom until a fire ravaged it in 1308. Leo set the date of the Sacro Processo for April 11, the anniversary of his capture at the battle of Ravenna. And so the procession served the dual purpose of holy rite and commemoration of Leo's sly worldly triumph. He spent the remaining days of March and early April with Paris de Grassis, lovingly arranging the costly details of the festival. Now Pope Julius, despite all his expensive wars and commissions to artists, had been a prudent financial manager, and he had left the Vatican treasury with more money than it had had since the death of Pope John XXII in 1335. On the Sacro Processo that marked the beginning of the Leonine Age, Leo unstintingly squandered a fourth of Julius' hoard. "God has given us the papacy," a Venetian quoted Leo as saying. "Let us enjoy it."

The Florentines were already relishing the pleasures of the Leonine Age. They had begun on March 11, when rumors reached them that Leo had been elected pope, with bonfires and bell-ringing and shouts of *Palle!*, the old rallying cry of Medici partisans. Then, when the rumor was confirmed, according to the diary of the Florentine shopkeeper Luca Landucci, "If there had been bonfires and rejoicings before, they were redoubled now, and in a different spirit; with innumerable bundles of brushwood, great branches, baskets, barrels, and whatever each poor man chanced to have in his house; all the smallest streets of the city did their part, without stint, and the people not yet being content, ran all over Florence to pull down the wooden roofs above the shops and everywhere, burning up everything. They put the whole city in great danger, and if the Eight [a government committee] had not made a proclamation that no more roofs were to be pulled down . . . on pain of the gallows, even the tiled roofs would have been destroyed and the shops looted. And this nuisance lasted all Friday and Saturday . . . with so much firing of cannon and continual cries of *Palle! Papa Leone!* that it seemed as if the city were upside-down, and anyone who had seen it from overhead would have said: 'Florence is burning down the whole city,' for

103

there was such a tumult of shouting, and fires, and smoke, and reports of the cannon, large and small; and on Sunday the same, and on Monday worse than ever. They placed up on the gallery behind the parapets of the Palagio, a gilt malmsey cask at each corner, full of firewood and other stuff to burn, and also on the ringhiera and in the Piazza many gilt casks were burnt, accompanied by the continual sound of the small guns. It was really incredible what a number of fires there were in the city. . . ." It had not quite dawned on the Florentines that the Medici family was now more than ever secure in their power in Florence and that this power would be used more for the Medicis than for Florence. "I am not surprised," a Genoese visitor remarked to several Florentines during the celebrations, "at your present satisfaction, since your city has never yet produced a Pope, but when you have once gained this experience, as has been our case in Genoa, you will grow to realize a Pontiff's dealings with his native land and the price his fellow-citizens have to pay for the honor." Nor could Leo have failed to notice that the Florentines took his election as an occasion to bedevil those poor remaining few Piagnoni, the last remnants of the followers of the reforming monk Savonarola who had seemed such an irresistible force not long before—until a bull of excommunication turned him over to the people and to their fire. Leo had developed a healthy cynicism about the crowd, who could be easily kept in line by lavish doses of bulls and circuses.

April 11 was a sweet spring day, warm and sunny, ideally suited to a parade. The marchers assembled in the piazza in front of St. Peter's and from there crossed the muddy Tiber, meandered through Rome to San Giovanni in Laterno, and returned to St. Peter's—in all a distance of about five and a half miles. First to set out from St. Peter's were the men-at-arms, dressed in scarlet, marching on foot; then came the members of the cardinals' households and the prelates of the court; then the standard bearers, the captains of the Rioni, the ancient divisions of Rome; the gonfalonieri, with the banners of the pope, Leo's bastard cousin Giulio as Knight of Rhodes, a favored Medici now and soon to be even more favored, as were the pope's other friends and supporters that the crowd picked out among the marchers; more horsemen with banners; 100 equerries of the court, nobles all, in scarlet robes fringed with ermine, the last four of them carrying the crowns and miters and other jeweled symbols of the papacy; then 100 mounted Roman barons, the old and bitter rivals Fabrizio Colonna and Giulio Orsini prominent among them, riding side by side in token of new harmony under the new reign of peace and tranquillity; armed servants, dressed in the liveries of their masters, followed each noble; the chief citizens of Florence, relatives and friends-in-exile of the new pope; sacristans and pages in red velvet; the Sacred Host, borne on the back of a horse, over which is held a cloth-of-gold canopy; priests and clerks by the hundreds, the bureaucrats of the curia who kept the vast and scattered business of the Vatican moving (slowly), in black and purple and crimson; 250 bishops and abbots; then the cardinals, each superbly mounted and accompanied by eight chamberlains holding the depending white trains; the Duke of Ferrara, enemy of Julius II, now apparently restored to favor in the court of Leo X; the Conservators of Rome, representatives of the Senators of ancient Republican Rome; the Swiss Guards, 200 strong, in their harlequinade uniforms.

Finally, back in St. Peter's piazza, a vast hulk of vestments and new pope was lifted into the saddle of a white Arab stallion. The horse was adorned with white silk and gold, and above horse and rider was held an embroidered white silk canopy. The pope wore white, heavily bejeweled white silk and white gloves and was perfumed and decorated with pearls. And the massive tiara pressed down on his brow. The men who rode with him told the near-sighted pope what banners and triumphal arches were to be seen along the route of procession, and Leo, purple-faced, with perspiration rolling off his face, smiled happily.

At the Castel Sant' Angelo, just before crossing the Tiber, Leo received a book of the Law from a rabbi and, according to tradition, opened it, read a word or two, and said, "We confirm your privileges [to live in the Holy City], but we do not consent to your faith," and let the book fall from his hand. The procession crossed the bridge, and the throngs cried out, "Leone! Leone!" The pope gave the crowd his benediction, and the two chamberlains following with bags of money showered the crowds with gold and silver coins—the seemingly inexhaustible wellspring of Leo's Golden Age.

The streets were strewn with Aphrodite's myrtle, symbol of mirth, joy, and love, and with box, the symbol of firmness in adversity; and the procession moved over the aromatic carpet with a strange, dreamlike hush to its steps. The houses were festooned with holly, for foresight, and laurel, for success. Velvets and brocades in a riot of color were draped from windows, the statues of pagan gods were set proudly alongside those of Christian martyrs in the niches of triumphal arches. Some of the fountains had been made to flow with wine, and the Romans toasted the new pope, and his family, and his friends, and all of Christendom, and the new pope again and again.

Agostino Chigi, a Sienese and one of the wealthiest merchants in Rome, erected an eight-columned arch on which he had inscribed a Latin couplet to the effect that Venus and Mars, Leo's two predecessors, had fled, and now Pallas held sway in a new, intellectual reign. A goldsmith in his neighborhood countered by putting up a statue of Venus and inscribing under it that Mars had fled, Pallas had come, but Venus reigns forever. There were more arches and inscriptions and Medici heraldic devices to beguile the pope and his admirers. The artists in Rome had dutifully turned themselves into set decorators: There was little sense yet that artists should not stoop to such things.

The procession made its majestically awkward way past the few new Roman palaces, eschewing the slums and dark alleyways, past the upturned bowl of the Pantheon, past the Capitoline Hill, that ancient Roman center of government, past the still half-buried Roman Forum where an inscription glumly reminded the new pope that men die but the church lives on, past the Palatine Hill dotted with farms and the rubble of emperors' palaces, past the crumbling Colosseum, now a stone quarry for the new palace builders, its stones sprouting enough plants to keep any Roman amateur botanizing for a lifetime, out to the edge of civilization, where San Giovanni in Laterno stood in forlorn glory at the frontier that had been reclaimed since the days of ancient Rome by thickets and brambles and boars.

There the pope was taken off his horse and escorted up the steps of the basilica. In the chapel of San Silvestro, the nobility was permitted to kiss his feet. The bishops and cardinals were more favored in their privilege to kiss the pope's hand. Leo gave each of the bishops a silver medal in commemoration of the event and one silver and one gold medal to each of the cardinals. The inevitable banquet took place in the palace of Constantine, and then, while the marchers assembled to return to St. Peter's, Leo took off his tiara and lay down, stupefied by exertion and pleasures, for a brief rest.

The golden afternoon yielded to dusk and dark on the return trip. Torches now cast a fitful glare on the silks and ermines of the weary marchers and their stumbling horses. Leo could not manage the last quarter mile of the journey, and when he reached the dinotherian castle of Sant' Angelo he was taken in for the night as a guest of Cardinal Alfonso Petrucci, one of his principal supporters in the recent conclave. Leo was delightfully entertained by his charming and flattering young host in a "gilded and painted chamber" directly above the huge basement vaults where, four years later, Petrucci would be strangled on the order of the pope.

"In thinking over all the pomp and lofty magnificence I had just witnessed," the Florentine physician Gian-Giacomo Penni wrote home, "I experienced so violent a desire to become Pope myself, that I was unable to obtain a wink of sleep or any repose all that night. No longer do I marvel at these prelates desiring so ardently to procure this dignity, and I verily believe every lackey would sooner be made a Pope than a Prince."

Leo set about the serious concerns of the papacy with fervor. His old poet-companions Pietro Bembo and Jacopo Sadoleto were made his pontifical secretaries. His nephew Innocenzio Cibò was made a cardinal. And, of course, he elevated Giulio de' Medici and Bernardo da Bibbiena to cardinalates. In this mood of warm generosity, Leo also pardoned several Florentines—Machiavelli among them—who had been discovered in a confused, half-baked attempt to conspire against the Medici government in Florence. Since Cardinal Francesco Soderini stepped aside in his opposition to Leo's election, Leo now recalled the exiled former gonfalonier of Florence, Pietro Soderini, to live under the protection of the pope. To replenish Pietro's finances, Leo arranged a marriage between one of his own nephews and a niece of Pietro. More offices and favors and little grants of money and lands trickled through his white-gloved fingers. Like a man who has come upon a chest of ancient coins and jewels, Leo plunged his hands into the riches and sifted through them; and when the trinkets cascaded this way and that, he was pleased to see how brightly they glittered. The treasure of the church, in money as in grace, seemed infinite.

Aside from his urgent personal concerns, Leo once again took up the habitual war with Louis XII of France. In this encounter Leo reached all the way to England to enlist the young Henry VIII in the cause. Henry drove the French from Italy; King James IV of Scotland seized on the moment to invade Northumberland; James was killed at the Battle of Flodden. The carnage involved in church politics had by now become so common as to be tedious. Leo wrote Henry to congratulate him for his victories: ". . . although it was certainly very painful to me to hear of such an effusion of Christian blood," the pope lamented according to form, "the destruction of so many thousands of the people of our common Lord, and the death of a Christian king of great fame and undoubted courage, the husband of your sister, who has fallen under the sword of a Christian king so nearly allied to him; yet I could not but rejoice in this victory over an enemy who sought to deter you from the prosecution of the commendable cause in which you are now engaged [that is, the last, small duties in concluding Leo's part of the war with France]. On this account I have already, on my knees, offered up my thanks to

God, who has thus crowned your arms with a double victory, and laid the foundation of that future glory which you have so well begun, in undertaking at so early a period of life the defence of His church."

All of the essential characteristics of Leo's pontificate can be seen in the events of 1513: the backroom politics, the love of ostentation, the golden age nourished by showers of coins, the court that rewarded poets above priests, that sweet sense of high —and sometimes rank—civilization, the threat of family feud and gangster savagery that underlay Vatican politics, the battles with France, the vast, proteiform power of the temporal institution— power so great that it was naturally thought to be invulnerable— the involvement with international diplomacy and warfare that had become absorbed as a part of the ordinary ritual of the church—carried out with smooth dexterity but without much spirit. To say that the church was worldly does not begin to describe it. It was very successfully worldly in one of the worldliest of times. And while it was often criticized for being spiritually derelict, the church was understandably impervious to such caviling. As Leo's great-grandfather Cosimo had said, "States are not ruled by pater nosters."

VIII

LUTHER: THE RIGHTEOUSNESS
OF GOD

In justitia tua libera me. Martin Luther, pedantic thirty-year-old professor of Biblical studies and guilt-obsessed sinner, was terrified by a word in Psalm 31—"righteousness." "In thy righteousness deliver me." Righteousness, justice, filled him with panic. For surely if God is just, then Martin Luther was damned. He had confessed his sins, repented, confessed again— and still he was a sinner, with no hope of ever having a pure soul. "*In justitia tua libera me*—I was horror-stricken and felt deep hostility toward these words, God's righteousness, God's judgment, God's work. For I knew only that *justitia dei* meant a harsh judgment. Well, was He supposed to save me by judging me harshly? If so, I was lost forever." And so, Luther said, "since the sole purpose of life and religion is salvation, I did not love a just and angry God, but rather hated and murmured against Him." "I knew Christ as none other than a stern judge, from whose face I wanted to flee, and yet could not." "I used to turn pale when I heard the name Christ." "I have often been terrified by the name of Christ, and when I saw him on His cross, it was like a lightning stroke to me." Terror at *justitia*. Yet, as a lecturer, Luther was bound to face that despised word in the psalm again and again. When at last he reached a new understanding of *justitia dei* and gave to it a new definition, he had defined "Lutheranism" and the Protestant Reformation.

He reached his new understanding as he had reached most of his conclusions—by an arduous process of argument and refutation.

A passage of the Bible would be confronted, past exegetes quoted, compared, rebutted. Luther's own thoughts would be put forth, and he would test them, pick them apart, wait for others to refute them. But now his contending inner voices were made public. Preaching four times a week in church and lecturing twice a week to his students, Luther had begun to forge his theology through the spoken word.

"He was a man of middling height," one of his students recorded, "with a voice both sharp and gentle: it was soft in tone, sharp in the enunciation of syllables, words, and sentences. He spoke neither too rapidly nor too slowly, but evenly and without hesitation, as well as very clearly, and so logically that each part flowed naturally out of what went before." Heavy-boned, sturdy, with a furrowed brow and strong, stubborn chin, as time went on he assumed a posture that made him appear as though he was bending slightly over backwards, while at the same time his chin had an imperious lift to it.

At six o'clock in the morning on Tuesday, August 16, 1513, Luther entered the lecture room at his monastery. "Good sirs, fathers and brethren, you have come, as I see," Luther began, after a year's preparatory study, "with great and benevolent spirit, to do honor to the famous prophet David." The opening was irrefutable. Luther stumbled on. "I feel very surely the weight upon my neck of this task, which for a long time I was reluctant to undertake (all in vain) and to which I yield only when compelled to do so by order. For I confess plainly that to this day there are some Psalms I cannot understand, and unless the Lord enlighten me with your merits, as I hope, I cannot interpret them."

The Psalms contain nearly all the joy and anguish, the wrath and hope that warred in Luther himself. "For a man's heart is like a ship tossed on a wild sea," he said later on, when he had begun to find his voice. "Here it is buffeted by fear, and care about causing disaster: there grief and sadness come along in present evil. Here comes a breeze of hope. . . . Such tempests teach us to speak with earnestness, they open up the heart and reveal what is at the bottom of it. . . . What is the greatest thing about the Psalms, but this earnest speaking amid these tempests of every kind?" Just as Luther found a kindred turbulent spirit in Augustine, he found the words that expressed the range of his torment in the Psalms.

Luther prepared for his lectures in the small tower room in which he worked his entire adult life. The Augustine cloister was made up of a mean and chilly dormitory, an old chapel made, according to a visitor, of "a very rickety frame building propped up on all sides, about thirty feet long and twenty feet wide," which "had a small, old, rusty choir gallery in which at a pinch twenty persons could stand, and on the south wall a pulpit about five feet above the floor, made out of old rough boards. In short, it had in all respects the appearance of those pictures which artists paint of the stable in Bethlehem where Christ was born."

In the courtyard, which opened onto the street, was a pear tree where Luther often met and talked with Staupitz. On one side of the court was the brewery of the old monastery. Connecting the brewery and the monks' dormitory was a building with a tower-like top story. There, in a small but heated room, Luther parsed and analyzed the Scriptures.

As was customary, Luther had a local printer run up an edition of the Psalter for his students and himself. He used two copies. One was for the *glossae*, the explanation of individual words and critical comments from past exegetes. His interlinear and marginal notes crowd the pages in neat and exceedingly small handwriting. Here Augustine is cited, there Nicholas of Cusa, there Father Stapulensis or Cassiodorus or Reuchlin, again Augustine. The young professor prepared his course with exhausting thoroughness. The second copy of the Psalter he used for his *scholia*, the more free-ranging notes that pose interpretations, debate with opponents, and draw upon contemporary events for illustration or support of an argument. Rummaging through the library for references, Luther filled the margins of the standard textbooks with the same neat handwriting, dismissing unhelpful scholars as "pig-theologer!" or "maggots!" or "fetid logicians!"

The traditional method of exposition that Luther followed (one he later said "interpreted ineptly almost all the words of the Bible") was fourfold: literal, allegorical, tropological, and anagogical. Or, as Luther said, "So Jerusalem means literally the city that has that name, allegorically the struggling church, tropologically the clean conscience, and anagogically the heavenly fatherland of the Church triumphant." He droned on in this way to drowsy students in the early morning twice a week, sometimes supplementing his morning lectures with another at midday, for two years.

"Justice," he posited, "recompenses to each his due . . . equity distinguishes between merits, justice rewards. God judges the earth with equity (because He is the same to all, willing that all should be saved). He judges with righteousness, because He gives each one his deserved reward." It was a manner of exposition that must have sorely tried the devotion of students. Henry of Langenstein apparently held the record for marathon exegesis. He took thirteen years to cover four chapters of the Bible.

Yet, for all his excruciatingly persistent attention to detail, Luther could not face Psalm 31. When he came to the phrase "Deliver me in thy righteousness," he quickly jots down, "not in mine which is nothing" and moves on, still too fearful of *justitia* even to pause over it for a moment in the lecture room. The model professor, though his students may not have realized it, was battling with the Devil in his tower room every night. "Where sin is," Luther wrote, "there is no good conscience, but only insecurity and incessant fear of death and hell, with which no joy or pleasure can abide in the bottom of the heart, but as Leviticus says, such a heart is terrified at the rustling leaf."

For Luther was plagued by fear and doubt and the Devil, by his own anger, his hostile feelings toward God, his rebelliousness—and by constipation. And somehow, getting rid of one problem was linked to getting rid of them all. "A Christian should and could be gay," he once said, "but then the Devil shits on him." When he was more confident he would say, "I can drive away the Devil with a single fart." But the battle was never finally won, and Luther fought the Devil and strained toward salvation with citations from Augustine, with syllogisms and mystical insights, with some of the foulest language the Devil must ever have heard, and with his fists. "Note this down," Luther would say to the Devil, "I have shit in the pants, and you can hang them around your neck and wipe your mouth with it." Luther would shit in the Devil's face and "throw him back into my asshole where he belongs." In his tower study the Devil would throw black ink at Luther, and Luther would throw ink back at the Devil as he contended with the righteousness of God. The Protestant Reformation was the result of Luther's pedantic insistence on *justitia*— but it was no polite academic nicety by which Luther won his struggle; it involved all of him, from head to foot, in a paroxysm of spiritual and personal passion.

Luther proceeded psalm by psalm, and before he reached Psalm 71, in which *justitia* occurs once again, he had begun to work toward his revelation. Help came first from Staupitz. "I remember, Reverend Father," Luther later wrote his mentor, "that in one of your delightful and wholesome talks [no doubt under the pear tree] . . . the word 'repentance' was mentioned. I received your word as coming from Heaven when you said that repentance is not genuine unless it begins with a love of righteousness and God, and that what the torturers consider to be the end and consummation of repentance is rather its beginning." Indeed, according to Staupitz, confession played a very minor role in the achievement of salvation. "Start with the wounds of Christ," he said, and "set Christ carefully before the mind's eye. That takes care of predestination—God foresaw the suffering of His son for sinners. He who believes in Him is predestined, he who does not believe is not. . . . We are justified by the blood of Christ, for that innocent blood was shed for the remission of our sins."

With these and other remarks Staupitz led Luther to a personal faith in the forgiveness of sins through Christ. Luther had thought he must first perfectly repent for his own sins and fulfill the commands of the Old Testament law and only then would Christ's sacrifice on the cross atone for his sins and assure his salvation. Staupitz taught, on the contrary, that *first* Luther must

have faith in Christ, then Christ's sacrifice atoned for his sins, and
then, at last, repentance began.

The crucial word *justitia*, as Staupitz taught Luther, referred
not to the righteousness of a judge deciding whether his law was
fulfilled but rather to the righteousness, or virtue, of God that
God *shares* with men. God, through grace, heals men; then, and
only then, does the process of repentance—a process, as it were,
of the convalescence of a sick man—begin. Then through good
works men became justified and shared in God's righteousness.
Thus they are predestined for salvation. To share in God's grace
man needs at first only to have faith. No man can *earn* this grace
from God through good works or contrition or in any way. No
man can be worthy of it. Man can prepare to receive grace,
however, by admitting his full guilt and unworthiness, by
complete humility and self-condemnation, by faith and total reli-
ance on God. Anguish and terror, Staupitz told the distraught
young man (Luther would read much the same in the works of
his favorite mystics such as Johann Tauber), were not signs that
Luther was destined for hell; quite the opposite: They were the
way in which God draws men to Christ and prepares them to
depend on God's righteousness.

In effect, Staupitz utterly reversed Luther's idea of the way to
achieve justification before God. In place of Luther's "active"
view of justification—that is, man is acceptable to God if his
actions are just—Staupitz taught that man is both passive and
active in becoming justified: He passively receives God's grace,
and only then does he actively do good works. Repentance came
last, not first, and came after the complete faith in Christ that had
already prepared him for the renewal of his soul. The idea was
not yet as clearly developed as it soon would be—nor had Luther
added the ultimate twist that would depart entirely from Catholic
teaching. But Staupitz's words were liberating to the young professor, and Luther turned quickly to his old companion Augustine.

In Augustine's treatise *On the Spirit and the Letter* Luther
found confirmation first of his new notion of God's righteousness:
The passage, according to Augustine, "does not say the righteous-

ness of man or the righteousness of his will, but the 'righteousness of God'—meaning not that whereby He Himself is righteous but that with which He endows man. . . . 'Being justified freely by His grace.' It is not, therefore, by the Law nor by their own will that they are justified; but they are justified freely by God's grace —not that justification takes place without our will; but our will is shown to be weak by the Law, that grace may heal its infirmity, and thus healed, it may fulfill the Law.

"Now it is freely or gratuitously that man is justified thereby, that is, he has no previous merits of his own with which to earn this favor, 'otherwise grace is no more grace,' since it is bestowed on us, not because we have done good works, but that we might be able to do them—in other words, not because we have fulfilled, but in order that we might be able to fulfill the Law." It is grace alone, Augustine insists, "that separates the redeemed from the lost," and permits the redeemed, through repentance and good works, to attain their predestined salvation, "all having been involved in the common origin"—that is, man's descent from Adam.

On the morning that Luther took up Psalm 71 he was able to speak of righteousness with confidence: " 'In thee, O Lord, do I put my trust; let me never be put to confusion. Deliver me in thy righteousness, and cause me to escape; incline thine ear unto me, and save me. . . .' The righteousness of God," Luther announced, "is wholly this, namely, that one humbles himself profoundly. . . . Here he [i.e., the prophet David] speaks properly of Christ, who is the power and righteousness of God through the greatest and profoundest humility." Having found his voice, Luther continues firmly, "He does not say that he desires to be freed by something else besides righteousness. For we are delivered from unrighteousness by righteousness, just as we are delivered from sickness by health, and from ignorance by knowledge.

"We are always sinning," Luther continued cheerily, "we are always impure . . . wherefore we who are righteous are constantly on the move, always being justified. . . . The starting point is sin, from which we must constantly depart. The goal is righteousness, toward which we must move unceasingly." Yet for all his apparent confidence and good cheer, Luther was still troubled—now by the thought of *becoming* righteous. God's grace was a miraculous and good start; Christ's atonement for man's sins was a great boon; but still man is not righteous until he completes the work by fulfilling the law. And so, if one becomes righteous, in some sense one must become predestined. Yet, either a man is or is not predestined for salvation. Now, in his tower room, Luther gnawed uneasily at the notion of becoming righteous.

He had already determined to follow his lectures on the Psalms with a series of lectures on Paul's Epistle to the Romans, and he set doggedly to work with Augustine to analyze Paul. Again Luther came across that word *justitia*, and the neat formulations of Staupitz and Augustine failed to reassure him. Again, Luther was plunged into doubt and confusion. "I was astray for a long time," Luther later said. "My inner condition was a mystery to me. True, I was aware of something, but what it was I did not know until I came to the passage in Romans I: 'The righteous shall live by faith.' There I found help. Then I saw what Paul had in mind when he spoke of righteousness. There in the text stood 'righteousness.' I related the abstract and the concrete and became certain of my cause, learning to distinguish between the righteousness of the Law and of the Gospel. I had considered both to be the same and Christ to differ from Moses only in time and perfection. It was when I discovered the difference between the Law and the Gospel, that they were two separate things, that I broke through."

Elsewhere, Luther wrote, "Day and night I tried to meditate upon the significance of these words: 'The righteousness of God is revealed in it, as it is written: the righteous shall live by faith.' Then, finally God had mercy on me, and I began to understand that the righteousness of God is that gift of God by which a righteous man lives, namely, faith, and that this sentence: The righteousness of God is revealed in the Gospel, is *passive*, indicating that the merciful God justifies us by faith. . . ." Soon Luther would say more clearly: by faith *alone*, *sola fides*. There was no

WHITE ROBE, BLACK ROBE

process of healing, of becoming. There was no utility whatever to good works. No one, no thing, stood between man and God. "Justification," Luther said, "does not take place through works, but by faith alone, without any works, and not piecemeal, but completely at once. The testament, that is, the Gospel promise, includes everything in itself: justification, salvation, inheritance, and blessing. It is appropriated by faith completely at once, not piecemeal. Truly it is plain, then," Luther repeats enthusiastically, "that faith alone brings such good things of God, that is, justification and salvation, and makes us instantaneously, not gradually, children and heirs, who then freely do good works of all kinds."

With that, Luther had his creed. His more squeamish followers were always embarrassed about the place where his revelations occurred: "These words 'righteous' and 'righteousness of God' struck my conscience as flashes of lightning, frightening me each time I heard them. . . . But by the grace of God, as I once meditated [perhaps while fighting off the vulgar attacks of the Devil] upon these words in this tower and *Cl.* . . . there suddenly came into my mind the thought that . . ." and so forth. The *Cl.* was an abbreviation for *cloaca*, or toilet. And so it would appear that Luther found spiritual and physical relief simultaneously— and "instantaneously, not gradually." For one whose theology was that of the "whole man" it was as appropriate an occasion as could be imagined; the fusion of humanity and spirit that he saw in Christ, he lived himself. He turned traditional Catholic teaching upside down. He solved his dilemma this time not by going over someone's head but rather by going behind the church fathers' backs to reclaim what he understood to be Paul's original teaching. The ironies and poetic and theological and personal correspondences abound. In any case, although Luther would be troubled by his digestion all his life, at this moment he evidently won a decisive battle against the Devil.

Now fear and repression, muteness, inhibition, constipation all gave way to an eruption of talk and writing and exuberant work. "I felt as though I had been reborn altogether and had entered

Paradise. In the same moment the whole of Scripture became apparent to me. My mind ran through the Scriptures, as far as I was able to recollect them, seeking analogies in other phrases, such as the work of God, that which God works in us, the wisdom of God, by which He makes us wise . . . the salvation of God, the glory of God. Just as intensely as I had before hated the expression 'the righteousness of God,' I now lovingly praised this most pleasant word. This passage from Paul became to me the very gate to Paradise."

Preoccupied and thrilled as he was by what his revelation meant to himself, the self-absorbed young professor did not quite seem to realize yet that in his scheme of things the pope was irrelevant —or worse.

IX

ROME, THE ENCHANTED CITY

"AVOID the Epistles of St. Paul," Papal Secretary Bembo advised Papal Secretary Sadoleto, "lest his barbarous style should spoil your taste." Just why Bembo thought the admonition was necessary is a complete mystery, for Sadoleto was no more likely to read Saint Paul than was Leo X. The priests of Rome were flamens, and they no longer forgave the sins of dying men but rather appeased "the powers of Hades." God the Father was Jove, or Jupiter *Optimus Maximus*; Christ was Apollo or Aesculapius; and the Virgin Mary was Diana. Sermons were praised or not depending upon just how Ciceronian in style they were, and when Christ's death on the cross was mentioned, the inevitable comparison was to Cecrops, Menaecius, and Iphigenia, who sacrificed themselves for the welfare of their country. Socrates and Phocion were invoked—and Epaminondas, a great man forced to defend himself against criminal charges. Scipio, after all, had suffered exile. Hymns composed by Marullus praised the ancient deities of Greece and Rome, and "persuasion" was used interchangeably with "faith."

Through all these elegantly composed sermons Leo sat perspiring. "He is indeed gross," his master of ceremonies, Paris de Grassis, observed of Leo at mass, "and has a fat body, and so then, as always, he was in a sweat, and never did anything in the midst of his ceremonial duties but wipe away the perspiration dripping from his head and face and throat and hands with a small linen cloth." By 1514 Leo had ordered the master of the palace to make certain, on pain of excommunication, that no sermon exceed a half hour in length, and several years later he instructed Paris de Grassis to remind the master of the palace that the council of the Lateran had declared that no sermon should exceed fifteen minutes.

The eighth deadly sin, in Leo's view, was tedium, and his court was dedicated to avoiding it at all costs. Leo doubled Julius' budget for the papal household, and more than 650 minions labored mightily to keep up with the succession of banquets and plays and carnivals and impromptu battles that Leo staged in which people gamboled up and down the banks of the Tiber assaulting one another with oranges. His hunting parties lasted for weeks, sometimes months, and he thought nothing of inviting 1,000 or 2,000 select friends to accompany him on the hunt. On the spur of the moment the pope would invite the cardinals in for cards; the doors would be thrown open and Leo would toss his winnings over his shoulder to the crowd of spectators. He loved chess and was an excellent player, very quick in his moves and shrewd in his tactics. He disapproved of dice as "injurious to morals"—though that seems a ruse to excuse himself from a game in which the canny tactician had to trust too much to chance. Leo had a fine ear for music, too, and after Raphael completed his tapestries for the Sistine Chapel, Leo could often be found sitting there under Michelangelo's ceiling with his eyes closed, his lips pursed, his white hands folded delicately in his lap, listening and humming as the finest choristers from France or Greece or Mantua—whom he had imported, at wonderful cost—sang the offices. A Spaniard named Gabriel Merino had an excellent voice and a good knowledge of church music, and Leo rewarded him for his accomplishments with the archbishopric of Bari. Similarly struck by the musical talents of a man named Francesco Paolosa, Leo made him an archdeacon.

The pope was very much a religious man, certainly just as religious as Luther was. But whereas Luther's experience of religion was intellectual and concerned with a sinner's guilt before God, Leo's experience of religion was entirely sensual and apparently utterly free of guilt. He could not tolerate hearing those interminable, meaningless sermons, much less, like Luther, give one; but he could happily sit in the midst of the visions of Raphael and Michelangelo, listening to the music of the angels and be transported to communion with God. Though Luther might insist Leo's experience was esthetic, anyone who has been "in heaven" at the sound of well-done Gregorian chant—or an Indian raga— can attest that the experience is a religious one. Leo always made a clear distinction, and a valid one, between religion and theology.

A savage love of the hunt, a lamentably typical Florentine love of crude jokes, an exalted sense of music and poetry—Leo intended to taste all the delicacies life had to offer. He brought more than 250 artists to Rome and more than 300 poets, and he kept them well entertained and well fed and traded verses with all of them. One fellow who hastened to Rome in the hope of getting support from Leo had to wait for several days to gain an audience. He delivered himself of some Latin verses and stood back waiting to be showered with gold. Instead, Leo instantly improvised an equal number of Latin lines, and with the very same terminations. The poet recovered from his shock: "Had fortune from your verses repaid," he said to Leo, "the tiara would never have encircled your head." A fair retort, Leo thought, and opened his purse. He sent away a great many men with nothing, and he rewarded scores of mediocre parasites—yet few men in history have been such generous and enthusiastic patrons of the arts. When Bernardo Accolti paid his patron a visit, the irrepressible Leo cried out, "Open all the doors, and let in the crowd!" Accolti improvised his verses and, according to a contemporary, "when it was known in Rome that the celestial Bernardo Accolti intended to recite his verses, the shops were shut up as for a holiday, and all persons hastened to partake of the entertainment . . . on such occasions he was surrounded by the prelates and chief persons of the city, honored by the solemn light of torches, and attended by a numerous body of Swiss guards." It was only a poet's due, thought Leo.

In all this heady swirl of music and verse and good wines and

Cicero, the inner circle that formed around Leo shared his charm and graciousness, his wit and liberality. They were, many of them, old friends who had met at the court of Urbino under Duke Guidobaldo of Montefeltro. It was to Urbino that Leo's brother Giuliano had fled when the Medicis were driven from Florence. And there in the evenings he joined Bembo and Accolti and Bibbiena for long, erudite, and gentle conversations with the duke and his brilliant and sophisticated duchess Elizabetta Gonzaga. Raphael had been born in Urbino, and the old courtiers from that refined city-state naturally assumed the role of favored men in Leonine Rome. If Leo had a text—in the way that Luther had his text in St. Paul—it was *The Book of the Courtier*, then being written between banquets and outings and diplomatic vexations by Baldassare Castiglione.

Castiglione, another member of the old Urbino group, had been sent to Rome as ambassador to the Vatican by Guidobaldo's successor, Duke Francescomaria della Rovere. The consummate courtier, he was well born (his mother was a Gonzaga) and, judging from Raphael's portrait, politely good-looking, with a fine nose and calm, clear eyes and a well-trimmed, full beard. He was thoroughly schooled in Greek and Latin and able to compose a respectable verse. He had dabbled handsomely, but not brilliantly, in the military as a cavalry officer at the Battle of Garigliano in 1503, helping to lose Naples to Spain. He had a fine turn of phrase, a mild wit, a temperament of good cheer and easy grace, and a natural gift for making himself welcome in the world. He had a connoisseur's knowledge of music and painting and wine and appreciated the gentle influence of women in the world. Not surprisingly, his ideal courtier has all the elements of character that Castiglione himself had.

The Book of the Courtier was written to savor and memorialize those early years of the century at Urbino when the talk was always agreeable, the evenings enchanting, the ladies witty but demure, the men serious but never somber. "Amidst the pleasant pastimes," Castiglione wrote, "the music and dancing which were continually enjoyed, fine questions would sometimes be proposed, and sometimes ingenious games, now at the behest of one person and now of another, in which, under various concealments, those present revealed their thoughts allegorically to whomever they chose . . . poets, musicians, and all sorts of buffoons, and the most excellent of every kind of talent that could be found in Italy, were always gathered there." On the occasion that Castiglione chooses for his book, a spring evening in 1507, various games and topics of conversation are proposed by the members of the company and dismissed lightly one at a time, until Federico Fregoso proposed that they consider "what belongs to the perfection of Courtiership."

Either the duchess, or her constant companion, a heckling widow named Emilia Pia, would set the particular topic for the evening and choose the speaker, and no speaker was permitted to plead ignorance or dispatch his chores briefly. The ease of entering into intellectual exercise, the ability to improvise a well-made and engaging argument, was, after all, one of the essential qualities of the courtier. And so, as the conversation continued from one night to the next, other characteristics of the perfect courtier were added to those already remarked in Castiglione. The courtier must dress well, but not ostentatiously; he must be an accomplished horseman and know how to compete well in jousts, tennis, swimming, jumping, and running but avoid "vaulting on the ground, rope-walking, and the like, which smack of the juggler's trade and little befit a gentleman." Pride is appropriate to the courtier, but not egoism; he must have self-respect and mutual consideration for others. He should have a certain nonchalance and a proper appreciation of appropriateness: "Let him consider well what he does or says, the place where he does it, in whose presence, its timeliness, the reason for doing it, his own age, his profession, the end at which he aims, and the means by which he can reach it." And, later: "Let him not attempt those quick movements of foot and those double steps which we find most becoming in our Barletta [a dancer at the court], but which would perhaps little befit a gentleman. Yet privately, in a chamber, as we are now, I think he could be allowed to try this, and try morris

124

dances and *branles* [a Spanish dance rather like the cotillion] as well; but not in public, unless he is masquerading. . . ." In great ways and small, the courtier was conjured into being and courtliness given its most gracious definition.

The gentlemen at Urbino agreed, as Leo's father, Lorenzo, had decided with his Florentine coterie some years before, that the vulgar tongue was acceptable and, in some instances, even preferable to Latin. And, at Urbino, the men adduced precepts, proposed models (Petrarch and Boccaccio), and vied with one another in praising their native tongue. These digressions are what make *The Courtier* a readable book and not merely a laborious code of behavior. Is sculpture a superior art to painting? Which is the best musical instrument for a courtier to play? On what occasion may a courtier disobey the orders of his prince? "And what," Signor Gasparo asked, "do you say of the game of chess?"

"It is certainly a pleasing and ingenious amusement," said Messer Frederico, the prissy and prosaic scion of a noble Genoese family, "but it seems to me to have one defect, which is that it is possible to have too much knowledge of it, so that whoever would excel in the game must give a great deal of time to it, as I believe, and as much study as if he would learn some noble science or perform well anything of importance; and yet in the end, for all his pains, he only knows how to play a game. Thus, I think a very unusual thing happens in this, namely, that mediocrity is more to be praised than excellence."

Questions of ethics and dress, manners and morals were taken up, and it is evident that the participants relished such lofty discourse. Nor did Castiglione neglect to provide some relief from these refined topics. "We shall give messer Bernardo Bibbiena the task of discussing pleasantries," Signora Emilia said, and Leo X's masterful politician sensed the mood of the company in a trice. Passing over the more ordinary pleasantries swiftly, the seemingly innocent, self-deprecating bald Bibbiena observed that "laughter restores the spirit, gives pleasure, and for the moment keeps one from remembering those vexing troubles of which our life is full." And with that he launched nimbly into a string of stories droll, whimsical, quizzical, absurd, farcical, sportive, jolly, and facetious. He displayed his dexterity in the pun, the yarn, the riposte direct and the riposte indirect, in persiflage and epigram, the tease, the badinage, ignoring neither trifle, whimwham, nor fiddle-faddle. Indeed, he provided Castiglione with the most complete summary of Renaissance humor we have, leaving out only the blasphemous, the obscene, the salacious, and the offensive.

"You will not have forgotten the foolishness of that abbot of whom the Duke was telling not so long ago, who was present one day when Duke Federico was discussing what should be done with the great mass of earth that has been excavated for the foundations of this palace, which he was then building, and said: 'My Lord, I have an excellent idea where to put it. Give orders that a great pit be dug, and without further trouble it can be put into that.' Duke Federico replied, not without laughter: 'And where shall we put the earth that is excavated in digging this pit of yours?' Said the abbot: 'Make it big enough to hold both.'"

Hours passed, and Bibbiena continued to hold the company, yielding from time to time when another member of the group was reminded of a story. ". . . one day I asked Fedra why it was that on Good Friday, when the Church prayed not only for Christians but even for pagans and Jews, no mention was made of cardinals along with bishops and other prelates, he answered me that cardinals were intended in the prayer that says: 'Let us pray for heretics and schismatics.'

". . . the Archbishop of Florence said to Cardinal Alessandrino, that men have only their goods, their body, and their soul: their goods are harried by lawyers, their body by physicians, and their soul by theologians."

Giuliano de' Medici replied: "One might add to this what Nicoletto used to say, that we seldom find a lawyer who goes to law himself, a physician who takes physic, or a theologian who is a good Christian."

As the second evening drew to a close, the conversation turned by chance to women, and brash young Gasparo Pallavicino blundered into a slighting reference. And so, before the company retired, the duchess proposed that on the following night "a Court Lady perfect in every way should be imagined, just as these gentlemen have imagined the perfect Courtier." Emilia Pia added: "God forbid that we should chance to entrust this task to any fellow conspirator of signor Gasparo, who should fashion us a Court Lady unable to do anything except cook and spin." And the duchess declared that she would confidently entrust Giuliano de' Medici with the task of describing the ideal woman.

The ideal woman that Giuliano described was, predictably, the duchess—a woman of grace, intellect, wit, beauty, modesty, and in all ways the complement, if not the equal, of the ideal man. She was not to make a career in the military, to be sure, or be educated in the "manly" arts of jousting and wrestling; she was to be chaste and deferential toward men. Indeed, she was to be all that one used to call feminine—until the mid-twentieth century. In retrospect she may not seem quite so "liberated" as some feminists would wish. Yet, in the Renaissance woman was truly liberated from a role of mere chattel to one of dignity, and a man who lived without the gentle influence of a woman was thought to be not quite civilized. The duchess rarely enters into the conversation of *The Courtier*, but it is her spirit that suffuses the book. She presides, and her character greatly determines what the men feel they may say and believe. In ancient times women had been warriors, many had been brave, some had ruled states, though for the most part they remained in a completely inferior state, and the best woman, Pericles maintained, was one nobody mentioned. The Provençal poets—Bernart de Ventadorn, Guilhem de Cabastanh, Arnaud Daniel, and others—were the first to celebrate the romantic love of women: Guilhem once wrote (in a translation by Ford Maddox Ford):

> The pleasant fever
> That love doth often bring
> Lady, doth ever
> Attune the songs I sing

Where I endeavor
To catch again your chaste
Sweet body savor
I crave but may not taste.

The humanists of the Renaissance turned Provence's poetic inspiration into a fully articulated ideal of woman that has lasted (for better and for worse, for richer and for poorer) until the present day.

And so, Castiglione fondly hoped, it might be seen from his little book "how superior the Court of Urbino was to all others in Italy. . . . And if these were such, imagine what the other worthy pursuits were to which our minds were bent and wholly given over; and of this I confidently make bold to speak in the hope of being believed, for I am not praising things so ancient that I am free to invent, and I can prove my claims by the testimony of many men worthy of credence who are still living and who personally saw and knew the life and customs that once flourished in that court: and I consider myself obliged, as far as I can see, to make every effort to preserve this bright memory from mortal oblivion, and make it live in the mind of posterity. . . ."

The hectic life of Rome prevented Castiglione from putting his manuscript in final form and publishing his book until 1528. In the meantime he joined the Roman court that was dedicated to surpassing Urbino in every way. And it succeeded—in its love of beauty, its mutual respect of individuals, its openness to the arts and philosophy, its cultivation of poetry and music and fun, its appreciation for well-used leisure, its celebration of the powers of man, its respect for the moral values of Plato and Cicero and Aristotle, and in its fragility. That it was fragile, and in many ways overlaid with artificiality, should not obscure its excellent qualities. It had become brittle, but not hollow.

The Roman University, first conceived by Boniface VIII in 1303, languished and all but disappeared during the reign of Julius II, who had diverted the funds for its support to his wars. Leo set about reviving the university with his habitual extravagance. He hired nearly a hundred professors at ample salaries and established faculties in civil and canon law, logic, rhetoric, mathematics, moral philosophy, medicine, astronomy, theology, and the first chair in botany. "Having a most earnest desire," he wrote to Marcus Musurus in one of the scores of college-conjuring letters Bembo and Sadoleto churned out for him in their fine Ciceronian style, "to promote the study of the Greek language and of Grecian literature, which are now almost extinct, and to encourage the liberal arts as far as lies in my power, and being well convinced of your great learning and singular judgment, I request that you will take the trouble of inviting from Greece ten young men, or as many more as you think proper . . . who may compose a seminary of liberal studies. . . ." To house the young scholars, Leo bought the palace of one of the cardinals and turned it into a Greek institute.

Soon enough books began to issue from the presses. While Luther worked out his *scholia* for Saint Paul, Leo patronized *scholiae* on the tragedies of Sophocles and the works of Pindar, a revised and corrected edition of the idylls and epigrams of Theocritus. He set Varino to work on a Greek dictionary, and when a book appeared in Greek typography, Leo rose to the occasion and subsidized a Greek press at his university.

Leo supported droves of writers all but indiscriminately. There was Tebaldeo, the failing physician in his fifties, who presented Leo with a Latin epigram in the pope's praise and received a purse of 500 ducats for his labor. Francesco Maria Molza, a young man of a noble family from Modena, wrote tender little nothings in both Latin and Italian; when he heard of Leo's generosity to poets, he left his native city, his wife and family (his father later disinherited him for it) and joined Leo's disciples with true devotion. Vittoria Colonna, the daughter of the famous *condottiere* Fabrizio Colonna, wrote vivacious verses in ottava rima, and it was to her, some years after Leo's death, that Michelangelo wrote a good many of his love sonnets. Gian Giorgio Trissino wrote a romantic tragedy for the stage, *Sofonisba*, which is generally conceded to be the first notable Italian work in blank verse. And, of course, there was Bembo, who spent most of his time during Leo's pontificate writing letters for the pope. His most famous work, *Gli Asolani*, had been written earlier in the century. It was a widely influential work in praise of Platonic love (of a sort Plato would not have recognized but that nonetheless has stuck even today as our notion of Platonic love). Much of Bembo's work was summarized by Castiglione in his reporting of Bembo's conversations in *The Courtier*.

Of the artists associated with Leo, only a few stand out. Luca della Robbia, the master of terra cotta, worked a bit for Leo and produced his coat of arms among other decorations for the Vatican. The pope left the completion of his father's villa at Poggio a Caiano to a relative, who enhanced the Medici reputation by employing Andrea del Sarto and Jacopo de Pontormo. But Leo's attentions were concentrated on two artists: Michelangelo and Raphael.

Michelangelo had been taken into the Medici household when he was an adolescent by Leo's father, and he had been raised among the family, been taught his craft in Lorenzo's "sculpture garden," and enjoyed the company both of the Medicis and their coterie of artists and scholars. Because of this special relationship to his family, Leo turned spontaneously to Michelangelo when he came to consider what distinctive legacy he could leave to his native city, which had never previously been blessed with a native son as pope. He decided that he could do no better than refurbish the Medici family church of San Lorenzo, both inside and out, and particularly give it a magnificent façade. When he informed Michelangelo of the fitting project he had for him, the sculptor was dismayed at the thought of leaving Rome. He had first to finish Julius II's tomb, he insisted. Leo had no enthusiasm for ♦ wasting Michelangelo's talents on immortalizing his predecessor and commanded Michelangelo to go to Florence. He was obligated to the Cardinals Pucci and Grossi, Michelangelo said. Leo would satisfy the cardinals. Michelangelo set off for Florence with his customary grumbling, to which he added this time, according to Vasari, "weeping."

Michelangelo repaired to the quarries at Carrara to look for suitable marble for the work. But Leo had heard of a new source of marble at Seravezza in Florentine territory and instructed Michelangelo to go there. The sculptor protested; he would lose time. Leo was adamant; a new quarry in Florence to rival that of Carrara was too tempting a prospect to ignore. And so, as Vasari reports, "it was necessary to make a road of several miles through the mountains, breaking the rocks with maces and pickaxes, and driving piles in the marshy places. In fulfilling the pope's wish, Michelangelo thus spent many years, and at length obtained five columns of some size, one of which is on the piazza of San Lorenzo in Florence. . . ." Michelangelo finished a model for some windows at the Medici palace, some designs for the church, supervised the laying of foundations of the church, and had one marble column delivered to Florence. During Leo's reign that was the extent of Michelangelo's accomplishments; it was the least productive period of his life. And the church of San Lorenzo remains today without a façade, a unique memorial to Leo's stubbornness —and to Michelangelo's recalcitrance.

While Leo harassed Michelangelo, he indulged Raphael in everything, and it is to Raphael that we must turn for the paintings that form our image of Leonine Rome. It is Raphael who painted the portrait of Leo with two cardinals (his bastard cousin Giulio, the future Clement VII, standing on the left), in which the pope is shown with his gold-rimmed eyeglass and a richly illuminated book on the table in front of him. Our image of Castiglione was painted by Raphael, as were those of Elizabetta Gonzaga and of Bibbiena, looking at us out of the corners of languidly heavy eyelids with the hint of a knowing smile playing at one side of his mouth. It is Raphael who glorified Plato, Aristotle, Pythagoras, and Ptolemy in his "School of Athens" in the Vatican, and it is Raphael who painted in the Vatican Logge his so-called "Bible" —forty-eight frescoes illustrating the Old Testament and four frescoes showing the New Testament—the most ambitious Biblical commentary undertaken in Leo's Rome, though unfortunately of no use in debating with Luther.

Raphael was born in Urbino in 1483, and in his self-portrait he seems a fragile young man, with large almond-shaped eyes that are, perhaps, too passive and pretty, and with the pursed, nearly simpering lips that characterize so many of his paintings of women. He was a passing fair ladies' man and, although most of his paintings are characterized by well-draped females and well-muscled nude males, he did one portrait of a bare-breasted woman, La Fornarina, a baker's daughter. She, too, simpers—but with fuller, more sensuous lips, and, although she is not beautiful, she looks yielding and willing enough. Some historians maintain that this young woman was Raphael's mistress, a dubious assertion at best, since the master left most of the work on it to his assistant Giulio Romano and only added the finishing touches himself. The other candidate for Raphael's mistress is La Velata, a sumptuously arrayed woman with an ample body, penetrating eyes, and a small, soft, welcoming smile. When Agostino Chigi commissioned Raphael to do some frescoes in his villa, Raphael was unable to keep his mind on his work until Chigi agreed to bring the artist's mistress to live in the villa while the paintings were being done. A look at the two portraits leaves little doubt that it was La Velata who kept Raphael from his work.

Perhaps no artist has been as popular in his own lifetime as Raphael was. Commissions swamped him, his fees were prodigious, he was Rome's first painter, Safekeeper of Ancient Inscriptions, and he built himself a princely villa in Rome. In his later years he was less a painter than an impresario of the arts, sometimes giving no more than the most general suggestion for a painting or fresco to his assistants, which they then executed in the name of Raphael. Ever modest, ever sweet-tempered, Raphael was one of Rome's finest spectacles as he walked from his villa to the Vatican each day accompanied by fifty assistants and students and sycophants—painters, architects, engravers, woodworkers. And Michelangelo thoroughly detested him. "You walk as a general at the head of an army," he barked out at Raphael during one of those morning processions. "And you," Raphael replied to Italy's leading grouch, "as an executioner on the way to the scaffold."

Leo X put Raphael to work finishing the rooms begun at Julius' behest, and in the frescoes for the pope's bedroom Raphael promptly inserted a picture of Leo on his white horse in "The Meeting of Attila with St. Leo the Great." It was this perhaps legendary event that Leo intended to have serve as the keynote of his pontificate: the bold, but gentle Leo with pacifying, ringed hand raised in mild approbation stops the Huns at the gates of Rome. Saints Peter and Paul descend from above with swords drawn and, at the right, Attila recoils in horror and sends the Huns into frenzied disarray. As Raphael had it, nothing could have been easier than to repel an attack on Rome. Having so handily dispatched the barbarians, Raphael next set his army of painters to work on the "Incendio," in which the pope as Leo IV appears with upraised hand to quench a fire that threatens the Vatican basilica. Next Raphael set Giulio Romano loose on the "Battle of Ostia," in which the troops of Leo IV defeated the Saracens at the mouth of the Tiber. Then Penni and Raffaellino del Colle turned their hands, under Raphael's now bored eye, to the "Coronation of Charlemagne by Pope Leo III," in which we see that even the emperor owes allegiance to the pope. The literal meaning of the two levels of Raphael's paintings, the reference to events past and present, is always perfectly obvious. The real message, however, lies elsewhere; in Raphael, turbulent, swirling, consummate energy is contained in a composition that is exquisitely serene and, like the painter himself, sweet-tempered. His sweetness is, at times, cloying, and I prefer the unbridled gusto of Michelangelo. Yet, in his ability to harmonize energy and serenity, Raphael probably expressed better than any other artist the intellectual ideal of the "Renaissance man," who contained all passions and knowledge in perfect dynamic balance. Had frescoes been theological arguments, Rome would have been invincible; unfortunately, Luther had no taste for paintings.

Many were called, and many chosen—so many, in fact, that those excluded from Leo's inner circle must seem a more select group than those who enjoyed the pope's patronage. Machiavelli was out of favor by virtue of his having apparently condoned, if not actually joined, the conspiracy of 1503 against the Medici government in Florence. He spent his days now wandering over his meager estate talking to his workers, drinking and trading stories at a local inn, and writing fretful letters to his friends begging for some job in Rome or in the Florentine government. He was a master at offering unsolicited advice and wrote constantly to a friend in Rome about politics in the hope that his letters would be seen by Leo. He was certain that if Leo were to read only a paragraph or two of his trenchant observations the word would go out instantly to bring this genius Machiavelli to Rome to be the political eminence at the Vatican. As acute a political observer as Machiavelli was, he could not bring himself to realize that, since he was so remote from Rome and its concerns and sources of news, his advice was destined to sound naïve and impractical and even bewildering in its irrelevance. Yet he persisted. "When evening comes, I return home and go into my study. On the threshold I strip off the muddy, sweaty clothes of everyday, and put on the robes of court and palace, and in this graver dress I enter the antique courts of the ancients where, being welcomed by them, I taste the food that alone is mine, for which I was born. And there I make bold to speak to them and ask the motives for their actions. . . . And for the space of four hours I forget the world, remember no vexation, fear poverty no more, tremble no more at death: I am wholly absorbed in them. . . . I have written down what I have gained from their conversation, and composed a small work *De principatibus.* . . ."

The Prince, as Machiavelli's book is known in English, was intended to be a handbook for Italian princes. Some of its advice was so bizarre that later historians have assumed Machiavelli meant it as satire. But, no, the more he lost touch with the realities of politics, the more earnestly didactic he became. If anything, he simply embarrassed the politicians he bedeviled with advice. What prince did not know that alliances were made to be broken at their convenience? What Italian prince had ever blanched at the murder of a rival? Machiavelli made explicit what princes had

134

long taken for granted. In doing so, he made the princes blush, if they had a shred of repressed decency left, or else discount Machiavelli as a hopeless innocent.

But Machiavelli dedicated his book first to Giuliano de' Medici and, later, when Giuliano's nephew Lorenzo inherited the family's political concerns, to Lorenzo. Whether he was ever able to overcome his discouragement at the chilliness with which his advice was received and actually present *The Prince* to Lorenzo is not known. According to one story, he did give the handbook to Lorenzo, but the young prince had just been given a pair of greyhounds and was far more interested in his hounds than in Machiavelli's manuscript. In any case, the work was not printed in Machiavelli's lifetime, and he returned disconsolately to his study and wrote his *Discourses on Livy*, a play, a short story, and ever more sardonic letters to his friends.

Leo invited Leonardo da Vinci to Rome, and Leonardo arrived at the Vatican escorted by Giuliano de' Medici. Leo proposed a subject and suggested that Leonardo try some sketches if the theme appealed to him. According to Vasari, Leonardo "straightway began to distill oil and herbs to make varnish, which induced Pope Leo to say: 'This man will never do anything, for he begins to think of the end before the beginning.'" The two men could never understand one another. Leonardo was in his seventies by this time, and he devoted his last years to his special pleasures—experiments with balloons and lizards and one thing and another—and died in France in 1519.

Lodovico Ariosto hastened to Rome, along with the hordes of poets, and, as the admitted leading poet of the age and an old friend of Leo and Giuliano, he anticipated an easy life during Leo's pontificate. He was the pope's senior by a year, a man with bright eyes, rumpled good looks, and an amused smile that seemed to indicate he expected the world to be corrupt and foolish. Ariosto knelt before the pope, and Leo reached down and raised him to he feet and kissed him effusively on both cheeks. Ariosto left his audience assured of the pope's patronage. But after he had waited several days in Rome without further word from his old chum, Ariosto left Rome in a huff and vowed never to return.

Leo conferred one small boon on Ariosto: He issued a papal bull securing to the poet the sole right to print his epic poem—the finest literary product of the age, and one of the finest achievements in Western literature—the *Orlando Furioso*. Leo also advanced several hundred crowns toward the expense of printing the work, and the first forty cantos appeared in 1516 (the final version of forty-six cantos was not finished until 1532, the year before Ariosto died).

Orlando Furioso is a bodacious, bombastic, often unruly, and at times delicate and graceful invention in several thousand lines, with two plots and a plethora of incidental events, tourneys, miniature histories and biographies, love scenes, disasters natural and unnatural, wicked swords and profusions of blood, sorcery and betrayal that takes place everywhere from India to the moon, where Orlando, driven mad by his mistress' betrayal, drinks ". . . a liquor soft and thin,/which, save well corked, would have from the vase have drained," and the magic liquor restores Orlando's senses. The moon in Ariosto's vision is a delightful place:

> Here other river, lake, and rich champaign
> Are seen, than those which are below descried;
> Here other valley, other hill and plain,
> With towns and cities of their own supplied;
> Which mansions of such mighty size contain,
> Such never he before or after spied.
> Here spacious holt and lonely forest lay,
> Where nymphs forever chased the panting prey.

If any single theme can be said to dominate *Orlando Furioso* it is that of chivalric love. Here the promise of the Provençal poets and Castiglione and Bembo is realized—and crystallized into the very model of romantic poetry. Brave deeds and beautiful maidens triumph. A hero without his heroine is not merely, as Castiglione maintained, less than civilized: He has no purpose to his life.

Courage and love are all. There is nothing immortal or antireligious in all this, though it is manifest that Leo and his courtiers dwelled increasingly in a world that was as incomprehensible and alien to the rest of Europe as Ariosto's moon.

The most remarkable of all the men who remained outside Leo's court, however, was Desiderius Erasmus, the greatest scholar of the age, a learned theologian, a reformer, the author of *The Praise of Folly*, and, just at this time, of a scathing satirical attack on Julius II called *Julius Exclusus*—and a man devoted to peace, to the unity of the church, and very particularly to Pope Leo X.

The ornament of Germany, or the ornament of the world, as Erasmus was commonly called, was at the height of his career. Ulrich Zasius, a jurist of Freiburg, remarked, "I am pointed out in public as the man who has received a letter from Erasmus." By 1516 men were calling themselves *Erasmiani*, and Erasmus was forced to go out of his way to avoid becoming the leader of a faction within the church. "I hate those party names," he said. "We are all followers of Christ, and to His glory we all drudge, each for his part." Yet, despite his protestations, he had become, as Johan Huizinga observed, "the conscience of his times," the man to whom all others appealed in their controversies over ethics or religion or points of scholarship.

Erasmus was restless in these early days of Leo's reign and was casting about for a new patron. He had met Leo X in Rome in 1509, and now he addressed a laudatory letter to the pope: "Would that I were permitted to throw myself on my knees before you, and kiss those truly blessed feet! I see and hear, how in every part of the Christian world the highest as well as the lowest are congratulating themselves on the elevation of such a Prince." Following a breathless encomium on Leo's virtues, he then begs the pope to accept the dedication of a work he has just finished on Saint Jerome, "so completely the first among Latin theologians, that we might almost call him the one person worthy of that name."

Leo accepted the dedication happily and then permitted broad hints to be circulated that he would like to have Erasmus at Rome. Erasmus' friend Andreas Ammonius wrote, "Leo was wonderfully cheered by your letter, and inquired with much interest, where you were, what you were about, and whether the Bishop thought you would be willing to come to him, with many other signs of an affectionate regard for you; and that he afterwards turned to some very learned and eminent persons, who happened to be by, and handed them your letter, adding his own opinion of your rare genius and learning, and that thereupon they all vied with each other, which should praise you most. . . . Looking to your own advantage, I would have you lose no time in going to his Court. . . ."

Leo could not be expected to make a more direct invitation, for it would not do to be rejected by the scholar. But Erasmus was a proud man and exceedingly reluctant to commit himself to any one court, and so he ignored Ammonius' letter. That neither man could bring himself to petition the other was to have a critical effect on the church. Had he gone to Rome, Erasmus would have been the only theologian of sufficient learning and wit to answer the questions Luther was to pose. As it was, he contented himself with dedicating to Leo his edition of the New Testament, the first printing of the complete Greek text, accompanied by Erasmus' own Latin translation. The first volume appeared in 1516, followed promptly by the others, and the edition was a major event of the sixteenth century that excited scholars throughout Europe. Luther seized on it and went straight to the word *poenitentia*, which, he observed, was *metanoia* (or *metávoia*) in Greek. *Metanoia*, as it happens, signifies not merely repentance but a change of mind, an alteration. Thus, Luther's notion of the uselessness of penances was reinforced. Henceforth it was Erasmus' New Testament, dedicated to Pope Leo, that Luther used to redefine Christianity. Several years later Jerome Aleander would write to Cardinal Giulio de' Medici that Erasmus' translation had "brought forth opinions on confession, on indulgence, on excommunication, on divorce, on the power of the Pope and on other questions, which Luther only had to take over—save that Erasmus's poison is much more dangerous than Luther's." And save that Erasmus could defend his positions from the point of view of one who did not want to see the church divided and saw no reason, even given his variant theological interpretations, that the church needed to be split. Of the hundreds of men that Leo courted or patronized or commanded to Rome, not one was the person he needed most of all. That one—shy, proud, and devoted to the pope—remained aloof.

Leo X was a man who was able to hold myriad contradictions of character in himself with pleasant equanimity. He could admire Erasmus and keep buffoons at his court, he could romanticize women and look on unconcernedly at the thousands of harlots who populated Rome. "It must always be remembered," Stendhal once remarked, "that since the time of the appearance of Luther, the *proprieties* have made an immense stride every fifty years." Leo X, Stendhal observed, "was able to enjoy life as a man of wit; a great cause of anger for gloomy pedants." Leo's favorite buffoon was Fra Mariano, formerly Lorenzo de' Medici's barber. He aroused hearty laughter by sucking 400 eggs, or consuming a camel's hair coat, or, in lieu of genuine inspiration, running down the middle of the table and bopping cardinals on their pates.

According to a Welsh traveler in Italy in the 1540's (one William Thomas, the first to write an English book on Italy), "Briefly, by report Rome is not without 40,000 harlots; maintained for the most part by the clergy and their followers." By the time Thomas wrote, Rome had already been cleaned up. In Leo's day, therefore, the population (which numbered between 40,000 and 85,000) must have been composed solely of clergy and courtesans—assuming the good traveler did not exaggerate. There were many courtesans, to be sure, and many were highly cultivated women serving the role more of geishas than that of the common, garden-variety whore. They were expected to recite Petrarch and Cicero and Ovid and discourse with wit and charm on philosophy. They were required to be able to compose a verse or two, sing, dance, and play a musical instrument.

According to Montaigne, who visited Rome even later than our Welsh friend, one paid for the verbal intercourse as much as anything else. Contemporaries generally agreed that Imperia was the loveliest of all the Roman courtesans just before Leo's time. When the ambassador of the Spanish monarch paid her a visit he was vastly impressed by the elegance of her home, and he turned around at one point during his visit and spat in the face of one of his servants, offering the excuse that it was the only place he could see that was fit for his need.

Supported by Leo's generous court, the ladies lived well, dressing in silks and velvets and gold brocades, with pages in attendance, riding about in fine coaches and commissioning artists to decorate those places in their apartments where they could find room between the tapestries. Carol Maddison reports that ". . . Turkish carpets covered the floors and tables. The curtains were of satin. The large, elaborately carved chairs were upholstered in crimson velvet striped with gold. The beds had the most gorgeous hangings, the finest lawn sheets, and luxurious bed covers. There were carved screens, richly bordered mirrors, caskets and jewel boxes engraved or inset, cupboards full of silver, majolica, and Venetian glass, paintings, statues, precious vases, elegant arms, lutes, mandolins . . ." and so forth and so on. Their cellars boasted excellent wines, and the courtesans were a welcome adornment in the churches of Rome, where they ordinarily found their clients.

Leo's Rome provided a stupefying round of pleasures. At a dinner at Agostino Chigi's, the precious silver plates were thrown out the windows into the Tiber after each course so that the guests could be assured they were eating from clean silver. (Chigi had his servants place nets under the water to rescue the hoard.) All sorts of people popped out of pies, of course, and some of the pastries were better architecture than they were food. At one of Chigi's dinners, the guests were entertained in a new and finely proportioned hall hung with excellent tapestries. The pope and others of the company marveled at the hall—and at the fact that the silver plate was engraved with the armorial bearings of each guest. At the end of the dinner Leo complimented Chigi and expressed regret that the Vatican had no such sumptuous banqueting hall. Chigi had been waiting for the compliment. He gave a signal to his servants, who unfastened the ropes holding the tapestries. When the façade collapsed to the floor, stalls and mangers were revealed, and Chigi said humbly, "But, Your Holiness, this is not my banqueting hall; it is merely my stable!"

In all this amusing swirl one man kept his wits about him. Leo X stood back from the scene with a majestic smile on his face, genuinely appreciative of the antics going on about him—but he was never drunk, never involved with either woman or man, and he never for all his rotundity, gorged himself. His clear, and often cold, detachment was shown off at its best during Isabella d'Este's visit to Rome in 1514.

Leo was both disappointed in Giuliano's softness in administrating Florence and impressed by his nephew Lorenzo. As he groomed Lorenzo to take over the family's Florentine concerns, he removed Giuliano by appointing him captain general of the church. Then, not to waste Giuliano altogether, Leo began to cast about for some state for his brother to rule that would not require exceptional political talents. All the states he considered, however, affected Isabella d'Este, the wife of Francesco of Mantua, for her relatives had interests in Modena, Reggio, Parma, and Piacenza. The gossips speculated that Leo would take one combination or another of these small states, or all of them together, and Isabella, remote from the center of rumor, was in a swivet. She wrote her friend Archdeacon Gabbionetta in Rome for advice. He could not guess the pope's plans, he replied, because "His Holiness swears everyone with whom he negotiates to silence, under pain of excommunication."

Taking the matter firmly in her own hands, Isabella set off for Rome in the autumn of 1514, traveling conspicuously *incognito* with her train of attendants. By the time she reached the walls of the city of gossip, the Vatican was fully prepared for her. Giuliano, Cardinal Bibbiena, and a crowd of other cardinals met and embraced her at the city gates and took her to the Cardinal of Aragon's palace. Bibbiena presented her with 500 ducats. All her needs were to be taken care of by the pope. When she went to the Vatican for her first audience with Leo, the sly Medici used his well-tested courtesy of raising the suppliant from her knees and this time added the flourish of having Isabella sit next to him, his queen for the season. He inquired after her husband, her children, old mutual friends, her health—and before she could recall why she had come to Rome, Leo launched her into the hypnotic social swirl.

"Day after day," she wrote home, "I visit these Right Reverend Cardinals, our cronies, I mean, for I should have too much to do, visiting them all." Nonetheless, she had so much to do that she had no time to recite her prayers. She wrote and asked her secretary to take three ducats "to the Reverend Mother of San Paolo and ask her to say them for us, while we are away."

Leo saw to it that pleasure constantly interfered with business. He always greeted her with smiles, delighted to see her, amused by her conversation—but, in all those revels, always distracted. He would nod and smile, but it was evident he had not quite caught what she had said. And was she enjoying Rome? And what news from home? And how were her adorable children? And was there anything at all he could do to make her visit a greater pleasure?

"Yesterday," one of Isabella's attendants reported home, "the Very Reverend Cardinal Riario gave us a supper so extraordinarily sumptuous that it might suffice for all the queens in the world. We sat for four full hours at the table, laughing and chatting with the most reverend Cardinals."

"Sweet and savoury, pastry and game, were all served at one and the same time," Herbert Vaughan writes of these dinners, "whilst the spirit of vulgar ostentation was satisfied by endless courses of rich dishes, so that only the trained gluttons of the period, such as Fra Mariano, were able to do them justice. Merriment amongst the guests was commonly aroused by some such device as a huge pie filled with blackbirds or nightingales. . . . At other times, applause was easily evoked by such puerile absurdities as a dish of peacocks' tongues or by a monster pasty, whence a child would emerge to lisp some complimentary or indelicate verses to the assembled guests." Vaughan wrote, obviously, after the proprieties Stendhal remarked upon had grown apace.

At a dinner at Cardinal Cornaro's, according to a Venetian envoy, "there was an endless succession of dishes, for we had sixty-five courses, each course consisting of three different dishes, all of which were placed on the board with marvelous speed. Scarcely had we finished one dainty, than a fresh plate was set before us, and yet everything was served on the finest of silver, of which his Eminence has an abundant supply. At the end of the meal we rose from the table gorged with the multiplicity of the viands and deafened by the continual concert, carried on both within and without the hall and proceeding from every instrument that Rome could produce—fifes, harpsichords, and four-stringed lutes in addition to the voices of hired singers."

During Isabella's visit, Leo called for a revival of Bibbiena's play *Calandria* in her honor. One of the first prose comedies in Italian, *Calandria* was originally produced in 1513 at the court of Urbino with a prologue by Castiglione. In its revival at the Vatican, the sets were done by Baldassare Peruzzi, the costumes were suitably lavish, and there were four *intermezzi* between the five acts in which elaborate ballets were done on mythological themes. The plot revolves around two absolutely identical twins, "so alike in appearance, in speech, and in manner" that their own mother could not tell them apart: Lidio, an adolescent boy, and his sister, Santilla. Both had fled the Turks and come to Rome; each thought the other had been killed. Lidio now dressed as a young woman in order to gain entrance to his mistress, an older woman named Fulvia who was married to Calandro, the very essence of the foolish husband. (Calandro was drawn from a character of the same name in Boccaccio's *Decameron*, and by that time "Calandro" had already come to be used synonymously with "simpleton.") Santilla, in order to get along in a perilous man's world, had disguised herself as a man.

Lidio, dressed as a woman, sleeps with Fulvia. Then Santilla, mistaken for Lidio, is taken in to Fulvia. Calandro, assuming Lidio to be a woman, tries to have one of the servants bring him to bed with Lidio. Men dressed as women sleeping with women; women disguised as men sleeping with women; men mistaking men disguised as women trying to bed down with men. The sexuality is titillatingly confusing, and all the airs and variations on the possible liaisons are worked out in the course of the play. At the end Calandro discovers that Fulvia is having an affair with Lidio and brings Fulvia's brothers in to witness the adultery. But by that time Lidio and Santilla have discovered one another (their own relationship is uncomfortably warm, incidentally), so Lidio escapes out a window and Santilla takes his place—so that Calandro and the brothers, feeling Fulvia's lover to confirm the cuckoldry, discover—a woman! Santilla is married to Fulvia's son; Lidio marries a young woman to whom Santilla (in her previous disguise as a man) had become engaged, and so, one assumes, the deception goes on forever, with Lidio now able to pose as Fulvia's daughter-in-law and gain access to his mistress any time.

Calandria is not a great comedy by any means. The *doubles entendres*, the malapropisms coming from the servants, and a good many of the scenes are strained, even by the conventions of its own time. But it is, if not great, at least very good, and much of it is rollicking fun. The moral of the *Courtier* was stated once again by Lidio in his remark that "women are the greatest source of goodness and comfort in the world, and without them we would be useless, inadequate, harsh, and like the beasts of the field." And Lidio's servant Fessenio managed to turn respect for women into the Roman style of perversion in a town of robed esthetes without wives: "Everyone knows that women are so desirable that nowadays all the men go about imitating them and would willingly become women both in body and in soul." The play celebrates sexual love—and yet women keep turning out to be men and men, women, and during one long stretch of the plot both Lidio and Santilla are taken for hermaphrodites. Having aroused and praised the naturalness of sexual passion, the Vatican court did not quite know how to deal with it naturally. But the pope and his court were hugely entertained, and Isabella was shocked.

The Mantuan ambassador wrote Isabella's husband and expressed the opinion that "although the perfection of mind and purity of life of Madama" were manifest, nonetheless Rome did not seem a proper place for women. The marquis was inclined to agree that the city was too full of temptations, and he wrote to request his wife to return. But Raphael was showing Isabella the sights—"every day we visit the antiquities, and every day they seem more wonderful"—and, besides, the pope absolutely begged her to stay awhile longer. Then, in midwinter, Isabella heard that Leo had bought the Emperor Maximilian's rights to Modena. The confused and hurt Isabella left to recover her equilibrium in Naples.

She was back in Rome after six weeks, but by then events had taken another baffling turn. Louis XII of France had died, and Giuliano had gone to France to take the pope's greetings to the new King Francis I, to take the hand of Francis' aunt Filiberta of Savoy, and to receive the title of Duke of Nemours. Isabella had no idea what to make of it and decided she had best return home. But Leo would not hear of it. Surely she would stay for Carnival? Bibbiena, too, insisted.

"Yesterday," Isabella wrote her husband on January 29, 1515, "to make a beginning of the festivals and merrymaking of Carnival, His Magnificence Lorenzo de Medici invited us to dine at his house . . . where we saw a splendid bull-fight in which four bulls were killed. The performance lasted about three hours. When dusk set in, we fell to dancing for about three hours' space. At the festival appeared the most reverend the Cardinals of Aragon, Este, Petrucci, and Cibo, all masked; but the Cardinals Bibbiena and Cornaro, who were likewise supping there, went unmasked. . . . The banquet was very fine and choice, and lasted about two hours, after which we again set to dancing. . . ."

Isabella was given the place of honor for the procession of the triumphal cars and for the regatta on the Tiber. She was there with Leo's court when barrels with fat pigs in them were rolled at terrible speed down a hill, and at the bottom peasants fought savagely to get hold of the casks and take a pig home. On the last night she witnessed the festival in the Piazza Navona. Triumphal cars wound through the piazza under the torchlight—strange creatures, the she-wolf of Rome, pagan deities, all went dizzily by in the flickering light. Two hundred handsome and half-naked young men paraded by as ancient Roman soldiers, and camels and other creatures from the Vatican gardens were led through the piazza. At the end there were fireworks to light up the sky, and showers of confetti, and exploding rockets, and the eerily-lit, drunken, milling mob. Isabella left for home on the following day, February 27, 1515, to the intense disappointment of her friends in Rome. She had spent far too much. Economy would rule the court of Mantua for several years hence. And she had neither accomplished her mission of saving her family's little principalities from Leo nor even discovered at all what Leo had in mind. The figure of this highly attractive woman—one of the brightest and most perceptive women of the Renaissance—reduced to a figure of gentle mockery in the Piazza Navona has made many a tender historian weep. Yet she was not mocked; Leo and his friends relished her company and would have liked her to stay in Rome forever. It was simply that when it came to politics, and especially the advancement of his own family, Leo had no peer at genial dealings, secrecy, vacillation, and success. His victory over Isabella was no conquest of a helpless woman. He had dazzled and outmaneuvered the most self-confident woman in Italy. And he had done it without revealing to anyone what his intentions or commitments were.

Still, politics was often a mere plaything to Leo. He was too accomplished at it, and it easily bored him. The pope reserved his real passion—and a surpassingly strong passion it was—for the hunt. "He left Rome," Paris de Grassis recorded in anguish, "without his stole, and what is worse without his rochet, and what is worst of all, he wore long riding boots, which is most improper, seeing that then the people cannot kiss the Pope's feet!" His favorite spot was the Villa Magliana, five miles from the city on the road to Porto. The hunting lodge had been built by Innocent VIII, improved by Julius II, and apotheosized by Leo. It had all the comforts of home: dining hall, chapel, loggie, fountains, and arbors. With the neighboring estate that belonged to his relatives the Orsinis, Leo was able to put together a hunting area that bordered the Tiber on the south, the Isola Farnese on the north, the seacoast on the west, and the ancient Via Cassia on the east.

The pope would take his party of a hundred or so, or several thousand, out for several weeks, or months. Or, if the spirit moved him, he would go from the Villa Magliana to Viterbo or Canino or the estate of Cardinal Farnese, where the terrain was good for pheasant and partridge and quail, thrush, ortolan, and lark; not even robins nor goldfinches escaped the indefatigable sportsman. For fish there were the wooded shores of Lake Bolsena or the artificial saltwater pond near Ostia that was always kept well stocked. Or, for something to relieve the tedium, the party would journey to Santa Marinella, on the coast, where stags and goats and boars would be stampeded over the cliffs into the water, and the hunters would spear them from boats or leap into the water after them—Leo sitting in a barge amidst the boiling, bloody surf, following the action eagerly.

"My beloved Castellan," he wrote one day, "I shall be at Civita Vecchia on the 24th day of this month with a large suite. You must arrange for a good dinner with plenty of fish for me, as I am anxious to make a display of state before the men of letters and others who will be my companions. I shall reimburse all your expenses on our behalf. I command you to let nothing be wanting at this banquet, since I wish to entertain thereat persons of the highest consideration, who are very dear to my heart. We shall be 140 in number, and that will serve to guide you, so that there may be no mistakes nor deficiencies through ignorance. I bestow my blessing upon you. Your most loving Sovereign."

The beloved Castellan must have been relieved that the pope brought such a small party on that occasion. He was accustomed to set off with any number, and they rode out—Bernardo Accolti brandishing a spear, the cardinals with their kennelmen, Bibbiena in knight's garb, Castiglione hoping the hunt would be successful so that he could approach the jubilant pope with another request, Bembo jouncing along unhappily on his mule, Fra Mariano falling off his mule within the pope's sight to give his sovereign some mirth to start the day, and Leo in his litter, huffing and puffing and wiping the perspiration from his face, smiling down on all.

At the Villa Magliana the staff would check the pens—first the prey that were always kept on hand, the hundreds of jays, herons, and doves, then the merlins and goshawks, the rabbits, and the ferrets that provided more informal entertainment before and after the big hunts. On the day before the hunt beaters and others would go out to the chosen area—a small wooded valley was ideal for the purpose—and enclose it entirely with huge strips of sail cloth, twenty feet long and six feet high. Swiss Guards would be posted around the area, and they would make certain that the nets were well tended by the peasants.

On the day itself, the nobles and dignitaries, the cardinals and their retinues would ride out in their liturgical splendor, dogs yapping at heel, polished swords rattling. They assembled on the hillside, and then the party would descend to one end of the valley. Leo would raise his white handkerchief and lower it, and the horns would blast, the guns would sound, and the beaters would drive the animals toward the opening. They came in frantic, cacaphonous stampede—boar and wolf, goat and deer, rabbit and bustard to the waiting hunters. And the shouts would go up to meet the beasts, horns blowing, dogs barking, beaters shrieking, and the very reverend cardinals would throw themselves on the frightened animals in a frenzy of fear and joy. Here one of the party spears a shaggy hunting dog that he mistakes for a wolf. There Lancetto, Cardinal Cornaro's favorite kennelman, leaps on the back of a wounded boar and rides him through the melee, buffeted this way and that by the stampeding deer and goats. He falls and the boar turns on him and gores him from head to foot. There two soldiers fight over the possession of a boar and one takes the other's eye out. There young Valerio Orsini collapses on the ground in tears for having lost a stag he was pursuing. And over it all sits Leo on the white horse that carried him at the Battle of Ravenna and in the Sacro Processo; he sits up on the hillside out of the fray, his monocle held tight to his eye, savoring the scene.

The slaughter is stupendous, the valley is littered with crying animals and groaning men, the grass is slippery with blood. And once, or perhaps twice, during the day a stag or boar is entangled in the nets surrounding the area. Leo's attendants lead his horse down the hillside and lift him out of the saddle and place a spear in his hand. He is led to the wounded beast who struggles to get free of the net; with the spear in his right hand and his eyeglass in his left guiding his aim, Leo delivers the death blow, and the courtiers applaud. Then, lifted again into the saddle, he returns to his vigil on the hillside. In time, the barking of the dogs fades and the calls of the beaters are muted, and the sun begins to sink over the hill. The party comes together again, leaving the beaters to dispatch the last of the dying animals and bring them in, and the happy, exhausted courtiers ride back to the villa.

At the villa, as the dinner is being prepared, Fra Mariano does his pratfalls, wine goes all around. Then a buzzard is sighted in the sky, and a cardinal sets loose one of the peregrine falcons. The falcon darts up in a keen arc toward the buzzard. But then an eagle is seen. The eagle swoops sharply in on the falcon, and one blow sends the peregrine to earth. He was the cardinal's favorite, and he will be given a burial with full military honors.

After dinner, after more wine, after even the conversations recounting the day have faded, Grapaldo of Parma improvises Latin hexameters to his lute: Diana, he sings, surprised in her naked loveliness in the woods by the brash hunter Actaeon, turns Actaeon into a stag and he is torn to pieces by his own hounds. Sipping wine in front of the dying fire, Leo can be heard to mumble over and over again, "What a glorious day. What a glorious day. . . ."

The character of Leo is ripe, if not overripe, for psychological analysis. Thus far, however, those who have come to analyze have stayed to wonder. It was enough for his own courtiers to know —indeed, it was well known throughout Europe—that if one had a favor to ask of Leo, this was the time to ask it. After a good day at the hunt, Leo would grant nearly anything. Ultimately, it was his expansive geniality, whatever its cause, that proved to be his tragic flaw. His geniality was both his greatest virtue and his complete undoing. In addition to the hundreds of gentlemen and clerks of the court at the Vatican, the pope kept countless other attendants, valets, grooms, keepers of hawk and hound. And, so, every morning as he lay abed he would discuss with his datary which abbacies and bishoprics were to be given away—for each time a benefice changed hands, the newly created abbot or bishop would have to pay the pope some recompense.

Nonetheless, debts mounted. "It would be easier," one Florentine remarked, "for a stone to fly than for this Pope to keep together 1,000 ducats." Church offices were sold, kickbacks solicited, concessions on alum mines granted for considerations. Still the debts mounted. And Leo had just appointed Raphael architect to the Church of St. Peter, Christianity's greatest monument to the church triumphant; and Raphael told Leo the basilica would cost at least a million ducats. Coincidentally, Leo had just invested Albert of Hohenzollern with the archbishopric of Mainz. Since Albert already held the bishoprics of Halberstadt and Magdeburg and was only twenty-four years old, he had to pay dearly for his new office. He would apply for a loan to the German banking family, the Fuggers.

Leo then, in order to maintain cordial relations with that rich and useful source of money, arranged to have the Fuggers reimbursed. Julius II had set a precedent by issuing a papal bull in Italy that granted indulgences to those who devoutly contributed to the building fund for St. Peter's. In December, 1514, while Isabella d'Este was trying to fathom what was on the pope's mind, Leo appointed his staff of croupiers for the extension of the St. Peter's indulgences beyond Italy into Avignon, Bremen, Salzburg, and some other provinces of Germany. Half of the income from Germany was marked for the building fund and half for the Fuggers.

X

THE KEYS TO REVOLUTION

"**D**URING all this time, the small fire of the true faith began to die away, so that it was almost reduced to ashes, and seemed scarcely to emit a single spark. For simony was now practised without a blush, and usurers openly, by various arguments, extorted money from the people and from minors; charity expired . . . religion was trodden upon, and of no value; and the daughter of Zion became, as it were, a shameless harlot without a blush. . . ."

It sounds like the language of the Reformation, but, of course, it is not at all. This little indictment of the church was written in the middle of the thirteenth century by a quiet conformist monk named Matthew Paris. The corruption of the church had been a commonplace centuries before Luther was born. All of the condemnations of the clergy that we ordinarily associate with the Reformation had become numbingly humdrum clichés by then. Some would find it shocking when Luther called the pope Antichrist; but it was a tired old charge. It had hardly caused a stir when it was lodged by the Bishop of Orléans against the papacy in the year 991. Leo X's own father had dispatched his son to Rome with a monotonous litany on the evils of churchmen, and there was scarcely a peasant in Europe who did not *know* of a nunnery where the good sisters received young men from Oxford in their cells, or of priests who charged a mite too much for burial services or were ignorant of their religion or always drunk from tippling mass wine. A priest who was guilty of murder escapes punishment by "benefit of clergy." A bailiff of a local convent pimps for the nuns. Stories of Leo's Rome could not have been shocking to most Europeans: Their own parish priests engaged in the same debaucheries and hypocrisies, and on an unstylishly petty level. While the pope bilked the archbishops, the nuns of Godstow spread syphilis in England—and, what was worse, they spread it to their neighbors' husbands.

The corruption was remarked at all levels, and there was no form of sin the clergy left untried. Dante lambasted them, and Petrarch, and Boccaccio. And Chaucer, in his *Canterbury Tales* (written centuries before Luther was born), so takes for granted the corruption of the clergy that his satire barely has a sharp edge to it in his sketches of the prioress, the monk dressed in fine gray fur ("the finest in the land./ And for to fasten his hood under his chin,/ He had of gold ywrought a curious pin:/ A love-knot in the greater end there was"), or the wanton and merry friar, who turned a nice profit hearing widows' confessions and was fond of giving hairpins to "faire wives." The friar, according to Chaucer, knew the taverns in every town:

> And every hostler and gay tapstere,
> Better than a lazar [leper] or a beggere,
> For unto such a worthy man as he
> Accordeth nought, as by his faculty,
> To haven sith sike lazars aequaintance.
> It is not honest, it may not advance,
> As for dealen with such pouraille [offal],
> But all with rich, and sellers of vitaille.

All of this was common talk, and yet the devout people continued to pay their church tithes that dressed the prelates and stocked the larders of the monasteries; they attended mass and confessed their sins and hoped that these consecrated brokers of God's grace would somehow help them to salvation. They resented the churchmen deeply, and some attacked the church: John Wycliffe and John Hus, the Lollards and the Taborites. But despite the reformers and revolutionaries, despite the kings of European nations who sought to get their hands on those rich church lands, despite the conflicts in the church itself between the pope and those cardinals who clamored for councils, despite the Avignonese schism of the early fifteenth century, despite economic depression and emerging independent social classes, despite the growth of new nationalistic feeling and archbishops who defied the pope, despite war and plague and famine and fire and rage, the church of Rome remained the unrepentant Kingdom of God on earth, which none could change and few even dared to challenge. There was no thought of abandonment, for that way lay the road to hell; and most men, as always, were able to take the realist's view that the world was never meant to be perfect.

The astonishing aspect of all this would seem to be that the Reformation did not occur long before it did. And historians have labored mightily to explain how certain economic and social and political forces had to combine to produce the event—the readiness often seems to be all. However, in the effort to define the broad historical forces that were the necessary midwives of the Reformation, the poor baby has been unceremoniously dropped.

Despite all the forces that tore at the church, it remained invincible for one crucial reason apparent from the keys on the coat of arms of the papacy. It is on those crossed keys that the entire structure of the church rests. The pope may be a scurrilous bastard, but he still holds "the keys to heaven," and it is through the sacraments administered by his priests that men may be privileged to have those keys open the gates of paradise to them. Men had been waiting for centuries to wrest those keys from the hands of the pope, but that was a job that could not be accomplished by caviling with mere political arguments or moral arguments or economic arguments or any other secondary argument. The Reformation was, after all, a theological revolution, and it was a fundamental theological argument that went right to the very center of the church and cracked and shattered the institution. When Luther proclaimed that man is saved "by faith alone," there was, patently, no more use for the pope's gold keys or his whole gilded establishment, and resentful men everywhere rose up and assaulted the church with a vengeance.

Leo X had no idea that his structure could be smashed by theological nit-picking, and Luther was amazed when he discovered his scholarly questions struck at the whole complex financial and political foundation of his own church. Luther probably imagined himself to be following the example set by Johann Reuchlin, the Hebrew scholar who was then having a squabble with the establishment theologians.

Reuchlin was sixty years old in 1515. He was a shy ex-lawyer who had traveled about Europe a good deal on diplomatic missions. A tall, white-haired gentleman with a bent for dilettante scholarship, Reuchlin chanced on some Hebrew books in Italy and embarked on his studies "for rest and recreation after much hard work and the tumult of court life." The avocation matured with the man until it had become his vocation, and he was recognized as Europe's foremost Hebrew scholar. He fancied himself a philologist and not a theologian at all, though he naturally observed in correcting a rendering of Saint Jerome by Augustine that "our text reads so, but the meaning of the Hebrew is otherwise," and he pointed out that some commentaries on the Bible were in error because the fathers of theology had not used a correct text. But he scrupulously avoided entering any theological debate. He was intent only upon emending errors of translation.

All of this was modest and apparently harmless enough. Reuchlin published a Hebrew grammar and lexicon, and he would have lived quietly, breeding white peacocks on his little estate, in the enjoyment of the esteem of the young scholars who followed him, if only he had not been led into a controversy with Johann Pfefferkorn, a Jew who had recently converted to Catholicism and was now determined to extirpate Judaism. In his book *Judenspiegel*, Pfefferkorn recommended that Jews be brought into the Catholic fold by prohibiting them from practicing usury, burning all their Hebrew books, and forcing them to listen to sermons. In search for allies for his scheme, Pfefferkorn presented himself to the Dominicans, who judiciously advised him that the abolition of usury might inconvenience the church and that sermons might not

154

be the most potent force for conversion. They were, however, all in favor of burning the books.

With the approval of the Dominicans, Pfefferkorn set off to find the vague, hulking Emperor Maximilian of the vague, hulking Holy Roman Empire. Always in debt, always skipping town to avoid confrontations with innkeepers over unpaid bills, always dashing off to wars to expand the uncertain boundaries of his ramshackle empire, Maximilian was to be found encamped at the moment in Padua. (The Holy Roman Empire was such an amorphous, confusing hodgepodge of principalities and shifting borders that Margaret of Austria, the regent of the Netherlands, had to have her nephew explain it to her.) Maximilian listened to Pfefferkorn's scheme and—absentmindedly, one supposes—issued an edict to have all Jews deliver their books to Pfefferkorn, who would decide which of them ought to be suppressed.

When Pfefferkorn appeared in Mainz on his mission, the archbishop casually ordered his clergy to ignore him. When the crusader objected, the archbishop suggested that such important decisions required a panel of men to deliberate. Thus, after more haggling and bedeviling of the emperor, it was decided to seek the opinions of several universities, of one Victor of Karben, of the Inquisitor-General Jakob Hochstraten, and of Reuchlin to decide which Hebrew books should be destroyed.

There were two Jewish books that attacked Christianity, Reuchlin wrote in calm, dispassionate judgment on the case. They were the Nizachon and the Toldoth Jeschu (both of which, though Reuchlin somehow neglected to mention it, had already been disowned by the Jews). Of the others, while none were Christian texts, they could not be said to have been written as attacks on Christianity. Reuchlin then considered the Talmud, the Cabala, and other Hebrew texts, noting their contents and reaching the technical conclusion that none of these texts could have been written against Christianity. Indeed, Reuchlin observed, many of these works were useful to Christians in the study of theology and, further, provided arguments that could be used to convert the Jews. In any case, Reuchlin said, since the books had not been repressed in fourteen centuries, what was the use of burning them now? The conversion of the Jews would best be accomplished by maintaining a cordial relationship with them and showing by the Christian example the truth of Christianity. In order that men might better know how to engage in friendly discourse with the Jews, Reuchlin suggested disingenuously that the emperor ought to set up two chairs of Hebrew studies at all of the German universities, where young men would then learn wherein the Jews erred and how they might be corrected.

Reuchlin was alone in his opinion on the matter and, although he had thought he was writing a privileged letter solely for the emperor's eyes, Pfefferkorn got hold of it and published a book attacking Reuchlin as a man who had probably been bribed by the Jews to write such an opinion. Reuchlin did not understand the Talmud, Pfefferkorn said, and his books on Hebrew subjects had probably been written by someone else, since Reuchlin was too ignorant to have written them himself. At that the calm old scholar erupted. In a book called *Augenspiegel* he printed the full text of his advice to the emperor, with explanations of some of the passages, and then proceeded to point out thirty-four mistakes Pfefferkorn had made in Hebrew. The famous "Battle of the Books" was on.

Now that Reuchlin had committed himself to a position in print, the theologians were able to move in on him. The good doctors at the University of Köln parsed his text and sent him a number of propositions that they insisted he either explain or withdraw. Reuchlin responded with an appeal to public opinion by publishing a German translation of his book, and with that the controversy became the topic of the day. Ortwin Gratius published an attack on Reuchlin. Reuchlin wrote a "defense" to the emperor. The University of Paris, then the center of theological learning, condemned Reuchlin's book. Liberal humanists throughout Europe—caring nothing for the Jews, but seeing the controversy as one threatening freedom of inquiry—pronounced themselves in favor of Reuchlin. The Inquisitor-General Hochstraten

summoned Reuchlin to appear before him. Reuchlin appealed to
the pope, and Leo requested the advice of the bishops of Worms
and Speyer, who debated the issues while the theologians of Köln
burned copies of the *Augenspiegel*.

Asked by the Elector to give his opinion on the case, Luther
wrote: ". . . there is nothing dangerous in his writings. I marvel
greatly at his opponents, because they make out of something so
plain a tangle worse than the Gordian knot, regardless of his
constant protestations that he is not setting up articles of faith but
simply expressing a technical judgment. This in my view absolves
him so completely from suspicion that if he had made a collection
of every heresy in the world, in such a purely technical report, I
should still hold him sound and pure in the faith which he explicitly professes. If technical judgments are no longer to be free
from danger, these inquisitors will be able to pronounce a heretic
anyone they like, however orthodox he may be. . . . There are a
hundred real evils around us, wherever one looks idolatry is ramp-
ant. These are the things we need to fight with all our strength.
But no, we leave them be and worry about alien irrelevancies like
the errors of the Jews. Could there be anything more stupid?"

Europe was divided into two camps of Reuchlinists and anti-
Reuchlinists—that is, nearly all of Europe was. At least one man
remained aloof. Erasmus, viewing the brouhaha as the dire news
that war had been declared, wrote two mild letters to members of
the College of Cardinals. It was absurd, he said, that such a petty
matter should divide the church and cause a charge of heresy
against a distinguished scholar. Fearing Armageddon, Erasmus
then drew into himself and worked at his own scholarly projects.

In March, 1514, Reuchlin published a volume of letters written
to him by famous men in support of his case, *Letters from Illustrious Men*. In its attempt to show that a consensus of the
learned supported Reuchlin, the book set a strange precedent:
Reuchlin placed the consensus of individual scholars against the
opinion of the pope, of theological faculties of the universities, of
councils, of the Inquisition. Later Luther would follow the same
path: If a matter had not already been settled by an authoritative

expression of opinion, it was legitimately open to question. Then, like Reuchlin, he would ask what the proper source was for an authoritative opinion—the pope, a council, the fathers of the church, canons and decretals, the Bible, a consensus of learned men, or the individual conscience?

Shortly after Reuchlin's book was published, another compendium of letters appeared, *Letters of Obscure Men*. At first they appeared to be letters written by friends of Hochstraten and Pfefferkorn and their allies—but something was wrong. These letters were evidently written by grossly ignorant men. They were vulgar, ill-informed, packed with prejudice, riddled with silly questions about sin. It was satire, of course (Erasmus was the first to recognize the hand of Ulrich von Hutten), and when the joke got out a German translation of the book circulated quickly throughout the country. Here was the establishment, good, upright men, who were loyal to their institutions, who had grown up as their fathers would have wished, got their university degrees, and held comfortable and responsible positions in the world. They were not evil men, they wished to do good, and they were worried about questions of fairness and virtue. But they were shocked! They had heard that some fellow named Reuchlin had had the temerity to defy the opinion of the august University of Köln. What did this mean? In their good, well-meaning confusion, they write to their old teacher Ortwin Gratius to ask his advice on this and other questions about the troubling modern world.

"I, therefore, wish now to ask your opinion in the case of one who should on Friday, which is the sixth day, or upon any other fast day, eat an egg in which there is a chick. For we were recently dining at an inn in the Campo Fiore, and were eating eggs. And I, opening my egg, discovered that there was a chick within; but upon showing it to my companion, he urged me to swallow it straightway before the host caught sight of it, for otherwise I should have to pay a Carolinus or a Julius for a fowl, since it is the custom here to pay for everything the host places upon the table, because they will take nothing back. . . . And I immediately swallowed the egg and the chick at the same time, and afterwards it occurred to me that it was Friday. . . .

". . . by heaven, Master Ortwin, I am much disturbed, and I do not know what to do about it. It is true that I might take counsel with a member of the Papal Court, but I know that they have bad consciences. As for myself, it seems to me that chicks in the egg are meat, because the matter is already formed and shaped into the members and body of an animal. . . . It is otherwise in the case of worms in cheese . . . for worms are accounted to be fish, as I have heard from a physician. . . . I beseech of you earnestly to reply to my question. . . ."

Then there was the case of a young scholar who wanted to know the proper manner of addressing one who was about to receive the degree of master of arts. Since a full master was called *magister noster*, should a "near master" be called *magister nostrandus* or *noster magistrandus*? Then there was the case of a man who had said that he was a member of ten universities. "Now a body may have many members, but can a member lay claim to many bodies?" Or there was the disturbing question raised by one John Pellifex who had seen two men in black robes at the marketplace in Frankfurt and, mistaking them for masters of arts, doffed his hat to them. His companion was horrified: They were Jews, he said, and Pellifex was guilty of an act of idolatry. Should he, Pellifex wants to know, seek absolution of an ordinary priest, or must he receive episcopal, or even papal, absolution for such an offense? Then there was the man who, like most of the correspondents, expressed utter bewilderment over the pope's hesitation to condemn Reuchlin: "I would say that the Pope erred—if I did not fear excommunication."

With the letters full of chop-logic, tortured reasoning, wretched grammar, stunning hypocrisy, and self-satisfaction, the anti-Reuchlinists were reduced to figures of fun. Erasmus, it is said, laughed so hard that he burst an abscess. Much of the attack was coarse (even Luther was offended), and Erasmus was upset both by the personal nature of the attacks and by the fear that mockery of Hochstraten would lead to mockery of other officers of the church. But the book did unite public opinion in Reuchlin's favor.

Eventually Leo would decide against Reuchlin, but not until 1520, when more "squabbles" in Germany seemed to call for a firm hand. By then it was too late. The outcome in all cases of this sort was utterly predictable: If a great university did not crush a scholar such as Reuchlin very quickly, it was seen as a failure. And whatever the liberal men of the church might think, it was essential to keep the Dominican Inquisition from embarrassment. It was unthinkable for the pope to fail to back up his employees. And yet, amazingly, Reuchlin emerged victorious, at least temporarily. In July, 1516, a commission of eighteen conveyed their judgment to the pope: Reuchlin's *Augenspiegel* was free of heresy. Only one dissenting vote was recorded in the verdict, that of Sylvester Prierias, master of the papal palace, who several years later was to be the man who framed the indictment against Luther.

True to his nature, Leo procrastinated. He neither endorsed the findings of his commission nor set them aside. Instead, he ordered that no more action be taken in the case. By doing nothing, he gave the victory to Reuchlin, and an inspiring victory it was. It had been won by an appeal to the people, by writings in the vulgar tongue, and the new printing press could claim much of the credit for the victory. Luther would use the same tools in his scholarly debate.

Luther had been chewing over several "technical" questions himself, and these lively days of open debate seemed a good time to bring them out in the open to see what other scholars might have to say about them. The young professor was having the time of his life at Wittenberg. He was immensely popular, attendance at church had begun to rise, and the bright young man was actually attracting new students to the university. "I do almost nothing but write letters all day long," he complained with the enthusiasm of one who relishes being at the center of things. "I am conventual preacher, reader at meals, sought for to preach daily in the parish church, am regent of studies, district Vicar (i.e. eleven times Prior), inspect the fish ponds at Leitzkau, act in the Herzberg affair at Torgau, lecture on St. Paul, revising my Psalms . . . I seldom have time to go through my canonical hours properly, or to celebrate mass, to say nothing of my own temptations of the world, the flesh, and the devil. You see what a lazy fellow I am."

He was, in fact, too busy at the moment with his official duties and with sorting out his new insights about Saint Paul to ask any major questions, but several minor items came to his attention. In September, 1516, for example, he presided over a public disputation at which his pupil directly attacked the old Nominalist school of theology with a series of theses having to do with God's bestowal of grace on man, and Luther happened to mention, by the bye, that Augustine's *True and False Penitence* was a fraudulent document, a remark that caused a small uproar in Wittenberg. But Luther was elated when Andreas Karlstadt, another professor on the Wittenberg faculty, agreed with him. He sent his old professor at Erfurt, Jodocus Trutvetter, "the Prince of Aristotelians," a series of propositions attacking Aristotle. And he wrote exultantly to a friend, "Our theology and St. Augustine are going ahead, and reign in our University, and it is God's work. Aristotle is gradually going down, perhaps into eternal ruin. It is wonderful how the lectures on the *Sentences* are out of favor. Nobody can hope for an audience unless he professes this theology, i.e. the Bible or St. Augustine, or some doctor of real authority in the Church."

In the meantime a small parochial matter nettled Luther. As All Saints' Day, November 1, 1516, approached, Luther became increasingly disturbed about the question of indulgences. Elector Frederick's Castle Church, as it happened, had a special concession from the pope whereby a visit to the Elector's collection of relics (along with payment of a moderate entrance fee) earned a reduction of 1,443 years from a man's expected time in purgatory.

Luther had not spent much time sorting out his understanding of indulgences—nor, if the truth were known, was anyone in the church altogether clear about the subject.

The principles that governed the granting of indulgences that were commonly believed in Luther's day had grown up haphazardly, with no one caring for the theory since the practice was so lucrative. According to the teaching of the church, Christ's sacrifice on the cross paid for man's sins, so that in the "treasury" of the church there was a vast store of merits, compounded semi-annually, as it were, by the merits of the saints who, being better than they needed to be, had some leftover merits which could be disbursed to others. This treasury was something in which all members of the church were shareholders and from which, by making the proper investment, they could draw dividends. The pope controlled the dividends—it was his keys that opened the door to the vaults, it was believed, and so to heaven.

According to the teachings of the church, true repentance for sin brought divine forgiveness. Even though forgiven, however, a sin still had to be punished, or "paid for"—just as a man had to restore or pay for a stolen sow. Thus, the church established various terms of punishment or payment for sins to be worked out on earth—prayers, fasting, pilgrimages, and so forth. In 853 Pope Leo IV proclaimed that knights could work off a considerable amount of such payment by serving the church devoutly in the Crusades. But by that time a corollary to the practice of payment had developed. Originally a mere manner of speaking for pragmatic people of the world, the notion of "payment" had come to be taken literally. To deprive oneself of money is, after all, a sacrifice, a punishment of sorts, and in certain exceptional cases where men had been unable to go on a lengthy pilgrimage the church had accepted monetary sacrifice as a substitute. Leo IV applied the principle on a large scale and announced that those knights who were unable to participate in the Crusades could instead support the holy endeavor with money sacrifices. In time the practice of accepting money in lieu of other penance became more widespread as more and more people appealed to the clergy

162

to be indulged in this fashion, and the church increasingly came to rely on these money sacrifices to finance itself.

Theory always followed practice in the growth of indulgences. Many men died, after all, without having worked out all their penances and so had to spend time in purgatory before their souls were cleansed of all worldly dross. Although indulgences originally applied only to penance imposed by priests on earth, gradually they were extended to cover all temporal punishments that might be coming to a man, in purgatory as well as on earth. And whereas no doctor of the church had ever said that indulgences carried with them the *forgiveness* of sins but only release from the temporal *punishment* for sins, ordinary Catholics, ever indifferent to nice theological hairsplitting, assumed they were buying forgiveness. The indulgence sellers, the relic hawkers, and even the hard-pressed Vatican itself were happy to let the common folk believe whatever they wanted so long as the cash kept coming in.

Indulgences proliferated rapidly. Nobody lost, everybody won. New churches and new monasteries, new bridges and new roads, even the dikes of Holland were constructed by indulgence financing, so that, in a time when governments could not effectively tax their own people, the church tax pervaded the entire society of Europe, financing the Vatican, monasteries, banking families, princes, mining ventures, wars. Indulgences were an ideal way to finance an institution—only the modern government lottery begins to compare with it, and even then not too favorably, as a popular way of raising money. And the buyers loved them as much as the sellers. Were your father and mother suffering in purgatory? Buy a packet of letters of indulgence to "assign" to them, and up they go to heaven. Had you neglected to fast during Lent? You could buy a "butter letter." Did you *intend* to sin? You could buy a receipted indulgence from another and have your sin paid for in advance. So the indulgence peddlers said, in any case, and no one cared to disbelieve them.

Here were the greatest insurance policies of all time: insurance for salvation. And they came at precise prices for precise purposes, all invested with mysterious and potent magic numbers:

seven years' indulgence for one price and for a higher sum a staggering, mystically jam-packed, round 1,000 years off purgatory! In the Jubilee Year of 1300, Pope Boniface VIII granted *plenary* indulgence—*complete* remission of penalties (for which people read "forgiveness") for *all* past sins to any and all who made the pilgrimage to Rome and visited the graves of the twelve Apostles in two weeks. This fantastic offer would only be repeated once every 100 years, Boniface proclaimed; but the jubilee plenary indulgence was such a boon to the tourist income of Rome that the 100 years was revised 50 years, then 33 years (Christ's life-span), then 25. In time, it was announced that if a man could not get to Rome himself, he could send a proxy, and eventually one could obtain a plenary indulgence by simply forwarding to Rome a payment equal to the cost of the journey (Thomas Cook and Sons never had quite as lucrative a tour package). The church responded ever more handsomely to the welcome popular pressure to increase the variety of indulgences to invest in eternity. There was nothing wrong with the system —except that the world had come to depend on it so completely, and it had a theological flaw.

Luther was at first offended only by the practice of indulgence selling, the disgusting manner in which people had been allowed to misunderstand their nature, and a good many churchmen heartily agreed with him. Luther could not take the time to frame any formal remarks on the technicalities of the question at the moment, but he could at least warn his own parishioners about the foolishness.

On the eve of All Saints' Day, therefore, he preached a mild sermon reminding his parishioners that indulgences were useful only in excusing a sinner from those punishments imposed by a priest in this world. Repentance and forgiveness for sins were different matters. The true change of heart that brings salvation could come only through contemplation of the wounds of Christ, through true remorse, and through grace, which God freely gives to the believer.

The parishioners had expected to gain 1,443 years' worth of

forgiveness on the following day by visiting the relics at the castle church, and they were not pleased by the sermon. The popular young professor was treated coolly in Wittenberg, and the Elector, who had previously promised Luther a new gown, now withheld it. Nothing roused Luther's resistance so much as opposition—his father had learned that, the Elector was learning it, and the pope soon would learn it. Whereas before he had thought only about the misleading character of the practice of selling indulgences, now he bore down on the subject with a new tenacity, and it gradually occurred to him that according to his understanding of penitence there was something deeply wrong with indulgences. The triad of beliefs that underlay the Reformation were now taking shape in Luther's sermons and lectures: Man is saved "only through grace" which comes "only through faith" which comes "only through Christ." In that light, not only was the practice of indulgence-peddling corrupt, but the theory itself was theologically insupportable.

XI

THE POLITICS OF INDULGENCES

L EO and Luther are not yet aware that they will clash in another chapter or two, but with that marvelous foresight
that comes of hindsight, we can see that trouble is not far
off. We must pause a moment now and anticipate them, for
when the conflict begins in earnest we shall have no more time
or opportunity than they did to sort out some of their assump-
tions and aspirations. We must not imagine that the pope was
powerless when Luther reached so rudely for the "keys to
heaven." When the time came to silence Luther's tentative academic nit-picking, Leo had an awesome range of weapons he
could muster to swat the gadfly: decretals, the teachings of the
doctors of the church, tradition, canon law, sanctions, the discipline of the religious orders, bulls of excommunication, financial
coercion of Luther's immediate superiors, and the whole political
machinery of the continent. None of these weapons was simple
to mobilize, but all of them can be directly and easily understood
—all, that is, save the political resources of the pope. While
Luther sorted out the ambiguities and contradictions of theology,
Leo steered a quicksilver course through the politics of Europe
in a manner that bewildered absolutely everybody—except himself.

Winston Churchill once remarked of Russia, "It is a riddle
wrapped in a mystery inside an enigma: but perhaps there is a key
... Russian national interest." The key to Leo's mysterious political ways lies in his ambitions for his family. Since the days of

Giovanni di Bicci de' Medici the family had made a steady, though often perilous, progress to eminence in Italy. By the time of Leo's father, they were the first family in Florence and one of the first on the peninsula. By some imperative most men resist settling back and counting their blessings. During the Renaissance, when everything was in motion from political alliances to the diaphanous robes that swirled around Botticelli's women, and when men believed in the wheel of fortune as firmly as nineteenth-century industrialists believed in progress, stasis was a heresy. Men were either on their way up or on their way down. In the circumstances there was nothing for Leo to do but devise a way for the Medicis to become the first monarchy of Italy. Alexander VI had tried for the Borgias, Julius II for the Della Roveres. It was a treacherous business, but it was the business for which Leo had been prepared by his family.

Although Leo failed to establish a Medici monarchy, he did rather better than any other man of the Renaissance. Where Borgias and Della Roveres reached too high too rashly, Leo had the old Medici patience and caution, and Medicis were to be dukes of Urbino and Florence, grand duke of Tuscany, and, of course, Leo's great-niece Catherine married France's King Henry II. Seen as a dynast, perhaps all of Leo's contradictions fall away. Genial, good-humored, generous to a fault, never able to refuse anyone anything, the antithesis of selfishness—all is a mask to conceal hard ambition. The enthusiast for games, the lover of crude jokes, the pope who loved a party—he took nothing seriously, it seemed. Did he have ambitions? Not at all; his only passion, it was widely conceded—with embarrassment—was the hunt. Leo's pontificate was all bread and circuses: The old tricks are always the best. Very few of Leo's contemporaries saw what his wan smile concealed.

Since Leo had perceived that his brother Giuliano was not sufficiently firm and flexible as a ruler, he placed Lorenzo in charge of Florence, with the immediate goal of annexing Urbino, Ferrara, and Modena and ultimately of creating a unified state of all Tuscany. Nonetheless, Giuliano had to be put to some use, and

167

Leo held his brother in reserve for the more tenuous scheme of a southern state. Ferdinand of Naples was in bad health, and Leo kept Giuliano about to learn something of politics so that he would be ready to assume control of Naples. The Medicis were nervously aware of their shortage of male heirs—cousin Giulio was being nurtured, successfully, to succeed to the papal tiara— and all the family intently husbanded their strength.

When Lorenzo's mother heard he intended to take part in a tournament, she had her secretary write her son a stern letter:

> Your mother has been informed that you practice yourself in tilting, wearing heavy armor, and managing the great horse, which may in all probability be injurious to your health. I can scarcely express to you how much she is dissatisfied with these proceedings. In the greatest distress, she has enjoined me to write to you on her behalf, and to observe to you, that although your ancestors have displayed their courage on similar occasions, yet you should consider who and what they were. When Piero di Cosimo appeared in a tournament, his father, who governed the city, was then living, as was also his brother. At the time Lorenzo exhibited, his father was also in being, and he had a brother, Giuliano, the father of the most reverend Cardinal, and when the same Giuliano tilted, Lorenzo himself governed. When your father appeared in the lists, he had two sons and two brothers; notwithstanding which he did not escape blame. You are yet young, and the magnificent Giuliano and yourself (both of you yet unmarried, and he infirm in his constitution) are the only support of the family. You cannot, therefore, commit a greater error than by persevering in such conduct, and she recommends that you should rather engage others in the contest, and stand by to enjoy the entertainment; thereby consulting your own safety and preserving the hopes of your family.

The Medicis indulged in high-spirited, spontaneous fun only when they could do so safely.

Beginning with Giovanni di Bicci's advice to "be as inconspicuous as possible," Medici ambition had long been cloaked under republican pretense, personal modesty, well-placed generosity, and the most private of dealings. Until Leo's time, the family's aspirations were also kept close to home. Though Leo's father was at pains to store up some goodwill from Louis XII of France, the credit was always against the future, never to be called upon in the early days of the Medici dynasty. The Medicis worked restrainedly within the confines of Florence and tentatively, through marriage and polite suasion, within the bounds of Italy.

By Leo's time, however, Italy had become the battleground on which French fought Spanish. While Leo had, therefore, to keep the appallingly fragmented Italian forces in balance (with the sort of treatment he gave Isabella d'Este), he had, too, to cope with the redoubtable forces of England, Spain, France, and the Holy Roman Empire. In truth, since he could not raise an army to establish a Medici monarchy in Italy—Julius had shown the futility of that, and Leo was, in any case, a subtler politician—he had to rely on the armies of other nations to accomplish his designs for him. While he balanced D'Este against Colonna against Sforza in Italy, he maneuvered the "superpowers" into battles in which he would be the winner. His only weapons were the tenuous influence of the papacy (always in danger of evaporating if the pope showed himself too ambitious) and his own cleverness.

Leo destroyed one alliance by arranging a marriage. When France, Spain, and the Emperor Maximilian talked of alliance, which would have brought three huge forces together in a way Leo could not manage, the pope persuaded Henry VIII to have his sister marry Louis XII. Next, he invited Louis XII to invade Italy and take Milan with the assistance of the papacy. At the same time, in the event Louis XII proved unreliable as an ally to conquer Naples, the pope arranged with Venice to join him in an alliance against France. When Louis died, having split one alliance by marriage, Leo cemented another, with France, by having Giuliano marry Filiberta of Savoy, the aunt of the new king Francis I. Again, he invited the French to invade Milan, promising not to bring allies against them, in the hope they would afterward drive the Spanish from Naples and give Naples to Leo. At the same time, he sent a meager contingent to join the Swiss, who fought against the French, which kept his Italian alliances in order. Leo's troops were led by Lorenzo, and Leo instructed Lorenzo not to engage in battle. That, in any case, was part of that plot. He was, of course, simultaneously dealing with the Spanish and the Holy Roman Emperor and bringing a different pressure against France through England, while at the same time he worked Henry VIII around by holding up ecclesiastical appointments, and—well—and so forth. Leo was on all sides of all controversies, a Cheshire cat who mystified his friends and enemies but amazingly never offended them.

Because news travels so notoriously rapidly in the twentieth century, we imagine that the pace of all things has accelerated. Yet, in the restless days of the Renaissance, the political scene changed more often than the weather. "As I know that M. Pietro Ardinghelli has continually apprized you of the most important occurrences," Cardinal Bibbiena wrote Giuliano, "I have not for the last ten days troubled you with my letters." Then he continues urgently, "Tomaso [the code name for Leo X], on going from home, left your Baccio [Bibbiena] to expedite many affairs of importance. With Ghingerli [the King of Spain], and with him who wishes to be related to Leonardo [Leonardo was Maximilian, and he "who wishes to be related" is Giuliano], an intimate friendship and good understanding has been concluded; they being fully inclined to do the same as the rest whom Leonardo knows, if that which Tomaso wishes for Leonardo be granted, which it is hoped will be done." Bibbiena apparently means that both Maximilian and the King of Spain were willing to let Leo keep his possessions in Lombardy. Bibbiena goes on in this fashion for several pages and then apologizes. "Bartolommeo, who has the cypher, is not at home. I must therefore express myself without it; particularly as this will be sent by our own messengers." Bibbiena touches on the kings of France and England, on archdukes, on the duchy of Ferrara and the cities of Parma and Piacenza, and on other pressing questions and then admonishes Giuliano: "You have never yet informed us whether you have excused yourself to the duke of Milan; whether you have sent to the Swiss and the Cardinal of Sion, as was spoken of and advised: or whether you have had any communication with his most Christian majesty. Respecting all these matters it is requisite that his holiness should be fully informed."

France, Spain, and England were by this time relatively well-united nations with central governments and capital cities, and Leo could therefore consider them in his schemes as well-defined units with predictable aims. The Holy Roman Empire, on the other hand, was a frightful mess, and it consumed the greater share of Leo's attention and patience.

In theory the Holy Roman Empire was a continuation of the ancient Roman Empire. The fathers of the church had maintained that when the Roman Empire finally collapsed it would signal the collapse of the great cycle of empires and begin the reign of Antichrist. Obviously, since Antichrist had not come, the empire still existed. Over the course of centuries, beginning in the reign of Augustus, the Roman emperor increasingly assigned "sacred" qualities to his office. It was understood that just as God reigned over men's souls in heaven and had as his vicar on earth the pope, so too was God the Lord of the earth. Thus, He had a second earthly representative, the emperor. The emperor's primary duty was to protect the church, its lands, and its clergy, to see that people obeyed the spiritual dictates of the priesthood, and to punish heretics if need be just as he would put down civil rebellion. In the tenth century the empire actually worked in this fashion (with the emperor taking slight precedence over the pope), and the two rulers were seen to hold tandem sway over the entirety of western Europe. Then as civil wars tore apart the secular institution and the emperors had to bow to election by a college of seven electors, Italy fell from the grasp of the emperor and the papacy grew to assume its own worldly authority, at least partly in self-defense.

In truth, by Leo's time all that remained of the old empire was a bit of the magic of the imperial name. Whereas the emperor had once commanded the allegiance of the rulers of Denmark, Hungary, Poland, Italy, Burgundy, France, Spain, and England, now he labored in vain to keep his obstreperous electors under the

171

impression that they were his vassals. Where once the empire had seemed strong because all its enemies were weak, now the newly united nations of England and France and Spain defied the empire with impunity. While once labor had been abundant and feudal ties easy to maintain, the plagues of the fourteenth century had decimated the population, and workers gave grudgingly of their labor and performed their tasks poorly. Agriculture and the social organization that had been built upon it went haywire. Landowners turned to other ways of exploiting their lands. Princely wars, bad harvests, and the uncertain beginnings of capitalism amidst a widespread depression in the fifteenth century all led to the growth of a wandering, unhappy, sometimes riotous proletariat. The emperor could not collect taxes, or keep a standing army, or support a police force. For that matter, it is a moot point just what laws police could have enforced. There was an imperial court of justice, but it had the scantiest of funds and few obeyed its mandates in any case. The emperor was an infamous figure, the scourge of innkeepers, because he could never afford to pay his bills. Sigismund, who reigned in the fifteenth century, skipped town one day and left his table linen behind, which the innkeeper was not able to sell because it was covered with garish imperial eagles.

The empire had no discernible boundaries and no center. The Habsburg family had seized on the imperial crown in 1273 and held it still in the person of Maximilian. Maximilian was the feudal overlord of Switzerland, Swabia, and Alsace, the count of the Tyrol, duke of Styria and Carinthia, and archduke of Austria. His titles indicate not the great strength of the emperor but his pathetic weakness: His empire was an omnium-gatherum that added up to a web of family ties and a hopeless confusion. Other noble families fought the Habsburgs, and the cities fought the nobles. Cities conducted their own affairs, made trade alliances and political alliances, declared war and concluded peace, just as the Italian city-states did. Sometimes a bishop or archbishop would press a claim to a city—not in the name of the Roman church or in the name of the emperor, but simply as another worrisome independent power. In the cities themselves plebeians, displaced farmers, wandering mercenaries, and unemployed craftsmen would rise against their princes in the cause of food or liberty. Small rebellions erupted here and there, and the sense of anxiety and fear of vast upheaval were palpable. This was the time that Dürer's terrifying series of woodcuts on "The Apocalypse" circulated about Germany, along with his disquieting "Melancolia I" and his "Knight, Death and Devil," in which a fully armored knight rides with a fixed smile past a hoary figure of Death and a mad, swine-snouted cross-eyed Devil. The landscape is marked by rotted stumps and exposed roots, and a moldering skull lies to one side. In a picture Dürer made to try out the then new technique of etching he portrayed a drunken woman unconscious at one side, a hard-mouthed, naked man holding a stein, a barren landscape, and a naked man at the center frenziedly tearing his hair out.

Superimposed on this world of dreadful chaos was the precise order of the financiers and the merchants. The bankers were able to maintain safe communications, transfer letters of credit, insure safe conduct for travelers, levy tolls, and exact duties; and, as usual, since they held the purse strings, they constituted the only stable form of "government" that extended throughout Germany.

Augsburg, which stood at the center of trade routes from the Alps, the Low Countries, and the Baltic, was one of the centers of the empire's invisible government. A town of industry as well as bustling trade, it produced the family of Fugger, servants of the Habsburgs and so efficiently rapacious that for a time the name Fugger replaced Croesus in the popular phrase "as rich as. . . ." By the time Columbus discovered America, Jakob Fugger had control of the Tyrol silver mines and a nearly complete monopoly of European copper and was beginning to finance Maximilian's hapless wars and lay hold of Habsburg lands when Maximilian defaulted on his loans. One important source of Fugger working capital came from the indulgence trade. Thus, added to Leo X's other lines of influence in Germany was the direct economic clout he had with the Fuggers, who in turn had the

Habsburgs very much in hand. In their turn, the Habsburgs *should* have had their electors under control.

The so-called Golden Bull, issued in 1356 by the King of Bohemia, defined the electors of the Holy Roman Empire as they existed in Leo's day. There were the three Rhenish archbishops (of Trier, Cologne, and Mainz) and four lay leaders (the King of Bohemia, the Margrave of Brandenburg, the Palatine of the Rhine, and the Duke of Saxony). As it happened, two of these offices now belonged to a single family, the Hohenzollerns. Not yet the preponderant power they were to become in German affairs, the Hohenzollerns were nonetheless a family on the way up. Joachim was the Margrave of Brandenburg and now, by virtue of having purchased the archbishopric of Mainz, Albrecht became the second Hohenzollern elector. This unforeseen turn of events put Elector Frederick of Saxony considerably out of sorts. The House of Saxony was considered Germany's leading dynasty in Luther's day. Frederick's brother had been archbishop of Magdeburg. First he had lost that office to Albrecht, and now Albrecht took Mainz as well. Frederick had been outmaneuvered by his rival, and thus Frederick and the Hohenzollerns entered a feud that was to have unfortunate consequences for Leo.

Described as a "fat dormouse" by one of the papal nuncios, Frederick was, in fact, more the size of an adolescent hippopotamus. Fully dressed for a German winter, with his full beard and ample fur collar, he made an imposing figure. He never married, he detested conflict and discord, he was a devout Catholic who had once made a pilgrimage to the Holy Land. When he brought back his first superb relics for his collection at Wittenberg, he was as devoted to the sacred objects for themselves as for the tourists they attracted to his town. Despite his phlegmatic character, he was known as Frederick the Wise. He looked after his own concerns with care and determination, and he had a sharp eye for painters. He came upon Dürer in Nuremberg in 1496, when the artist was still little known, sat for his portrait, and ordered two triptychs for his castle chapel in Wittenberg. The so-called Dresden altarpiece was done for Frederick. He brought Lucas Cranach

174

to Wittenberg in 1505 and set him to work designing coins and costumes and palace rooms, and as some indication of Frederick's fierce pride, he set Cranach hard to work on portraits: In one year alone Cranach turned out sixty portraits of Frederick.

Dürer worked for Albrecht of Brandenburg briefly, too, and in his portrait of the archbishop Albrecht appears to be a dull-witted, paunchy man, with a double chin and drooping lower lip. Albrecht was a man who was fond of starting out on grand schemes and then letting them collapse as he changed his mind, became fearful of the outcome, vacillated—and then embarked on yet another new plan. He employed Mathias Grünewald as his court painter and flirted with the reformers—Ulrich von Hutten was one of the resident humanists at his court. But, like the Holy Roman Empire, Albrecht had no center: He toyed with the idea of marriage, dallied with mistresses, kept a good table, and by virtue of his manifest inadequacies stuck the more firmly in Frederick's craw.

Curiously, Luther owed both these men allegiance. Wittenberg was in Saxony and under Frederick's rule, but the Archbishop of Mainz was the "primate of all German archbishops" and therefore Luther's superior in the church. It was precisely this contradictory set of authorities, so typical of the Holy Roman Empire, and the rivalry between Albrecht and Frederick that would later make it so difficult for the pope to bring a mere monk to heel. Leo's ambitions for his own family reached all the way to Germany and there became embroiled in the rivalry between the House of Saxony and the Hohenzollerns. While they bickered, Luther was held aside by Frederick as a political weapon and so spared a burning at the stake.

But now we anticipate our heroes too much. On March 17, 1516, Giuliano de' Medici died in Florence after an extended illness. It was said, as a matter of course, that he had been poisoned, but it appears more likely that he succumbed to some unknown disease. Leo's intentions for Lorenzo were consequently pursued with a new zeal. The pope trotted out some old grievances against the Duke of Urbino—the duke had murdered the

Cardinal of Pavia some years before—and found occasion to excommunicate the duke and deprive him of all his lands and titles. Lorenzo led 14,000 men into Urbino, including 1,000 light horse, and took possession of the town with only the slightest difficulty. Not until January, 1517, was the Duke of Urbino able to gather an army to regain his city. With 5,000 Spanish infantry, 1,500 light horse, and several thousand Italian mercenaries, the duke set out for Urbino. Once again, an outnumbered defending force quietly slipped away—and the duke was once again installed in his own territory.

When Leo heard of the loss of Urbino, he "warmly remonstrated" with the French ambassador, complained to Maximilian and to the King of Spain, and issued papal briefs calling upon all Christian princes to join in punishing the traitor duke who had taken up arms against Christ's vicar on earth. Leo was, by now, a far more useful friend to all the warring factions of Europe than the powerless Duke of Urbino, so all came to his defense: 400 lances came from Naples, 300 lances from France; Gascons, Germans, Swiss, and Italians lined up behind the pope, and the two armies took to the field. Siege, march, countermarch, flanking maneuvers, assaults on small towns—both armies engaged in those elaborate strategies of Renaissance warfare whereby both try to avoid direct conflict and wait for the other to tire, disintegrate in quarrels, or run out of money to pay mercenaries. In this instance the duke ran out of money first and surrendered Urbino to Lorenzo.

It was said that Leo spent a million ducats on the "war" of Urbino, and it is useful to recall what a ducat was worth in his time. Reuchlin paid one ducat an hour in Rome for tutoring in Hebrew. Fifty or 100 ducats could buy a painting by Botticelli. A man could live moderately well for a year on 200 ducats. Leo's average expenditures in the course of a year amounted to nearly 600,000 ducats. Balanced against these expenditures was an income of some 420,000 ducats a year, which produced a lamentable deficit which Leo worried about from time to time. Leo's budget can be contrasted with that of Sixtus IV, whose income during his reign from 1471 to 1484 was about 290,000 ducats. Both popes had to rely for income on alum mine concessions, the salt monopoly, grain export licenses, rents, tithes, and tributes from the papal states, and the datary, money from the sale of venal offices and indulgences. In Sixtus' day, the datary contributed only 40,000 ducats to the treasury. But in order to make up for his increased expenses Leo required 144,000 ducats from the datary—three and a half times what Sixtus thought he could squeeze out. Like most Europeans, Leo had come to rely far too much on indulgences.

The pope watched with particular interest, therefore, as the agents of the Fuggers made their way across Germany. An indulgence campaign was prepared with all the elaborate plans and shenanigans of a modern advertising or political campaign. After protracted negotiations that took into account all the various demands of princes and prelates, the pope issued a bull of indulgence setting forth the purpose of the campaign and the types of indulgences granted. Commissioners were appointed, who appointed subcommissioners and assistants; the local archbishop, in this instance Albrecht of Brandenburg, issued his own statement, complete with pep talk and advice on tactics and salesmanship. Then the salesmen were drawn from the ranks of experienced preachers. The better preachers commanded a high percentage of the take, and they were accompanied by their own retinue of assistants, front men, flacks and claques, and body servants if they were among the stars of the circuit. All of these people took some cut of the proceeds based on sliding percentages, and there had been grumbling for decades among the people who wondered where the money really went. Often the fees and kickbacks and rake-offs and salaries consumed the entirety of the sums collected. Just what percentage of the indulgence sale Leo got from all the activity is questionable. To raise as much money as he did from indulgences is some measure, however vague, of the vast sums the indulgence sellers harvested—and some measure of how crucial indulgence money had become to the economies of Europe.

The salesmen hit town with the hoopla of a traveling circus.

177

The front men went out ahead with the message "The grace of God and of the Holy Father is at your gates," and the town's church bells rang and priests and nuns led the welcoming procession with their lighted candles to the edge of town. There they met the preacher and his retinue and escorted him to church. Leading the way was the papal bull of the day, held aloft on a velvet cushion, and the people sang and chanted and prayed through the town. If the parish was rich enough to have an organ, that too boomed out as the party entered the church. Then, at the altar the large red cross was set up and the pope's coat of arms was suspended from it, and the preacher mounted the pulpit and opened his pitch. Once he had worked the parishioners up to the proper state of mind, he set them on the confessionals. In the confessionals the priest charged with this aspect of the campaign asked, "Tell me, on your conscience, how much money you can give away, in order that you may obtain so complete a pardon?" Albrecht had specified in his instructions: "This question ought to be put at that moment, so that the penitents may be the better disposed to contribute." Indulgences were priced according to economic class and specific sin. Heads of state, princes, archbishops, and bishops were required to pay 25 ducats for an ordinary indulgence. The price to abbots, counts, and barons was 10 ducats. Lesser nobles and clergy paid 6, and those with an income of 200 ducats a year paid half a ducat. It was, in fact, a very inexpensive way to salvation. Different preachers varied their prices based on what they thought the traffic would bear, but the price for polygamy was routinely figured at 6 ducats, for theft from a church or perjury 9 ducats, the practice of magic 2 ducats, murder 8 ducats. The money was placed in boxes that were heavily girded with iron bands and opened only in the presence of the preacher, a civil authority, and a representative of the Fuggers, who divided and disbursed the money: so much for Leo, so much for the salesmen, so much for the campaign organizers, so much for Albrecht to pay for his archbishopric, so much for the Fuggers.

One of the most famous indulgence salesmen in Germany was

178

The Politics of Indulgences

Johann Tetzel, a cherubic Dominican, the son of a goldsmith, who was now seventy-three years old. He had been in the indulgence business steadily since 1502 and established himself as one of the most accomplished pitch artists in the church. He was an outstandingly good organizer, politic with the local authorities, and an efficient administrator of his large staff. He had a monthly allowance of 80 ducats—a handsome salary then—and an unlimited expense account. He traveled with a carriage and three horses and an imposing retinue of servants and assistants and the more polished representatives of the Fugger bank. His "by gains," as the saying goes, exceeded his salary considerably—recall Chaucer's pardoner who gave special rates in casual encounters with widows. It is said that in 1507 he made 2,000 ducats in two days.

Tetzel has become a legendary figure in the history of the Reformation, a scapegoat to whom all the vices have been attributed. He had several illegitimate children, it was said, and he was reputed to be a raucous tavern-goer. But he was probably no worse than most of the salesmen, and he apparently believed that he was doing a good job in a good cause. Rome's only complaint, relayed to Tetzel through Albrecht, was of low income and high expenditures. But even though the Vatican goaded Tetzel, he was recognized as a valuable salesman. And however much townspeople might complain about his habits in the taverns, he enjoyed a special status. He was a direct representative of the pope, able to bestow the same favors as the pope himself, and so he was something of an illustrious figure in the small towns of Germany. He was, to be sure, a far more impressive figure than any local monk.

No authentic record of Tetzel's sermons survives, and so it is impossible to know precisely how he spoke. In later Reformation reports of his words exaggeration was the goal, and no doubt words were put in Tetzel's mouth that would have horrified the poor fellow. Yet from the archbishop's instructions and Tetzel's own later defenses of his sermons something of the old sermons can be pieced together.

"Indulgences," Tetzel proclaimed from the pulpit, "are the

most precious and the sublimest gift of God. That cross," he would intone, pointing to the red cross, "has no less efficacy than the very cross of Jesus Christ.

"Come forward, and I will give you sealed letters, in virtue of which even the sins which you may have a *wish* to commit in future, will all be forgiven you. I would not exchange privileges with St. Peter in heaven; for I have saved more souls by my indulgences than the apostle ever did by his preaching. There is no sin so great but that the indulgence may procure its remission; nay, should anyone, an impossibility no doubt, should anyone have done violence to the holy Virgin Mary, mother of God, let him but pay and it will be forgiven him."

Having got his audiences' attention with that claim (he denied he ever made it later, but it was an unconvincing denial), he would work himself into a swivet and play airs and variations on his theme. Having sold all the indulgences he thought he could to the living, he then turned to their deceased relatives, who could be sent to heaven instantly. As the popular ditty went: "Once you hear the money's ring, the soul from purgatory is free to spring."

"Priest! Nobleman! Merchant! Woman! Boys and girls! Hark how your parents and other friends who have died, call to you from the depth of the abyss: 'We are suffering a horrible martyrdom! A small sum, given us as alms, will deliver us; it is in your power to bestow this, and yet you will not!'

"Oh weak people, and little better than the beasts, who do not comprehend the grace richly offered you! . . . Now is heaven everywhere open. . . . You have it now in your power to deliver so many souls! . . . Hard-hearted and neglectful man! For twelve groschen you can deliver your father out of purgatory, and you are ungrateful enough not to save him!"

Then Tetzel would advance to a selfless theme to touch the religious feeling in his audience. "Know you wherefore our most holy Lord distributes this grace among you? It is intended that the ruined church of St. Peter and St. Paul should be rebuilt. . . . That church contains the bodies of the holy apostles, Peter and Paul, and a multitude of martyrs. These holy bodies, in consequence of the present state of the building, are now, alas! . . . continually knocked about, put under water, soiled, dishonored, and reduced to rottenness by the rain and by the hail. . . . Ah, shall these sacred ashes remain any longer in mud and in disgrace?"

Those who failed to make some contribution were harassed, insulted, threatened; and those few, very few, who dared criticize were given a ready retort: "All those who criticize my sermons and indulgences will have their heads ripped off and be kicked bleeding into hell; heretics I will have burned until the smoke billows over the walls."

Tetzel was prevented from appearing in Saxony. The Elector Frederick had his own collection of relics that carried indulgences with them, after all, and he did not care to see his trade harmed. Nor did he wish to have any money go from his subjects to help Albrecht of Brandenburg pay the duty for Albrecht's new archbishopric. But the people of Wittenberg could not be stopped from going to Tetzel, and Tetzel set up a campaign in Jüterbog, just four miles over the border from Wittenberg. As men and women from Luther's parish flocked over the border to buy salvation and returned with stories of marvelous bargains, the theologian's dismay grew daily. Surely the pope did not know what pernicious stuff was being preached in his name?

XII

1517

FOR some people in Rome the burning question of 1517 was whether Raphael had chosen the best colors for his frescoes in Cardinal Bibbiena's bathroom. For others—Michelangelo, for instance—the question was whether Raphael would do well or embarrass himself with his fresco for the pope, the "Oath of Pope Leo III." For Leo X the question was how to extricate himself from a plot on his life, a plot originated in, of all places, the College of Cardinals.

However friendly Leo may have been, he never lacked enemies. Although he had charmed and bamboozled them into docility most of his life, in 1517 everyone lost patience with the pope. The young Cardinal Alfonso Petrucci, who had entertained Leo at Castel Sant' Angelo on the evening of the Sacro Processo, was the first to grow bitter. His brother, the ruler of Siena, had been deposed, and a pro-Medici party took over Siena, confiscating the Petrucci estates in the process. Alfonso played with the notion of stabbing the pope in a public place in the mode of ancient republican heroes. Then, from fear either for his skin or his soul (to assassinate the pope would be sacrilege), he determined on a plan that would leave his own hands technically clean. When the pope's physician was absent from Rome, Alfonso urged the pope to have his anal fistula treated by a well-known Roman surgeon, Battista da Vercelli. According to the scheme the two worked out, Vercelli was to treat the pope with poisoned bandages.

Leo's sense of delicacy saved him from Vercelli's poison. Averring that he could not permit a stranger to treat him, the pope stoically waited for his own doctor to return. But Alfonso could not suppress his rage and complained indiscreetly against the pope's ingratitude. Vercelli, fearing discovery, left town but continued to take an interest in the plot and wrote often to his secretary, Antonio Nino, urging him to go ahead with the plan if an opportunity should arise. Some of the letters were intercepted, and Leo requested Petrucci to come to Rome (at the time the cardinal was out of town conferring with his deposed brother) to discuss some business. Petrucci, fearing the worst, demurred; Leo, expressing surprise that the cardinal should think he had anything to fear, guaranteed him safe conduct and, in order to impress Petrucci with his intention to keep his word, solemnly promised the Spanish ambassador that the safe conduct would be observed. Thus, with the additional guarantee of the Spanish ambassador, Petrucci came to Rome. On his arrival he was given an audience with the pope and then escorted from the pope's chambers by an armed guard to the Castel Sant' Angelo, where he was clapped into "the most horrible of its underground dungeons, full of a cruel stench." Cardinal de Saulis, a relative of the deposed Duke of Urbino, was also implicated in the plot, and he joined Petrucci in the dungeon. One need not, Leo explained to the outraged Spanish ambassador, keep faith with poisoners.

It was a routine affair—a malcontent and his accomplice put into prison. But then the surgeon Vercelli was caught and imprisoned. A man named Pocointesta, who had been in the service of the Petrucci family, was put in prison. As a matter of course, they were all put to the rack, and, predictably, they implicated more and more members of the College of Cardinals in the conspiracy. Leo called for a meeting of the cardinals in full consistory, intending to face down the presumed conspirators and force public confessions from them. But on second thought, he decided he had to eliminate the one cardinal who might be able to lead a faction against him.

On the morning of May 22, 1517, while the cardinals were assembled in consistory, Leo sent first, according to the diary of

Paris de Grassis, "for the Cardinal of Ancona, who continued with him about an hour. As we were surprised at this long interview, I looked through an opening of the door, and perceived in the chamber of the pope the captain of the palace, and two of the guards under arms. I was apprehensive of some untoward circumstance; but I remained silent. Seeing, however, the cardinals Riario and Farnese enter the pope's chamber with great cheerfulness, I concluded that the pope had called them to consult with him respecting a promotion of cardinals, of which he had spoken in the morning; but scarcely had the cardinal Riario entered, than the pope, who commonly walked very deliberately between two of his chamberlains, hastened out of the room with great precipitation, and, shutting the door, left the cardinal Riario with the guards. Greatly astonished at his haste, I enquired from the pope the reason of it, and asked whether he meant to enter the consistory without his stole. He was pale and much agitated. He then ordered me, in a more positive tone than usual, to send all the cardinals from the consistory, and afterwards, with a still louder voice, to shut up the consistorial chamber. I obeyed; and no longer entertained a doubt that the cardinal Riario was arrested." Thus Leo eliminated his chief rival in the previous election and the only cardinal who could have led a rebellion against him in 1517.

On June 8, he called the cardinals into consistory once again, and this time he did face them. Each cardinal was required to answer under oath whether or not he was guilty of conspiring against the pope. Francesco Soderini first denied any guilt and then collapsed in tears and admitted his offense. An old Medici rival, he had hoped Lorenzo would be wed to one of his relatives, according to Bibbiena's promise that had originally secured Soderini's vote in the conclave of 1513. Next Cardinal Adrian of Corneto confessed. It was said that he believed an astrologer's prediction that an Adrian would be the next pope, and he was interested in speeding the realization of the prophecy (indeed, another Adrian would be pope on Leo's death). He was also, and more to the point, a relative of the former Duke of Urbino.

184

That Petrucci was guilty there is little doubt. But what of the others? The rack could force confessions easily enough, but it was, perhaps, too handy in forcing confessions that involved Riario—to whom, I believe, Leo had promised the tiara after his own death—and partisans of the Duke of Urbino. Whenever cardinals were involved in plots, they were always quick to leave Rome. Yet, a very long time passed between the arrest of Petrucci and the confrontations with the other cardinals. Had they had guilty consciences, they would certainly have fled town the moment Petrucci was arrested.

What, then, of the "confessions" of Soderini and Adrian in the consistory? The record of the "trial" was kept secret, but its method is evident. Leo pressed those cardinals he wished to have confess to admit some animosity toward him. Any one of them, if pressed sufficiently, would have had something to confess. Leo had promised on his election in 1513 that he would create no new cardinals. Each new cardinal decreased the chances of any incumbent to be elected pope in the future and simultaneously increased the current pope's own faction in the college. Yet, by 1517 Leo had created eight new cardinals. The entire college felt ill will toward the pope. Leo only needed confessions, however, from his most dangerous rivals.

Leo genuinely may have feared that his rivals were conspiring against him, and he decided to take the opportunity to eliminate all of them at once—those who had taken part in the plot and those he feared might cause him trouble later. Whatever the truth of the matter, the pope gained handsomely by the plot. He declared that he would not have the conspirators executed but merely impose fines on them. While the college recovered, first, from the shock of the discovery of an assassination plot and, second, from the shock of Leo's magnanimous mercy, Leo created a new batch of thirty-one cardinals, all of them Medici partisans. It was the largest creation of cardinals in the history of the papacy, and Leo gained doubly by it. Henceforth, the college was utterly subordinate to his will, and in creating these new cardinals, he naturally required each of them to pay for his office. He made

500,000 ducats in the transaction to help make up the deficits of the Urbino war. Whether or not the cardinals had a plot to murder Leo, it was certainly nothing compared to Leo's plot to assassinate the college.

Leo was as good as his word with Riario, Soderini, and Adrian. He imposed a fine of 25,000 ducats. Well, he was almost as good as his word. When the cardinals found it easy to raise the money jointly, Leo said he had meant they had to pay 25,000 ducats *each*. Soderini and Adrian abruptly left town, Soderini to Fondi and Adrian to some unknown place. It was said that one of Adrian's servants murdered him for the money he had succeeded in taking along on his flight. Riario made a public confession and was restored to his ecclesiastical office. Soon, however, Riario considered it prudent to leave Rome, and he took up a more secure residence in Naples, where he died in 1520.

Cardinal de Saulis was pardoned but kept under a close watch, and he died in the following year, not without the usual rumors, probably unfounded, that he had been poisoned. Petrucci was strangled in the dungeon of Castel Sant' Angelo by one Orlando, a Muhammadan hangman of the Roman court. Antonio Nino and the doctor Vercelli were tortured, dragged through the streets of Rome, throttled, quartered with red-hot pincers, and finally hung up on the parapet of the bridge of Sant' Angelo, where they could be seen from the papal palace.

Among the new cardinals Leo appointed to the college were Lorenzo Campeggio of Bologna, who later went to England to decide with Thomas Wolsey the delicate question of the divorce between Henry VIII and Catharine of Aragon and who would be appointed to the see of Salisbury there; Niccolo Ridolfi, Giovanni Salviati, and Luigi Rossi, sons of three of Leo's sisters; Louis of Bourbon, from the important royal family of France; the seven-year-old son of the King of Portugal; the next pope, Adrian of Utrecht, a counselor of King Charles of Spain; one member each of the families of Colonna and Orsini; Francesco Pisani of Venice and Giovan-Battista Pallavicini of Genoa; Albrecht of Mainz; and the leader of the Dominican order, Tommaso de Vio of Gaeta, known as Cajetan, who had impressed Leo by writing a treatise *On the Power of the Pope* and who would soon be called upon to chastise Martin Luther.

In the summer of 1517, Johann Tetzel moved on from Jüterbog to other towns in his indulgence campaign, and the immediate cause of Luther's aggravation over indulgences was removed. But in the autumn of that year while Luther was preparing his lectures for the new term he happened on a small handbook issued under the imprint of Albrecht, Archbishop of Mainz, that contained sample sermons for indulgence preachers. Luther looked through the book and became irritated once again. It seemed evident to him that the corrupt practices in indulgence selling were no mere idiosyncrasies of Tetzel but that misunderstandings in the business were rife—they reached right up to the archbishop himself. Luther decided he would cause a little fuss and get the matter settled. He had no thought of creating a big furor, but certainly a boisterous little fuss.

He spent odd moments through the autumn of the year preparing a set of questions about indulgences. He made no positive assertions. He was scrupulously correct in preparing his theses for academic debate. He was not ready to challenge indulgences in themselves. He was not yet sufficiently certain of his theological ground; he had not finished working out all his notes and conclusions on fundamental matters. In the ninety-five theses he finally worked up for debate he neither questioned the rightness of indulgences themselves nor challenged the authority of the pope; he merely pointed out certain *claims* made by sellers of indulgences that he was willing to debate. He had found no formal judgment by the church on these questions, and thus he assumed, as was customary in the circumstances, that these were permissible questions for debate.

When he had finished writing out his ninety-five theses, he took them across the street to a printer named Johann Grünenberg, who ran off a few copies. Then, on October 31, 1517, the eve of All Saints' Day, he and a friend named Johann Schneider took a midday stroll over to the castle church. The church door served much the same role as a bulletin board at a university. Eventually everyone in town passed through those doors, and so that was where notices of special events were posted, personal messages, schedules of lectures and church services, subjects of talks, and theses for academic debates. Luther tacked up the Latin text of his theses along with a brief introductory note: "In the desire and with the purpose of elucidating the truth, a disputation will be held on the subjoined propositions at Wittenberg, under the presidency of the Reverend Father Martinus Luther, Augustinian Friar, master of arts and doctor of sacred theology, and ordinary lecturer upon the same in that place. He asks those who cannot be present and discuss the subject orally to do so by letter."

That Luther knew he was about to cause trouble is apparent from the fact that he did not dare tell either his mentor Staupitz or the Elector Frederick what he had done. He was aware that his theses would cause a local stir. To make certain they had the proper effect he sent off two other copies of the theses, one to the Bishop of Brandenburg, in whose diocese Wittenberg was, and the other to the Archbishop of Mainz.

"Pardon me, most reverend Father in Christ, and most illustrious Prince," he wrote Albrecht, "if I, who am but the dregs of men, have the rashness to write to your sublime grandeur. The Lord Jesus is my witness, that feeling how small and despicable I am, I have long delayed doing so. . . . May your Highness, meanwhile, allow a look to fall on a grain of dust, and in the spirit of episcopal gentleness, graciously receive my request.

"The papal indulgence is carried hither and thither through the country in your Grace's name. I wish not to accuse the vociferations of the preachers, not having heard them, so much as the false ideas of simple and gross-minded persons among the people who, in purchasing indulgences, think themselves sure of their salvation. . . ."

Luther's alternation between abject fawning on worldly men of power and vicious attack is a mark even of this early letter to Albrecht. As he moves into an exposition of his questions on indulgences, his passion overtakes him and he berates the archbishop: "Great God! The souls entrusted to you are prepared by their instructions not for life but for death. The just account that will one day be demanded from you, becomes larger and larger from day to day. . . . I can no longer hold my peace."

But then his own vehemence frightens him, and he subsides: "Most worthy Father in God, in the instruction of the commissioners, which has been published in your Grace's name (doubtless without your knowledge), it is said that the indulgence is the most precious of treasures . . . and that repentance is not requisite in those who purchase it. . . . Ah, I supplicate your Highness, by the Lord Jesus Christ, to bestow a look of fatherly watchfulness on this affair, to suppress this book entirely, and to enjoin the preachers to hold a different language to the people." In a postscript, Luther asked the archbishop to look over the theses he enclosed so that he could see "on what shaky ground the indulgence promulgations rest."

As we look back on that autumn day in 1517, we see the thunderous beginning of the Reformation, the heroic Luther nailing his theses resoundingly on the door of the church, his new theology issued as a bold challenge to the establishment. Nothing could be farther from the truth. Luther was ambivalent and fearful, abusive to the archbishop and fawning, desperately hoping for a little brouhaha and living in trepidation lest it should occur. And the theses themselves have only the barest hint of his new theology. He was again, as he had been so often before, asking for someone to answer his questions and put his mind at ease and take care of things for him so that he could have some peace. And yet, on the other hand—for there were always at least two precariously balanced sides to Luther's actions—he *did* hope he would unsettle a few people.

Luther's letter did not reach Albrecht's court counselors, who sat at the time at Kalbe, until November 17. Albrecht said he had no interest in the matter, though he did consider the monk's letter "insolent," and had the questions referred to the faculty of the University of Mainz. But he was in no hurry to answer and in the meantime no one came to debate with Luther—not a soul. Nor did anyone in Wittenberg take any notice of the obscure little proclamation tacked to the door of the church. Nor did anyone write Luther. And so the pattern of Luther's next several years was set. When he was ignored, when no one bothered to answer him, it provoked him. On November 11, since he had not heard from Albrecht (who had not yet even received his letter), he sent out the few remaining copies he had of the theses to some friends and asked their advice on whether they thought he should have them published. He had, he said, "waited patiently" for some reply from Albrecht.

In the first four theses Luther sets out a general understanding of penance and penitence. They hint at Luther's ultimate understanding of *poenitentia*, but he was not yet prepared to debate the more fundamental aspects of the matter. With scholarly rigor, he stayed to his main point, disputing the indulgence practices on their own terms:

1. When our Lord and Master, Jesus Christ, said "Repent," He called for the entire life of believers to be one of penitence.
2. The word cannot be properly understood as referring to the sacrament of penance, *i.e.*, confession and satisfaction, as administered by the clergy.
3. Yet its meaning is not restricted to penitence in one's heart; for such penitence is null unless it produces outward signs in various mortifications of the flesh.
4. True repentance lasts as long as a man is displeased with himself, that is, until he enters the kingdom of heaven.

In the following theses, Luther marked out the pope's authority over remission of penalties for sins:

5. The pope has neither the will nor the power to remit any penalties beyond those imposed either at his own discretion or by canon law.
6. The pope cannot himself remit guilt, but only declare and confirm that it has been remitted by God; or, at most, he can remit it in cases reserved to his discretion. Except for these cases, the guilt remains untouched.

Thus Luther distinguished between temporal penalties imposed by canon law and God's forgiveness of sin—the central point most people misunderstood. So far, all of the theses are unexceptionable. The pope had been careful to make the same distinction that Luther did in theses 5 and 6; only in Albrecht's instructions to his salesmen did an officer of the church willfully obscure the distinction. But, in a set of twenty-one theses, Luther next attacked one of the most significant appeals of indulgences, their efficacy in helping suffering relatives in purgatory:

> 8. The penitential canons apply only to men who are still alive, and, according to the canons themselves, none applies to the dead.

Since this matter of legal history had been conveniently overlooked by the indulgence merchants, Luther hammered repeatedly at it from several directions:

> 10. It is a wrongful act, due to ignorance, when priests retain the canonical penalties on the dead in purgatory.
> 11. When canonical penalties were changed and made to apply to purgatory [this had been declared very recently, by the Borgia Alexander VI], surely it would seem that tares were sown while the bishops were asleep.
> 12. In former days, the canonical penalties were imposed, not after, but before absolution was pronounced; and were intended to be tests of true contrition.

Luther here distinguishes between penalties that paid for sins and helped to "buy" salvation and penalties that were "tests" that signified whether the sinner was truly contrite. It was a short step to the proposition that true contrition and repentance and forgiveness existed quite independently of all the practices of the church. But Luther does not press that point now—that would be another argument. Rather he pushes relentlessly on to drive a wedge between the pope's authority on earth and his lack of authority over purgatory. These are the essential theses: If the pope has no authority over purgatory, then indulgences lose their appeal entirely as items the living may buy for the dead, and their appeal to the living, as storing up credits against time in purgatory, is diminished enormously. These are all merely points for debate, but Luther is staking out the essential part of his argument now, and he does so firmly:

13. Death puts an end to all the claims of the church; even the dying are already dead to the canon laws, and are no longer bound by them.
20. The pope, in speaking of the plenary remission of all penalties does not mean "all" in the strict sense, but only those imposed by himself.
21. Hence those who preach indulgences are in error when they say that a man is absolved and saved from every penalty by the pope's indulgences.
23. If plenary remission could be granted to anyone at all, it would be only in the cases of the most perfect, *i.e.*, to very few.
24. It must therefore be the case that the major part of the people are deceived by that indiscriminate and high-sounding promise of relief from penalty.

Next comes a foreshadowing of Luther's attack on the special powers of the pope, and it sounded ominous to a great many, even though it was buried in a set of tedious debating points:

25. The same power as the pope exercises in general over purgatory is exercised in particular by every single bishop in his bishopric and priest in his parish.

And, in concluding his attack on the utility of indulgences for the dead, he could not resist taking a few pokes at Tetzel's popular line:

27. There is no divine authority for preaching that the soul flies out of purgatory immediately the money clinks in the bottom of the chest.
28. It is certainly possible that when the money clinks in the bottom of the chest avarice and greed increase; but when the church offers intercession, all depends on the will of God.

After his scornful reference to Tetzel, Luther next moves on to eleven theses concerning the value of indulgences for the living. Again he draws his distinctions between contrition and forgiveness, penalties imposed by the church and true reconciliaton with God:

30. No one is sure of the reality of his own contrition, much less of receiving plenary forgiveness.
31. One who *bona fide* buys indulgences is as rare as a *bona fide* penitent man, *i.e.*, very rare indeed.
32. All those who believe themselves certain of their own salvation by means of letters of indulgence, will be eternally damned, together with their teachers.
33. We should be most carefully on our guard against those who say that the papal indulgences are an inestimable divine gift, and that a man is reconciled to God by them.
34. For the grace conveyed by these indulgences relates simply to the penalties of the sacramental "satisfactions" decreed merely by man.

Luther is repeating himself here, but having made his case against indulgences for the dead, he wishes to drive home his point about indulgences for the living:

35. It is not in accordance with Christian doctrine to preach and teach that those who buy off souls, or purchase confessional licenses, have no need to repent of their own sins.

And now Luther altogether annihilates the efficacy of indulgences:

36. Any Christian whatsoever, who is truly repentant, enjoys plenary remission from penalty and guilt, and this is given him without letters of indulgence.
37. Any true Christian whatsoever, living or dead, participates in all the benefits of Christ and the Church; and this participation is granted to him by God without letters of indulgence.

Luther might well have stopped right there. If he could successfully defend Thesis 37, he had completely undermined indulgences. Who would buy them any longer if all men shared in the benefits of Christ and the church without indulgences? Then Luther threw the indulgence trade a sop:

38. Yet the pope's remission and dispensation are in no way to be despised, for, as already said, they *proclaim* the divine remission.

The italics are this author's. Luther maintains that the indulgences do not bestow remission but that they "proclaim" it. They are, in other words, a symbol of a remission, a remission that may or may not be true, depending on whether a man is truly contrite. A high price to pay for a symbol that may or may not symbolize anything real. Luther had no hatred for indulgences understood in this way, and his next two theses try to save indulgences:

39. It is very difficult, even for the most learned theologians, to extol to the people the great bounty contained in the indulgences, while, at the same time, praising contrition as a virtue.
40. A truly contrite sinner seeks out, and loves to pay, the penalties of his sins; whereas the very multitude of indulgences dulls men's consciences, and tends to make them hate the penalties.

In the succeeding set of twelve theses Luther sets out a program of instruction for Christians that will teach them just how indulgences can be used within this new understanding of them:

41. Papal indulgences should only be preached with caution, lest people gain a wrong understanding, and think that they are preferable to other good works: those of love.
42. Christians should be taught that the pope does not at all intend that the purchase of indulgences should be understood as at all comparable with works of mercy.
43. Christians should be taught that one who gives to the poor, or lends to the needy, does a better action than if he purchases indulgences;
44. Because, by works of love, love grows and a man becomes a

better man; whereas, by indulgences, he does not become a better man, but only escapes certain penalties.

45. Christians should be taught that he who sees a needy person, but passes him by although he gives money for indulgences, gains no benefit from the pope's pardon, but only incurs the wrath of God.

In effect Luther has outlined the tenets of Christian charity in this world, and these last several theses betray that sweetness of disposition that often bubbled up in Luther's sermons. The sweetness now leads him to a rather touching bit of wishful thinking (though it is not without a barb concerning the pope's need for prayer):

48. Christians should be taught that, in granting indulgences, the pope has more need, and more desire, for devout prayer on his own behalf than for ready money.

Then he moves on to remark on the pope's motives, and these two theses, more than any other bit of information about Luther, make it evident that he truly believed the pope was ignorant of what was being preached in his name. Obviously Luther was not attacking the pope or the church at large, but simply trying to help the pope do his work in keeping his preachers honest:

50. Christians should be taught that, if the pope knew the exactions of the indulgence-preachers, he would rather the church of St. Peter were reduced to ashes than be built with the skin, flesh, and bones of his sheep.

51. Christians should be taught that the pope would be willing, as he ought if necessity should arise, to sell the church of St. Peter, and give, too, his own money to many of those from whom the pardon-merchants conjure money.

The suspicion must have then occurred to Luther that the pope might, in fact, know what the preachers were saying. So, for good measure, to settle that ghost and to make certain that by allowing indulgences to creep back into church practices he was not understood to say they had validity in the old sense:

WHITE ROBE, BLACK ROBE

52. It is vain to rely on salvation by letters of indulgence, even if the commissary, or indeed the pope himself, were to pledge his own soul for their validity.

In his next set of theses, numbers 53 through 80, Luther gets in his cracks at the indulgence preachers who usurp the pulpit and forbid any other priest to take up time with preaching the gospel while sales are in progress:

53. Those are enemies of Christ and the pope who forbid the word of God to be preached at all in some churches, in order that indulgences may be preached in others.
54. The word of God suffers injury if, in the same sermon, an equal or longer time is devoted to indulgences than to that word.
55. The pope cannot help taking the view that if indulgences (very small matters) are celebrated by one bell, one pageant, or one ceremony, the gospel (a very great matter) should be preached to the accompaniment of a hundred bells, a hundred processions, a hundred ceremonies.
56. The treasures of the church, out of which the pope dispenses indulgences are not sufficiently spoken of or known among the people of Christ.

In speaking of the proper way of preaching Luther digresses about the content that needs to be taught, and here his own theology begins to emerge, the theology of Christ's merits, of faith in Christ being sufficient for salvation, of the supreme importance of the Bible:

60. We do not speak rashly in saying that the treasures of the church are the keys of the church, and are bestowed by the merits of Christ:
61. For it is clear that the power of the pope suffices, by itself, for the remission of penalties and reserved cases.
62. The true treasure of the church is the Holy Gospel of the glory and the grace of God.

Having gone so far, Luther draws himself back to the narrow focus of his disputation. He has lost some of his sense of orderly progression here, and apparently it occurs to him that he is flirting with excommunication. Once again he goes over his central tenets on indulgences, covering himself as he goes against the possibility of condemnation for heretical views:

69. Bishops and curates, in duty bound, must receive the commissaries of the papal indulgences with all reverence;
70. But they are under a much greater obligation to watch closely and attend carefully lest these men preach their own fancies instead of what the pope commissioned.

Is it clear that he has not presumed to attack indulgences *per se* but only the abuses that result from misunderstanding their character? He will make it perfectly clear:

71. Let him be anathema and accursed who denies the apostolic character of the indulgences;
72. On the other hand, let him be blessed who is on his guard against wantonness and license of the pardon-merchants' words.

Luther must have liked that pair of theses; he had protected himself against the charge of heresy and managed to call himself blessed for attacking indulgences. But perhaps he is harming the pope's trade in indulgences now that he has shown them to be so nearly worthless? Again he protects his flanks:

73. In the same way, the pope rightly excommunicates those who make any plans to the detriment of the trade in indulgences.
74. It is much more in keeping with his views to excommunicate those who use the pretext of indulgences to plot anything to the detriment of holy love and truth.

Thus Luther placed himself on the side of love and truth. Secure now, he placed Tetzel on the side of the plotters against love and truth:

75. It is foolish to think that papal indulgences have so much power that they can absolve a man even if he has done the impossible and violated the mother of God.

76. We assert the contrary, and say that the pope's pardons are not able to remove the least venial of sins as far as their guilt is concerned.

And on to another claim of Tetzel's:

77. When it is said that not even St. Peter, if he were now pope, could grant a greater grace, it is blasphemy against St. Peter and the pope.
79. It is blasphemy to say that the insignia of the cross with the papal arms are of equal value to the cross on which Christ died.
80. The bishops, curates, and theologians, who permit assertions of that kind to be made to the people without let or hindrance, will have to answer for it.

Beware, Albrecht! Tetzel is a blasphemer, and you will answer for it: *That*, Luther must have thought, will make the archbishop take notice. Luther is drawing near the end of his theses, and as a parting shot the man who so loved to use parables of sows in his sermons now opposes the wisdom of the common man to the chicanery of men like Tetzel. If the common men who were to read these theses could not understand the theological points Luther had raised in the earlier theses, they could certainly understand this next set of theses. And they could respond enthusiastically to the bold young monk who did not fear to speak out in this way and voice their complaints and give dignity to them in the form of theological arguments written in Latin. Luther attacked the indulgences from all angles and on all levels, but here were the theses that caused his attack to spread like a brush fire throughout Europe:

81. This unbridled preaching of indulgences makes it difficult for learned men to guard the respect due to the pope against false accusations, or at least from the keen criticisms of the laity;
82. They ask, *e.g.*, Why does not the pope liberate everyone from purgatory for the sake of love (a most holy thing) and because of the supreme necessity of their souls? This

would be morally the best of all reasons. Meanwhile he redeems innumerable souls for money, a most perishable thing, with which to build St. Peter's church, a very minor purpose.

84. Again: Surely this is a new sort of compassion, on the part of God and the Pope, when an impious man, an enemy of God, is allowed to pay money to redeem a devout soul, a friend of God; while yet that devout and beloved soul is not allowed to be redeemed without payment, for love's sake, and just because of its need of redemption.

86. Again: Since the pope's income today is larger than that of the wealthiest of wealthy men, why does he not build this one church of St. Peter with his own money, rather than with the money of indigent believers?

87. Again: What does the pope remit or dispense to people who, by their perfect penitence, have a right to plenary remission or dispensation?

88. Again: Surely greater good could be done to the church if the pope were to bestow these remissions and dispensations not once, as now, but a hundred times a day, for the benefit of any believer whatever.

And then Luther warns that he *will* be answered—a warning that went, disastrously, unheeded:

90. These questions are serious matters of conscience to the laity. To suppress them by force alone, and not to refute them by giving reasons, is to expose the church and the pope to the ridicule of their enemies, and to make Christian people unhappy.

And, again, he affirms that he believes a proper answer can be made to him, and he takes pains to save the pope's face:

91. If, therefore, indulgences were preached in accordance with the spirit and mind of the pope, all these difficulties would be easily overcome, and, indeed, cease to exist.

In the concluding several theses, Luther departs from the form of topics for debate and writes what sounds more like the opening of a manifesto:

92. Away, then, with those prophets who say to Christ's people, "Peace, peace," where there is no peace.
94. Christians should be exhorted to be zealous to follow Christ, their Head, through penalties, deaths, and hells;
95. And let them thus be more confident of entering heaven through many tribulations rather than through a false assurance of peace.

Luther distilled centuries of resentment and grumbling against indulgences in these ninety-five theses, and he added the one necessary ingredient to turn grumbling into revolt: a denial, on the basis of theology and canon law, of the usefulness of indulgences. To be sure, he said that indulgences "proclaim" the remission of sins; and he did believe that men had to pay some penalty for their sins after they had been forgiven, though "works of love" or gifts to the poor were better payments than indulgences. But that was all he had to say in their favor. For all his pronouncements that "the pope rightly excommunicates those who make any plans to the detriment of the trade in indulgences," Luther retained indulgences in this system only to damn them with the most astonishingly faint praise. He had offered the theses as topics for debate. But what was left to debate?

The copies of the theses that he sent out to his friends were printed and reprinted. They were translated into German and, as Luther later recalled with undiminished amazement, "Within a fortnight, they had run throughout all Germany." The Bishop of Merseburg had them posted on his churches and monasteries. Before the end of November, Thomas More had seen a copy in England. Dürer got copies in the Netherlands and was so delighted with the theses that he sent Luther some woodcuts and engravings. Erasmus got a bound copy of the theses in Basel in December. And the poor, the princes and prelates throughout Germany, and intellectuals everywhere wrote ecstatically to the monk. It tries the imagination to conceive of a little leaflet moving so quickly even in the twentieth century, and it utterly unnerved Luther. He had not really investigated the questions he had raised with anything like the thoroughness with which he had probed the Psalms. "I myself did not know what the indulgences were," he said later, "and the song threatened to become pitched too high for my voice."

When word of the disturbance on the remote frontiers of the Holy Roman Empire reached Leo X in Rome, his mind was still on the conspiracy of the cardinals. "Thank God," he was rumored to have said, "the axe has been taken from the root and laid to the branches."

XIII

1518

"WITHIN three weeks I shall have the heretic in the fire," Johann Tetzel announced in the new year of 1518, and his confidence seems humorous in retrospect. But Tetzel was not the only comical figure of 1518. The theologians of the church now arrayed themselves against Luther with cries of "infamous, blasphemous scoundrel," "Bohemian heretic," "son of a bitch," "leper with a brain of brass and nose of iron," and other standard phrases of academic debate in the sixteenth century. The ineptness of the church in serious theological matters was flamboyantly displayed by a proud, bumbling trio that came jauntily forward to crush the *fraterculus*, or "mini-friar"—Tetzel, still fuming and bragging; the seventy-year-old master of the papal palace, Prierias, a fox terrier in disputation; and, finally, Cardinal Cajetan, fastidious and condescending. Each of them lost his battle with Luther, each in his own way, and together they drove Luther farther outside the church.

The uproar was perceived at first as a rivalry between Augustinians and Dominicans. It is said that Leo X remarked, "Luther is a man of talent; these are only the squabbles of monks." But, then, the pope is also quoted as saying, "Never mind, it is only a drunken German. He will feel differently when he sobers up." Taken together, the two remarks cancel one another out, but still leave the impression, widespread at the time, that most onlookers saw the business as a petty fight between the two religious orders. At the Dominican convention at Frankfurt on the Oder, 106 countertheses were drawn up against Luther, and the convention took the additional, highly inflammatory step of deciding to denounce Luther formally in Rome as a heretic. Tetzel sent 800 copies of the countertheses to Wittenberg where, to the dismay of Luther, the students manhandled Tetzel's messenger and made a bonfire of the countertheses.

In the meantime, in his own leisurely fashion Albrecht of Mainz passed Luther's theses along to Rome with a note saying that the Augustinian monk was causing trouble with the indulgence sale and that he ought to be told to hold his tongue. In Rome the Cardinal de' Medici suggested to his friend Gabriel della Volta, the promagistrate of the Augustinians in Rome, that the rivalry between the two orders was unseemly, and Volta passed the word on down the line to Staupitz to tell the monk to be quiet.

Luther, meanwhile, was working on a set of "explanations" of his theses. These explanatory notes, which he called *Resolutiones disputationum de indulgentiarum virtute*, he very properly sent off to Bishop Schulze of Brandenburg, with the request that the bishop should correct or delete anything he found objectionable. The bishop replied weeks later that he could find nothing wrong with the resolutions. It is questionable whether the bishop ever troubled to read them. Or, if he did, his bland response indicates once more how remarkably ignorant the officials of the church were about theology. The bishop asked Luther to hold back publication for the time being, however; and Luther obeyed the bishop's request so strictly that Schulze soon allowed him to publish once again.

Luther's *Resolutions* were published in Latin, and a précis of his arguments was printed in German under the title *Sermons on Indulgences and Grace*. It was his first direct appeal to the people in the German language, and the little book went quickly into more than twenty editions. Each time Luther explained himself, he got deeper in trouble. For each time he adduced new arguments to buttress the old ones, he went deeper into his own theology, into the discoveries he had made in the Psalms and Saint Paul. It was in his *Resolutions* that Luther disputed the church's understanding of *poenitentia*. In Latin, Luther said, this means "do penance"; but in the Greek *metanoia*, the meaning is "be penitent," or, more simply, "change your mind." Thus, Luther moved from an attack on indulgences to an attack on the sacrament of penance itself and on toward his belief in salvation through faith alone. Next, Luther tossed off an aside: "Suppose that the Roman Church were as once it was before the days of Gregory I, when it was not above the other churches, at least not above the Greek." That little explanatory digression would send a chill down the spines of the Roman prelates. The primacy of the Roman Church, Luther said, was merely an historical development, not the result of some divine purpose. Thus, when the defenders of the church came to insist Luther must deny his arguments because the Roman Church is supreme and may alone interpret doctrine, Luther had already "explained" that the Roman Church's primacy was a simple quirk of history.

Leo X knew nothing of all these resolutions as yet, and he would have been mightily surprised, as would the other European leaders, to hear that anyone doubted the primacy of the Roman Church. As Duke George of Saxony would say in the heat of debate later on, "What difference does it make whether the Pope is pope by divine right or human right? He is pope just the same, isn't he?" Leo, pope just the same, spent the spring of 1518 commissioning Raphael to paint his frescoes in the Vatican *loggie*, seeing the shipment of Raphael's tapestries for the Sistine Chapel arrive from Brussels, and settling an academic dispute in Rome over one Longolius, who had, some years before, compared Augustus to Charlemagne and found Augustus wanting. There were some who said Longolius should not be given Roman citizenship because of his untoward remark. Leo amiably maintained that the mistake was to be attributed to Longolius' youth and should be forgiven.

In April, Lorenzo de' Medici was sent off to Paris to marry Madeleine de la Tour, daughter of John, Count of Boulogne and Auvergne, and, through her mother's side of the family related to John, Duke of Vendosme and thus to the royal family of France.

The Medicis were at the crowning point of their social climbing. and although the feckless Lorenzo would ruin all for his own family by dying in little more than a year, it was from this marriage that Catherine de' Medici, who ruled France through three of her monarch sons, would issue. Lorenzo arrived in Paris to serve on April 25 as baptismal sponsor for the king's newly born son. The wedding celebration that followed was suitably impressive. Leo's own spendthrift gifts to the bride were estimated at a value of 300,000 ducats, including a bed made of tortoise shell and mother-of-pearl among other things, the lot being transported to Paris by a train of thirty-six horses.

Just as the Dominicans had had their convention in January, so the Augustinians called a convention of the order in 1518. On April 26, the day after the son of the King of France was baptized, Luther arrived in Heidelberg for the annual disputations, socializing, food, and drink. Luther had trudged to the convention on foot and after four wearying days on the road he wrote back to Wittenberg: "I am properly contrite for going on foot. Since my contrition is perfect, full penance has already been done, and no indulgence is needed." Because he was already a notorious public figure and in danger of being seized as a heretic and shipped off to Rome, he traveled incognito. But when he arrived at Heidelberg, he discovered he was the celebrity of the hour. Staupitz appointed him chairman of the disputations, and the indulgences were not mentioned in public. The disputations were taken up with Luther's "new theology."

For these disputations Luther drew up a new set of theses, which embody more of his fundamental beliefs that "God is not found except in sufferings and in the Cross" and "The law says 'Do this,' and it is never done. Grace says 'Believe in this one' and forthwith everything is done." He attacked the old Aristotelian Nominalists and put forward the theology of the cross, Saint Augustine, and the Bible. He split the convention between the generations, and although the older men did not attack him, they shook their heads, or held them, at the sight of the roaring young man. "I have great hope," Luther said, "that as Christ went over to the Gentiles when the Jews rejected Him, so this true theology will be taken up by the younger generation though it is rejected by opinionated old men." Indeed, the young men responded enthusiastically: Johann Brenz, who would later lead the Lutheran party in Württemberg, and Martin Bucer, who was to lead the movement at Strassburg, instantly embraced Luther as their leader. "Their wiles were not able to move him an inch," Bucer wrote of the older men's arguments against Luther. ". . . his sweetness in answering is remarkable, his patience in listening is incomparable, in his explanations you would recognize the acumen of Paul, not Scotus: his answers, so brief, so wise and drawn from the Scriptures, easily made all hearers his admirers." And then Bucer added the ultimate accolade. "That which Erasmus only insinuates, Luther speaks openly and freely."

After years of self-doubt, after months of nettlesome opposition and cold neglect, Luther found himself the champion of the hour, and he reveled in it. "The Count Palatine, too," he wrote back to Frederick's chaplain Spalatin, "has been treating me extraordinarily well. He entertained me with Father Staupitz. . . . We had a wonderful time together, conversing happily, eating and drinking, and viewing all the treasures of the chapel and the armoury, and being shown over this whole, truly royal and remarkable castle. Nothing was omitted that kindness could prompt. The doctors heard my disputation with evident pleasure and debated with me so modestly that they made themselves very dear to me. For although the theology seemed strange to them at first, they discussed it perceptively and skillfully. . . ."

No complete record of the Heidelberg disputations survives, so it is not possible to say with certainty just how much of the new theology Luther introduced at the convention, but arguments always pushed Luther deeper into his ideas, and there is no doubt that he spoke of *poenitentia* and *metanoia*, of the righteousness of God as righteousness that God freely bestows on man. He placed Scriptures above the accretion of later interpretations by the fathers of the church. He attacked "good works." The full Lutheran doctrine was beginning to unfold, and Luther was jubilant at its reception. Staupitz insisted that the star of the convention could not return to Wittenberg on foot, so Luther was treated to a wagon ride back home. In the wagon he found himself sitting next to an old Erfurt teacher and, still ebullient from his triumph at Heidelberg, the young man badgered his old teacher incessantly while the wagon jounced back toward Wittenberg. "I talked with him," Luther reported, "and tried to persuade him, but I do not know with what success. I left him pensive and dazed." When his self-doubt left him, Luther could be unbearable. Still euphoric after his return to Wittenberg, he summed up his journey for the folks back home in words worthy of a conquering general: "I went on foot. I came back in a wagon."

Momentum carried Luther forward now. It is a rare man who confidently believes that he has got a hold on the truth and a rarer man still who, believing he knows the truth, can preserve his sense of modesty and moderation. On May 16, the day after Luther returned from Heidelberg, he preached a sermon on excommunication—not that the pope had threatened excommunication, but Tetzel and his supporters were calling for it, so Luther anticipated them. "I preached a sermon," he wrote to a friend, ". . . on excommunication and its virtues. I rebuked the tyranny and ignorance of the whole filthy pack of officials, commissioners and vicars. Everyone was aghast, they had never heard anything like it; now they are all waiting to see what evil will befall me as a result. I have lit a new fire, but this is what happens with the word of truth."

Having snatched the carrot of indulgences from the pope, now he took away the stick. Like the sale of indulgences, the practice of excommunication had grown ludicrously corrupt. Originally reserved for important enemies of the church, excommunications were, in Luther's day, laid down wholesale on recalcitrant petty princes, on archbishops who had neglected to pay for their offices, on town councils who attempted to put a tax on the beer produced by monasteries, on peasants who did not pay their tithes, on townsmen who defaulted on debts. At harvest time, when most tithes naturally came due, the excommunication bans "fly about

207

by the hundreds like bats," Luther said. If a man were not brought to heel by a ban, his family was excommunicated, and if the family did not pay up, a whole town would be placed under the interdict. The practice had been extended to cover not only the excommunicate's exclusion from the sacraments of the church but also eviction from his house and prevention from engaging in business.

As it is with indulgences, it is a wonder that the practice of excommunication had not long since caused a revolution in the church. Yet, again, Luther's attack was not lodged on mere political grounds. He went at the theological foundations of the matter. According to his understanding of his religion, men had communion with God, personal communion, direct, and unaffected by any intermediaries. That communion with God depended solely upon the individual's faith, not on anything external. Thus, "No man, no bishop, pope, nor even an angel can give or take away this communion." What did it mean if a man were excommunicated for not paying a tithe or declining to buy an indulgence? Not a thing. He was not excommunicated from his communion with God—by which, alone, he was saved. From that, all else followed: If he were excommunicated for voicing unorthodox views, it was nothing to him. "If you are unjustly banned for the sake of truth and right, you may by no means stop doing what has drawn this upon you. If in consequence you die without the sacrament, if your corpse is thrown into unconsecrated ground . . . happy are you! Blessed is he who dies under such an unjust ban! For inasmuch as he has remained faithful, he shall gain the crown of life." The pope had neither the authority to save through indulgences nor damn through excommunication. So much for the pope.

It turned out that some Dominicans were in the congregation that Sunday morning, and they took notes on Luther's sermon and forwarded the notes to Rome, claiming them to be a true and faithful copy of Luther's sermon. Luther fulminated against the "abominable spies" when he learned of their treachery some time later, and the Dominicans had, in truth, embellished Luther's words and added some gossip of their own. But even if they had not been exaggerated, Luther's words were sufficient to provoke the pope. The sermon, along with other writings by Luther, took a prominent place on the agenda for the Dominican convention scheduled for June. There is no way of knowing, of course, but one can well imagine that there was a good deal of lip-smacking in the Dominican Order in May, 1518.

Despite all he had said, Luther was, as he insisted again and again, a loyal son of the church who only posed topics for debate and stood ready at any time to be corrected. This may sound implausible at this point, yet it was true. Luther saw no reason that the church could not get along very happily and prosperously in spite of all he said. It would get along much better, in fact, if the popes and bishops would not make insupportable claims but would content themselves with what God had meant them to be. What Luther did not understand—and what Leo X understood to the exclusion of all else—were the political, economic, and social consequences of his actions. Could the pope be revealed as a minor helper in man's quest for salvation without making the church a weak, impoverished prey to rapacious kings and princes? If one of the pope's spokesmen had candidly told Luther the facts of life, would it have caused Luther to move more quietly and allow the church to work out other ways of dealing with the world? Well, it is extremely doubtful, though it is impossible to know with certainty. What is certain is that in the middle of 1518 all the pope's courtiers and all the pope's priests got together and pushed Martin Luther farther and farther into the role of champion against the church.

"I lay my work at your feet, Holy Father," Luther wrote at this time to Leo X, "with the utmost confidence." He enclosed a copy of his *Resolutions* to prove that, whatever the Tetzelites might be saying about him, he was a good Catholic, ready to accept the decision of the pope—ready, that is, providing the pope's decision "have its origin in Jesus, without whom you cannot propose or state anything. . . ." The old ambivalence careened through this letter to Leo. Luther knew he was right, yet he bowed to the will of the church. But the will of the church needed to be "His will." Nonetheless Luther only posited debatable theories about "His will." But the theories were proven in Luther's view. However, he would argue with some learned theologian or submit his views to the faculties of several universities and welcome anyone who could prove him wrong. There was still room to answer Luther, if only his theses would be taken seriously and debated fairly. "For my own protection, let my book go out under the safeguard of your name, Holy Father, so that everyone may realize with what pure intentions I have sought to fathom the nature of ecclesiastical power and in what reverence I hold it. . . . Most Holy Father, I cast myself at your feet. . . ." At the end, damn him, Luther added, "I cannot recant."

Leo had not time to sort through Luther's *Resolutions* or even to spend much time looking after the Vatican theologians who did. Sultan Selim, after murdering his father, Bajazet, had seized the direction of the Ottoman Empire, had his brother publicly put to death, conquered Persia, and annexed the well-established and powerful Egyptian Empire. It was said that Selim enjoyed reading books about Alexander and Julius Caesar, and the old Italian fear of Turkish conquerors was revived. Leo called the cardinals together in consistory and proclaimed a truce among all the powers of Europe; any prince who disobeyed the truce was, naturally, to be excommunicated. He then dispatched his ambassadors to the European rulers. "It is folly to sit still and suppose that these ferocious enemies can be conquered by prayers alone," Leo said. "We must provide our armies and attack them with all our strength." For the purpose of raising armies, Leo announced that voluntary contributions would be sought from all sovereigns of Europe, a compulsory tax would be levied on their subjects, and, of course, those who balked could be excommunicated. He proposed to raise cavalry from the Poles and Hungarians, infantry from the Swiss and French, fleets from Spain, Portugal, and England. Germany would provide a vast army, and the pope himself would join the campaign, disembarking from Ancona at the head of 100 ships of war. Leo would restore the eastern empire to the

sway of Rome, recapture the Holy Land, and avenge Turkish
atrocities against Christendom.

The grand strategic planning was worthy of Churchill, the
dream itself comparable to the grandest schemes of any pope. The
project dwarfed the designs of Leo's predecessors for rebuilding St. Peter's. If it had actually come off, Leo would no doubt
have been pleased. At the very least, however, he would raise
enormous sums of money; and if the campaign never got started,
he could still use the fortune he hoped to bring in. Like Luther,
Leo was ambivalent. There is no reason to believe that he had at
this early date quite made up his mind what he wanted most: the
glory of reclaiming the Holy Land, or some more spending
money. He had no reason to make up his mind prematurely. He
could wait and see what the proceeds were. Perhaps the flurry of
organizing a campaign would be sufficient to deter the Turks.
Perhaps he could regain the Holy Land on the cheap and have
both his glory and his fat purse. There were many possibilities,
and he pursued his plans—which, in any form, stood to bring him
something good—with cheerful enthusiasm. He dispatched no less
an emissary than Cardinal Bibbiena to France, and Cardinal
Wolsey returned to England on the mission. The Luther controversy was referred to the seventy-year-old Prierias, master of the
holy palace and the only man who had voted against Reuchlin in
that prior dispute.

Prierias' attack on Luther made Tetzel look like a pedantic,
careful scholar. He took up Luther's theses one by one, which
gave his deposition a spurious semblance of answering the challenge. But his arguments were superficial in the extreme. He
stated that the church was represented, quintessentially, by the
Church of Rome; that the Church of Rome was represented by
the College of Cardinals and, in turn, by their elected head, the
pope. Thus, the pope represented the church, and he could no
more err than could the church itself. Having tossed that off,
Prierias then indulged himself in invective and innuendo, calling
Luther a "bastard" and insinuating that he would have found
everything to his liking if the pope had given him a bishopric. The

church's authority "is greater than that of Scripture," Prierias maintained, without bothering to prove it, and "The Pope's word is the oracle of God." The master of the holy palace looked at what he had made and found it good, and so he wrote an introduction boasting that he had only taken three days to write his screed. When the matter at last came to Leo's attention, he is said to have remarked woefully, "He would have done better to work on it for three months instead of three days."

Luther was at first stunned when he realized he had provoked a response from no less a person than Prierias. But once he began to read he was relieved—and then scornfully amused. "Our Lord God was merciful," he said, "for that bacchant wrote such rubbish one could only laugh." He was so pleased with the amateurishness of Prierias' paper that he reprinted it in full in the reply he wrote to it. It was too stupid to take altogether seriously. "You see, Reverend Father," Luther said to the pope in his rebuttal, "I have given you my answer in all haste, in two days." On August 7, the smart aleck received a citation from the pope to appear in Rome within sixty days to answer to charges of heresy. Prierias might be a dolt, but he was the pope's dolt, and Leo would not have Luther toy with him.

Then politics intruded on Luther's life once more. The Diet of the Holy Roman Empire assembled that summer in the prosperous little walled town of Augsburg, its wealthier section dominated by the Fugger palace. There the electors assembled with their retinues, clerks, legal aides, messengers, advisers, and body servants. There Cajetan appeared to proclaim the pope's campaign against the Turks. The cardinal rode into town on a white horse draped in purple, trailed by his own band of diplomats, ecclesiastical lawyers, clerks, and other hangers-on, all dressed in satins and velvets, and Cajetan insisted that his own rooms at the palace be lined in purple satin. He would only eat off silver plate and complained of the bad wine, the coarse bread, and the barbaric cuisine of the Germans and spent his free hours in his room working on a study of Aquinas and shivering in the German summer.

Maximilian had two aims at the Diet of 1518: to promote the pope's tax and take some of it for his own needs, and to ensure that he would be succeeded as emperor by his grandson, Charles V, King of Spain. Cajetan carried the argument for the new tax, though he did so with orotund dignity, declining to mention such distastefully mundane matters as money. At solemn high mass, during which he presented Maximilian with a sword symbolizing the ancient unity of pope and emperor, he surveyed more than 1,500 years of history: the old struggles against the infidels, the blessed Crusades, the new threat to the survival of Christendom, regret over the lost Holy Land, the new opportunity for heroism in a fight with the Turks, the prospect of a final defeat of the enemy that would make the world safe for Christendom. The electors nodded and looked glum. The old war cry was pitched too high for them. The Bishop of Liège, Erhard von der Mark, replied at the Diet. The crimes that the Roman Church had perpetrated on the rest of Europe were well known, he said, and in an indictment that struck at the political and economic issues of which Luther was unaware he detailed the vast sums of money that had poured into Rome from Germany for dubious purposes, the abuses against patronage rights and charges for church appointments. "These sons of Nimrod grab cloisters, abbeys, prebends, canonates, and parish churches, and they leave these churches without pastors, the people without shepherds. Annates and indulgences increase. In cases before the ecclesiastical courts the Roman Church smiles on both sides for a little palm grease. German money in violation of nature flies over the Alps. The pastors given to us are shepherds only in name. They care for nothing but fleece and batten on the sins of the people. Endowed masses are neglected, the pious founders cry for vengeance. Let the Holy Pope Leo stop these abuses." The bishop was followed by other speakers who took the emperor to task for his incessant wars, his inability to administer imperial concerns, the insecurity of the countryside, violent eruptions in the towns, rising prices: All the stored-up resentments flooded out and drowned the Crusade decisively.

Gradually it became clear to Maximilian that he was likely to lose his other goal, too. The emperor was an old man at age fifty-nine, exhausted by his grandiose and feckless schemes. Before he died, he planned to have Charles V crowned King of the Romans. To be King of the Romans was a precondition of becoming Holy Roman Emperor. It was a formality that Maximilian had never gone through himself, since it involved an inconvenient trip to Rome to be crowned. Yet if Charles could be made King of the Romans, on Maximilian's death he would naturally succeed to the old man's office. The pope had reason to dislike the idea of Charles as emperor: that would combine, under the Habsburgs, the rule of Austria, the Netherlands, Spain, and—if Charles were successful in pressing another claim—Naples. The electors, it appeared, were also fed up with the Habsburgs. It was said that Frederick of Saxony was a possible candidate, and Francis I of France, with papal backing, was at work on his own campaign for the office.

With Maximilian in bewildered retreat from his electors, Cajetan persuaded him to help in the church's skirmish with Luther. The cardinal's primary job at Augsburg that summer was to sell the Crusade, but the curia had decided to take advantage of his presence in Germany to settle the Luther controversy. The monk had been summoned to Rome, and he needed to be delivered. Cajetan sought the emperor's help with two arguments: first, that by cooperating with Rome on this matter, he might expect the pope's favor in the question of Charles V; secondly, that since the electors had used the unheard-of argument that "the people" would oppose the tax for the Crusade, this monk Luther was obviously dangerous for the threat he held to all constituted authority. Rebellion was breaking out on all sides, and Luther must take some of the blame for it.

Thus, on August 5 (two days before Luther received his first citation to appear in Rome), Maximilian wrote to Leo. This Luther was preaching pernicious stuff, inflammatory nonsense. The Reuchlin controversy had fed the fires of revolt in Germany, and this business of the indulgences was raising havoc in the

214

empire. Old principles were questioned. Even the princes rebelled now! Authority itself was under attack, and unless Luther were stopped instantly, excommunicated for the damnable heretic he was, there was no telling where it all might lead.

Most historians have seen Maximilian's letter as striking fear into Leo's heart, but it is doubtful that the pope was afraid of the emperor's extravagant panic. Leo had seen how heretics were handled many times in the past; the condemnation of Savonarola was fresh in his mind, and he was simply following a proven old method for dealing with troublemakers. The civil authorities must beg for action; then, when the church answers the plea, no onus attaches to the remote Vatican authorities and, at the same time, the pope is assured that whatever bulls he may issue will be enforced. To move without such assurance was to risk embarrassment. Maximilian took Cajetan's bait, and the curia moved with practiced efficiency now.

On August 23, far short of the sixty-day deadline the pope had first given Luther to reply to his citation, a triple warrant went out for the monk's arrest. One copy went to Cajetan. "We charge you," Leo's letter to Cajetan read, "to cause to appear personally before you, to prosecute, and to constrain, without delay . . . the said Luther. . . . If he return to himself and crave pardon for [his offenses] . . . we grant you power to receive him into the unity of the holy mother, the Church. . . . If he persist in his obstinacy, and should you fail to bring him into your power, we authorize you to proscribe him in all parts of Germany, to banish, and curse, and excommunicate all who adhere to him, and to command all Christians to shun their presence. And to the end that this plague may be more easily extirpated, you shall excommunicate all prelates, religious orders, universities, communities, counts, dukes, and potentates, except the emperor Maximilian, who fail to seize the said Martin Luther. . . ." Cajetan must have been wryly amused at Rome's lack of understanding of the situation in Germany. Excommunicate hundreds for the sake of getting at Luther? His directions were foolish, but he would bring Luther to heel in his own way. A second copy of the warrant went to Frederick, with another, milder letter: "Dear Son, when we think of your noble and praiseworthy race," and so forth and so on. The pope complimented the politically useful elector. The other business followed crisply. Let the elector deliver Luther to Cajetan, "lest the godly of the present and future times should come to lament and say: 'The most pernicious heresy that ever afflicted the Church of God, owed its rise to the assistance and the favor afforded by that high and praiseworthy house' " of Frederick's. A third letter went to the vicar-general of the Saxon Augustinian Order with the terse instructions to have Luther bound hand and foot and delivered to Cajetan. Luther was on his way to Rome, it seemed, from which few travelers of his sort returned.

When Luther had received his first summons to Rome he had written Frederick and requested that the elector intercede for him and insist that he be given a hearing on German soil. It happened that in the course of the politicking at the Diet five of the electors had been persuaded to endorse, however reluctantly, the candidacy of Charles V. Only one elector had refused outright, and that was Frederick. The pope recognized immediately that he had a valuable ally in Frederick, and so he took pains to avoid antagonizing him. Thus when Frederick spoke to Cajetan about Luther's request and Cajetan forwarded the appeal to Rome on August 29, the news came back promptly: The pope had decided to award the Golden Rose, the highest honor the pope could bestow on a temporal ruler, to Frederick, and the papacy would happily accede to Frederick's request that Luther be heard by Cajetan in Augsburg. The tax for the Crusades had been lost, both princes and prelates in Germany were rebellious, Maximilian had an outside chance to ensure the preponderant power of the Habsburgs —but Leo had an ally in Frederick. Frederick had never met Luther and knew little enough of what the monk was about, but he was proud of his university and he had some prideful interest in seeing his professor treated with respect. It was a tenuous, quirky set of circumstances that came to Luther's rescue. Luther hadn't the vaguest notion just how tenuous, or how completely unrelated to his own concerns his rescue was.

Another set of instructions were sent out to Cajetan telling him that Frederick's wishes were to be obeyed. Then yet another set of instructions arrived saying Frederick was to be jollied along and kept happy but Luther was, nonetheless, to be delivered to Rome if he refused to recant. Cajetan had enough instructions by that time to deal with a dozen heretics, and he decided, naturally enough, to ignore them all and do his best. On September 25, Luther received the order to appear in Augsburg before Cajetan. As letters flew back and forth between the cardinal and Rome, the Diet broke up in Augsburg in a flurry of equally contradictory goings-on. Maximilian did not yet quite comprehend what was happening in his empire, and he continued to shift his ground with the breeze. He set out from Augsburg to go hunting and left the parting advice with Frederick to look after Luther, who "might be useful one day" against the pope.

Luther started out bravely for Augsburg on September 27. "I am like Jeremiah," he said, "a man of contention and strife; but the more they multiply their threats, the more do they augment my joy. . . . They have already torn to pieces my honor and reputation," he announced grandiloquently. "One thing only remains to me: it is this miserable body: let them take it." Then, in a remark well designed to be a famous last word, he said, "He who would bear Christ's Word in the world, ought to look for death every hour; for our husband is a bloody husband."

The journey south took twelve days, and each took its toll on Luther's confidence. He stopped at Augustinian monasteries along the way, where all the friars clucked about him and told him he was sure to be burned at the stake. Luther thought of it and said, "What a disgrace to my parents." At Nuremberg, the prior of the monastery gave Luther a new cowl to replace the threadbare one he wore, and it well may have occurred to Luther that his friends were anxious that he make a good appearance at his execution. While Luther walked to the confrontation, Cajetan spent the time reviewing the monk's arguments thoroughly and writing down refutations for each point. Luther was unaware, of course, of what care Cajetan was taking in preparation for the meeting, but he did realize that he was about to meet a genuine theologian. By the time he reached the outskirts of Augsburg, stomach cramps had prostrated him, and the young hero had to be taken the last three miles in a cart.

The prior of the Carmelite monastery in Augsburg put Luther right to bed, and it was several days before he recovered his strength. Some of Frederick's advisers were still in town and came to call, as did a number of the prominent townspeople. They arranged a safe conduct for the monk and talked of mutual friends. Cheered to discover that he had supporters even in this foreign city, Luther revived, and Cajetan made his first mistake. Prior to his meetings with Luther, Cajetan sent one of his retinue, Urban de Serralonga, to make a casual, ostensibly independent visit. Serralonga tried a mixture of amiable banter and friendly advice. Luther ought, really, to recant, Serralonga said. He need only speak a single, small word, *revoco*, and that would be that. Indulgences were not so important, after all, and even if some things were said that were not strictly true, the money came in and it was used for good causes. In the end, as Luther could see, indulgences produced some good. In any case, the pope could establish articles of faith or throw them out as he pleased. Luther demurred. Did Luther challenge the pope's authority, then? Did he imagine his elector would protect him, then? Luther did not think so. Then where would he go? "Somewhere under heaven," Luther replied. Serralonga was just the tonic Luther needed before his meeting with Cajetan. The argumentative juices had been got going again, and he wrote to Spalatin: "This go-between has put new heart into me. Give my regards to my friends in Wittenberg and tell them to be of good courage."

On the morning of October 12, Luther walked the short distance to the Fugger palace, accompanied by five other friars. The cardinal received the six German friars in a room swathed in crimson hangings and accented with the brilliantly colored costumes of the Italians of the cardinal's court. They must have seemed a foppish, simpering lot to Luther, who recalled that during the interview they tittered constantly. For their part,

Luther and his friends must have seemed a mangy bunch of uncouth barbarians. They entered awkwardly, gawking and uncertain. At the center of the room was Cajetan himself in his silk robes, his delicate slippers—a small man, prissy and punctilious. He had studied the writings of Thomas Aquinas from earliest boyhood, and he was a strict believer in the hierarchical order of the church and the authority of the pope. He had a keen memory for ecclesiastical law and could quote decretals with the best of the church lawyers. His greatest talent, however, lay in debate. He had a precisely logical mind, a talent for keeping cool, and an eloquent turn of phrase. He was well known for having bested the facile Italian humanist Pico della Mirandola in debate, and it was Cajetan who had been responsible for leading the debate against the "Arabian influence" of Averroës and having him condemned at the Lateran Council. Luther had never seen his like before and, for all the appearance of effeminacy in these Italians, the monk knew that he was now facing a formidable adversary.

Following the instructions Serralonga had given him, Luther prostrated himself in front of the cardinal. On the cardinal's direction to rise, Luther came to his knees. And on a further order, the monk came to his feet. The two men stared at one another silently, Cajetan perhaps assuming that Luther would blurt out a recantation or perhaps counting on his silence to intimidate the German. Finally Luther broke the silence: "Most worthy Father, in compliance with the summons of his papal holiness, and at the request of my gracious lord, the Elector of Saxony, I appear before you as a submissive and obedient son of the holy Christian Church, and I acknowledge that it is I who have published the propositions and the theses now in question. I am ready to listen with all obedience to the matters of which I am accused, and should I be in error, to submit to instruction according to the truth."

Cajetan replied with gentle condescension, saying that he understood Luther was learned in the Scriptures and then getting brusquely to the point, requiring him to "own your faults, retract your errors, propositions, and discourses . . . abstain in future from disseminating your opinions, and . . . engage to be more moderate, and avoid all that may grieve or unsettle the Church."

"I wish, most worthy Father," Luther replied, "that the brief of the pope, in virtue of which you have received full powers to treat with me, be communicated to me."

At that the Italians tittered and rustled: The monk intended to be legalistic! Cajetan, with his fistful of contradictory instructions from the pope, replied smoothly and without hesitation that he could not grant Luther's request.

"Be so good," Luther said, "as to let me know wherein I may have erred."

Again the audience was amazed and discomfited at the effrontery of the monk. Again Cajetan, confident in this of his own preparations, answered easily that Luther must retract two propositions: "The treasure of indulgences is not composed of the merits and sufferings of our Lord Jesus Christ, and, secondly, the man who receives the holy sacrament of penance ought to have faith in the grace that is offered to him." Cajetan had shrewdly chosen two propositions that covered, first, the principle of the pope's authority and, secondly, Luther's central notion of the necessity of faith. He would retract the statements, Luther said, if Cajetan could show him in what way they were wrong.

In the bull Unigenitus, issued by Pope Clement VI in 1343, Cajetan replied, "you have a statement by the pope that the merits of Christ are a treasure of indulgences."

Luther had always said in his writings that he would submit to the authority of the pope. He believed, he said, that the pope was simply ill-informed; when better informed, the pope would understand that certain practices and teachings of the church needed to be changed. He proposed to debate those practices and teachings. Yet here was Cajetan proposing not to debate these matters at all but to ask at the outset whether Luther accepted the supremacy of the pope in matters of faith. If the answer were yes, then Luther must retract and be silent. If the answer were no, Luther was manifestly a heretic and would be burned at the stake.

Luther did not want to answer either yes or no. He wanted to debate the issues he had raised and find the truth. So he squirmed, and Cajetan probed. Luther stalled, and Cajetan insisted.

Luther was relatively ignorant of ecclesiastical law, as he always admitted, and he said to Cajetan that he would prefer to base his arguments on Scripture. But, Cajetan answered, it is the pope who must interpret Scripture, and in the bull Unigenitus he had done so. But could Cajetan show him in the Bible where he had erred? Cajetan quoted more decretals and asked whether Luther would recant. Yes, Luther would recant, providing that the pope did not contradict Scripture in his decretal. The pope, Cajetan politely explained to Luther, could not contradict Scripture. The Bible needs "interpreting," and the pope is empowered to interpret it; the pope could not err in this matter—he was above the Scriptures, and above councils, too. Pope Nicholas V, Luther undoubtedly recalled, had condemned the council of Basel.

Luther: "The university of Paris has appealed against that."

Cajetan: "The gentlemen of Paris must pay the penalty for doing so."

The dialogue went profitlessly on and on in this course. Cajetan quoted decretals; Luther said he would recant if the decretals could be substantiated by Scripture. The pope interprets Scripture —and so forth, and so on. It was apparent to Luther that he could not make Cajetan see the point of what he wanted to debate, and it was equally apparent to Cajetan that Luther was obstinately refusing to see the logic of his argument that if the pope were supreme in interpreting Scripture there was no point to Luther's arguments. Luther had, in fact, been fairly trapped. If he were to have a chance to argue, he must first take the heretical position that the pope was not alone able to interpret Scripture definitively. If he were to declare that, then he had already lost the argument. He asked Cajetan for an opportunity to reply in writing, and Cajetan said he would hear his response on the following day.

On the next day Luther was accompanied by a larger band of friends and supporters, including two counselors of the emperor,

several of Frederick's legal aides, Staupitz, the renowned scholar
Konrad Peutinger, a knight, a doctor, a notary, and enough others
to bring a smile to Cajetan's lips when he saw the crew enter the
crimson-draped hall. The recantation, it appeared, would be
phrased in careful legal terms. The pope's scholar was ready for
it; he had already exhibited an incisive mind, an ability to get to
the heart of Luther's challenge to the hierarchical order of the
church, and a shrewd capacity for putting his antagonist in a
dilemma and holding him there. The opening of Luther's remarks
must have reassured Cajetan:

> I declare that I honor the holy Roman Church and will con-
> tinue to honor her. I have sought the truth in public disputations,
> and all that I have said I regard, even to this hour, as just, true,
> and Christian.

Luther was to keep his pride in recanting, it seemed.

> Nevertheless, I am but a man and may be mistaken. Accord-
> ingly, I am disposed to submit to instruction and correction in
> those things in which I may have erred.

The statement still sounded like a recantation, but then Luther
surprised the cardinal. Was the pope supreme? Luther's answer
was at once clever, naïve, and daring:

> I declare that I am ready to reply by word of mouth, or by
> writing, to all the objections, and all the reproaches, which the
> lord legate may bring against me. I declare myself ready to sub-
> mit my theses to the four universities of Basel, Fribourg, Lou-
> vain, and Paris, and to retract what they shall find erroneous.
> In a word, I am ready to comply with all that can be asked
> from me as a Christian. But I solemnly protest the course which
> has been sought to have given to this affair, and against the strange
> pretension of obliging me to retract without having refuted me.

When the arrogant, thirty-five-year-old, ill-mannered, loud-
mouthed provincial school teacher finished reading his statement,
Cajetan's courtiers tittered and Cajetan himself burst out in laughter. The affront to Cajetan was monstrous: Luther did not deign

to answer his arguments, or submit to his judgment, or bow to the representative of the pope. The brazen fellow would now set up his own court! Just how multifaceted Luther felt his statement to be we do not know, but it can be read on many levels. First, it was an insult to Cajetan. Second, it was a means of escape from his dilemma of the "yes-no" proposition on the pope's authority. Third, it was a means to gain a public disputation to argue his theories, since Cajetan was unwilling to debate the specifics of Luther's theses. Fourth, it was, in effect, Luther's reply on the question of the pope's authority: Some vaguely constituted panel of university scholars was to be preferred in interpreting the Scriptures.

Luther had not written a reply to the cardinal's points, Cajetan reminded the monk with cool civility. Would he care to reply now whether he accepted the pope's authority, the pope's judgment as expressed in the bull Unigenitus, and would he reply whether he recanted or not? Luther replied that in his opinion there was no need to get into all that, since they had had "quite enough wrangling yesterday."

Cajetan, reminded of his own august position by the impertinence of the lowly monk, replied sharply: "My son, I did not *wrangle* with you. I am ready to reconcile you with the church."

Luther had behaved badly—that much was clear, if not to him, then to his friends. He had asked for an argument; he had got one; and now he wanted to take the argument elsewhere. He should have been embarrassed, though, of course, he wasn't. Staupitz stepped forward and asked if Luther might again be extended the favor of a reply in writing on the following day. The favor was granted, and the Luther faction left the hall in unceremonious confusion.

That night Staupitz released Luther from his vows of obedience to the Augustinian Order—ostensibly to free Luther to debate as he chose, but at the same time to let Staupitz wash his hands of his unpredictable pupil. Staupitz did not know quite what was going wrong, but he knew Luther was courting disaster in bad fashion.

On the following day Luther appeared with only two brave

companions. The rest of his supporters, including Staupitz, had accounted the Fugger palace too dangerous a place to be in Luther's company. This time Luther read a prepared statement that came directly to grips with the cardinal's arguments. First, he said, "Christ's merits are not a treasure of indulgences exempting men from good works, but a treasure of life-giving grace. Christ's merits are applied to the believer without indulgences, without keys, by the Holy Ghost alone, and not by the pope." Secondly, "I have stated that no man can be justified before God unless by faith, so that man must believe with an entire assurance that he has obtained grace. . . . The faith of the righteous man is his righteousness and his life." Luther buttressed his argument with copious quotations from Scripture and yet another protestation that he would retract if he were proven wrong.

Cajetan replied with lengthy citations from Aquinas, decretals, and another reference to Unigenitus. He had prepared very thoroughly for this meeting, and while he was not supposed to debate with Luther, his pride of scholarship got the better of him and his eloquence carried him away. In Luther's report of it, the cardinal ranted on and on irrelevantly. In fact, from his own point of view, the cardinal answered each of Luther's arguments completely and cogently, dotting every iota as he went. Would he, Luther asked the cardinal, show him the passage in Unigenitus? Cajetan reached for a book and opened it to the page he had marked: "The Lord Jesus Christ has acquired this treasure by his sufferings."

Luther: "Most worthy father, be so good as carefully to weigh and consider that expression, 'He has acquired.' Christ has acquired a treasure by his merits; His merits then are not the treasure; for to *acquire* and to *be* are not the same; the cause and its consequence are two different things. Christ's merits have acquired for the pope the power of giving such and such indulgences to the people; but they are not the very merits of the Savior which the pontiff's hand distributes. Surely my Father is not under the impression that the Germans know no grammar."

The distinction Luther drew is agonizingly subtle. Some scholars insist the distinction was irrelevant—mere academic nit-picking of an embarrassingly impolite sort. We need not examine the subtleties Luther saw in his remark; Cajetan was sufficiently taken with it himself to write hastily to Rome and ask for a confirmation of his own interpretation. Suffice it to say that Luther brought the dialogue to a halt once again. Cajetan said he would forward Luther's document to Rome; in the meantime, Luther must retract his theses. The main thing, aside from all these scholarly questions, was to show that he accepted the authority of the pope—that was absolutely essential. But Luther would not retract until proven wrong. Did he, then, reject the authority of the pope? But, Luther asked, was the pope's decretal so very clear? Cajetan thought it was. Did Luther reject the pope's authority?

"I am not so audacious," Luther said, "that for the sake of a single obscure and ambiguous decretal of a human pope I would recede from so many and such clear testimonies of divine Scripture. For, as one of the canon lawyers has said, 'in a matter of faith not only is a council above a pope but any one of the faithful, if armed with better authority and reason.'" So, at last, Cajetan had provoked Luther to the ultimate logical extension of his thought. The pope, he repeated one last time, must interpret Scripture.

"His Holiness abuses Scripture," Luther replied. "I deny that he is above Scripture."

"I am authorized," Cajetan said, "to pronounce excommunication on you and on all who take your part and to lay all places that shelter you under the interdict. Recant!"

Luther declined. And so Cajetan thundered at him: "Go! Do not let me see you again unless it is to recant."

When Luther left, the cardinal told his companions that he thought he had at last shattered Luther's confidence. And Luther wrote to Spalatin, "His confidence was shattered, and while he still went on shouting, 'Recant! Recant!' I turned and went." Cajetan thought over the arguments Luther had presented, the old notion that councils were superior to popes in interpreting Scripture and all the rest, and said to his friends, "This Brother Martin should have brought fresher goods to market." And Luther thought over the tired old quotations from Aquinas and the obstinate dwelling on Unigenitus and said, "He may be a distinguished Thomist, but as a theologian and a Christian he is incoherent, obscure, and unintelligent, no more fit to judge this matter than a donkey is to play the harp." (The image of the donkey playing the harp would soon appear in cartoon form—with Leo as the harpist.)

In short, both men emerged losers from their confrontation. Luther had not managed to have his theses debated. The eminently logical Cajetan had led the unwilling Luther into declaring a clear heresy but he had not silenced the rebel. The whole meeting had been a vexing, unseemly hassle. Both men had lost their tempers and shouted; both had gone further in their arguments than they had intended. Both made another attempt to patch things up. That evening the cardinal invited Staupitz for dinner. Staupitz was a member of the old nobility and was at ease among men of the courts, and Cajetan thought he could talk to him sensibly. Could Staupitz induce Luther to retract his statements, the cardinal asked. "I must confess to you, my lord," Staupitz said, "that that is beyond my ability; for doctor Martin is my superior, both in intellect and in acquaintance with the Holy Scriptures. You are the Pope's representative. It is up to you." Cajetan offered as great a compromise as he could. His one sticking point was the authority of the pope, and he and Luther had made the "treasure of merits" the point over which that issue needed to be settled. If Luther would retract only that, Cajetan said, it would be sufficient.

Staupitz carried the message back to Luther. "Refute then," Luther said, "the declarations of Scripture that I have produced." Staupitz could not and said he could not. The older man evidently had no idea what to say to his adopted son. He admired Luther and was puzzled by him. No doubt he had another of those fatherly chats and induced Luther to compromise as much as he

226

could. On the next day Staupitz and several other of Luther's supporters fled Augsburg, urging Luther to follow quickly.

Luther sat down and wrote a letter to Cajetan. "I confess," Luther wrote, "that I have not . . . shown sufficient modesty, sufficient meekness, or sufficient respect for the name of the sovereign pontiff. . . . This greatly distresses me, and I beg to be forgiven for it." He told Cajetan that he would publicly, from the pulpit, acknowledge his error—and then, wonder of wonders, he promised silence. "I am ready to promise, without its being asked of me, not to say a single word more on the subject of indulgences. . . . But, in like manner, let those who have led me to begin, be compelled, on their side, to be more moderate for the future in what they say or else to hold their peace."

Luther had promised, in truth, nearly all that had been asked of him. Cajetan had insisted at first that he must retract his errors. Luther promised something at least as good: public avowal of his devotion to the pope, the acknowledgment Cajetan wanted above all of the authority of the pope. Secondly, Cajetan had insisted on silence in the future, and Luther had promised it. Thirdly, Cajetan had demanded that he be more "moderate" in future, and Luther readily agreed, providing his academic opponents would not take advantage of his silence and embarrass him, "professionally," as it were. Both men had backed very far indeed off their debating positions. Luther would never again concede as much.

Luther waited for four days for an answer from Cajetan, but the cardinal was now utterly silent. Silence always drove Luther wild. At the Carmelite monastery he stewed and speculated. Would he now be arrested in spite of his safe conduct? Would the cardinal accept his modified position? Luther still knew little of how cardinals behaved. Cajetan was finished with the monk. He had offered his compromise, and Luther had not accepted it to the letter. There was nothing left for Cajetan to do now but turn the matter over to the secular authorities for enforcement.

It was another opportunity missed, and it is from that missed opportunity that we may date Luther's definite break with the church. He wrote Cajetan once again, saying that his friends advised him to appeal directly to the pope. He was reluctant to do so, Luther said, still believing that Cajetan would deal with the matter. When that, too, was met with silence, Luther prepared his letter to Leo, "from the pope ill-informed to the pope better informed," pointing out that the doctrine of indulgences had never been formally declared and thus remained an acceptable topic for debate. He gave instructions to the prior of the Carmelite monastery to post the letter on the door of the Augsburg cathedral two or three days after he had left town, and in the middle of the night, on October 20, 1518, Luther was secretly bundled out through one of the city gates, where he was put on a horse, and he set out at an uncomfortable gallop on a stiff-legged horse for Wittenberg. He had never been on a horse before, and after he had gone for eight hours, he got off, found he couldn't walk, and collapsed in a pile of straw to sleep. While Luther slept, Cajetan was spending his time working up the draft of a bull for the pope to issue on indulgences. It was true, he realized in his debate with Luther, that the church had never declared itself on the matter, and he dispatched his draft speedily to the pope so that the oversight might be corrected.

It took Luther ten days to ride from Augsburg to Wittenberg. At Nuremberg he was shown the pope's earliest instructions (since canceled, contradicted, then issued again) to have him bound and sent to Rome. He said he considered the document a fraud, since he had not even appeared for his hearing by the time the pope's instructions were dated. "It is impossible to believe that anything so monstrous could have emanated from a sovereign pontiff." But as he bounced himself black and blue on his way to Wittenberg, losing his way just past Leipzig and then finding it again, he had time to consider just how badly treated he had been. The adventure had been filled with crises small and great, with fears that his safe conduct would be ignored as so many papal safe conducts had been, fears that he and his friends would all be arrested and sent to Rome, fears that he would be burned in Augsburg. He had been first outmaneuvered in argument by the

228

cardinal, then browbeaten, then threatened. As he rode away from Augsburg, he rode away from the church—and as he did, he gathered strength. His stomach troubles ceased, the Devil no longer battled with him, his writings became sure and sharp—no longer exaggerated, no longer, or very rarely, laced with the posturings of the lone warrior. What he had pretended before he had now become in fact. Threatened with the stake in Augsburg, he lived now as though he had died and been reborn. He arrived in Wittenberg on October 30, the first anniversary of his posting of the ninety-five theses.

Soon enough Cajetan's expected letter reached Frederick and called for Luther's delivery to Rome. Frederick passed the letter along to his professor and asked for a written reply. The response that Luther wrote was addressed not simply to Frederick but to Cajetan, the pope, and the German people, as well. His scholarship, his love of a fight, his gift for the direct and telling phrase all came into play now. And when he returned to the overworked subject of the "treasure of Christ's merits," he outdid himself. It was written nowhere in Scripture that Christ had endowed the church with this treasure from which the pope might dispense indulgences. And if a decretal existed, how old was it? It had not endured the test of time as the Scriptures had. "You are not a bad Christian if you deny the decretal. But if you deny the gospel you are a heretic. I damn and detest this decretal. The Apostolic Legate opposed me with the thunder of his majesty and told me to recant. I told him the pope abused Scripture. I will honor the sanctity of the pope, but I will adore the sanctity of Christ and the truth. I do not deny this new monarchy of the Roman Church which has arisen in our generation, but I deny that you cannot be a good Christian without being subject to the decrees of the Roman pontiff. As for the decretal, I deny that the merits of Christ are a treasure of indulgences because his merits convey grace apart from the pope. The merits of Christ take away sins and increase merits. Indulgences take away merits and leave sins. These adulators put the pope above Scripture and say that he cannot err. In that case Scripture perishes, and nothing is left in the Church save the word of man. I resist those who in the name of the Roman Church wish to institute Babylon." He offered in his letter to leave Wittenberg so as not to embarrass the elector, and there is no doubt he was prepared to leave with a light heart. He was as good as dead at Augsburg; henceforth, any time alive was a gift to Luther.

On November 8, after looking over Cajetan's draft on indulgences, Leo issued the bull Cum Postquam, which blandly stated that the pope could not forgive sins but that he could only grant indulgences for temporal penalties. He could release no merits from the "treasury" but only petition God to grant them. The bull stated precisely what Luther had posited the year before, and had it been written six months earlier, had it been the basis for Prierias' answer to Luther, it is conceivable that Lutheranism would have been stopped right there. But by now Luther had moved on, goaded by his antagonists. He looked at the bull and said that it was a perfectly good piece of work—though, of course, it did not go far enough.

Luther had not heard from Frederick about his offer to leave Wittenberg, so he took the elector's silence for concurrence and prepared his departure. He wrote an appeal for a general council ("Therefore from Leo badly advised and from his excommunication, suspension, interdict, censures, sentences, and fines, and whatsoever denunciations and declarations of heresy and apostasy, which I esteem as null, nay as iniquitous and tyrannical, I appeal to a general council in a safe place"), and invited his friends to a farewell dinner. On November 28, he got his answer from Frederick. The elector reluctantly agreed to Luther's plan to leave Wittenberg. On December 1, he sat down to dinner with his friends, and a message arrived in mid-course: why had Luther not yet left? And then, even before Luther had finished his meal, another message arrived: Luther was to stay in Wittenberg. The elector had some things he wished to discuss. He would let Luther know the time and place.

All of this was perplexing in the extreme to Luther, but that is only because he, like almost everyone else, could not comprehend just how Leo X engaged in politics. Viewed from Rome, the year 1518 was not puzzling at all. After Prierias' heavy-handed attack on Luther, Leo took a direct interest in the affair. If he did not fully appreciate the theological questions in the controversy, he did appreciate the political ones. To prevent the Habsburgs from controlling too much of Europe he needed to keep Charles V from succeeding Maximilian as emperor. To frustrate Charles V's ambitions, he needed Frederick as an ally. One must not suppose that he failed to see Luther as a challenge to papal authority. He did. But Luther had no power alone; his very existence depended upon the protection of either Maximilian or Frederick. Maximilian had already spoken. Now Leo only needed to secure Frederick's friendship for his political ends, and the Luther question would settle itself.

It is in this context that Leo sent the several contradictory messages to Cajetan. If Cajetan could silence Luther, well and good. But if he could not, Leo must not be suspected of trampling on Frederick's university instructor. Thus Leo armed himself with a set of contradictory instructions so that no matter what happened, he would have one set to show Frederick as his firm directive. Cajetan's head might spin, but that was no concern of Leo's. In fact, the cardinal was in very bad odor in Rome for not having handled his mission better.

The matter of Frederick's pride in his university remained, along with the quite real obscurity of dogma concerning indulgences. Leo solved both with the bull Cum Postquam. By issuing the bull Leo showed that he did not treat Frederick's professor lightly. He went to the unusual length of answering a "mini-friar" with a papal bull, so much did he respect Frederick's faculty. The bull also, so Leo evidently reasoned, cleared the theological air. Now that Luther was answered, he must either be quiet or else prove himself a truly recalcitrant fellow, whom Frederick could not then hesitate to deliver to Rome. The bull neatly served a third purpose as well: It completely undercut Tetzel. Tetzel, poor, devoted servant of the church that he was, was cashiered and died shortly afterward. He was abandoned even by his own

WHITE ROBE, BLACK ROBE

order. Luther alone wrote a letter condoling the pope's good servant.

Finally, there is the matter of those messages that kept interrupting Luther's dinner. The first message came as a result of Cajetan harassing Frederick. Frederick did not want to deliver up his professor, so he thought it better to rush him out of his jurisdiction. But Cajetan's head could keep spinning for all Leo cared. He had dispatched another messenger to countermand Cajetan's dictate. This messenger, a young man named Miltitz, arrived in the nick of time with a superbly Medicean array of bribes and threats. He was to give Frederick the coveted Golden Rose (provided Frederick still seemed a loyal son of the church). He also brought two dispensations annuling the effects of illegitimate birth, which the elector could apply to two of his children and thus entitle them to ecclesiastical benefices (providing he remained a loyal son of the church and did not want Miltitz to release the sheaf of seventy bulls of excommunication he carried with him). He also carried a packet of patronage notes for offices ranging right up to that of papal notary, which Frederick could help him to distribute. As for Luther, well, the pope was the most generous and open-minded of men. Miltitz was prepared to talk with him one last time. If he proved obstinate even then, Frederick would surely understand that he and the pope had no choice. Frederick understood. And so the second dinner-time message went out.

Viewed from Rome, everything was wonderfully clear. Nor had Leo noticed any crises to speak of. There had been some minor irritations. The setback on the Crusade had been a blow, to be sure, but there would be other ways to raise money. Prierias and Cajetan had caused him some bad moments, but the pope had cut through the mess, settled Luther's troublesome objections to indulgences, and was at the close of the year making certain of Frederick's allegiance. Should the monk prove a nuisance in the future, Frederick could be depended on to take care of him. Alas, what neither Frederick nor Leo knew as they arranged their political solutions was that Luther was already, once again, one more theological step ahead. "I whisper it in your ear," he said to a friend in Wittenberg, "the Pope may be Antichrist."

For Luther to call the pope Antichrist was no casual piece of polemics. The idea of Antichrist was an ancient one. According to some theorists, there were three great epochs in the history of the world corresponding to the Holy Trinity. The first had been the reign of the Old Testament and of God the Father; the second was that of the New Testament, of God the Son and of His church; the third would be a new era of the Spirit in which men would seek salvation without need of the church. Before the new age dawned, however, Antichrist would rule the world. He would compare himself to God, and he would send his messengers throughout the world spreading his pernicious doctrines. There would be confusion everywhere, and the church would be cast down for its worldliness. Such was the teaching of Joachim de Fiore, a monk of the twelfth century, whose prophecies had just been published in Bologna in 1515 and dedicated, strangely enough, to Cardinal Giulio de' Medici. According to Joachim, Antichrist would bring about a catastrophe, a huge convulsion in the world, and then the new age would be ushered in by a monk.

XIV

1519

TO tell the truth, 1519 was a boring year in most respects. The essential ingredients for an explosion had been brought together in 1517 and 1518, and a momentum alone should have carried Leo and Luther to a definitive clash in the following year. But 1519 unfolded instead with a tantalizing aimlessness and a curious, and ominous, calm. Leo and Luther drew warily back from one another, hesitated, and hardened their positions. The great public events of the year seem to have occurred with capricious pointlessness and served only to distract Leo and Luther and to knock the year into a lurching, disjointed rhythm. Several major characters had their exits and their entrances this year, but by 1519 they were all anticlimactic events. During the first six months of the year, Leo and Luther went through their duties and public events automatically—as we shall, briefly.

On January 4, Luther met Karl von Miltitz, emissary of the pope, a twenty-eight-year-old strutter and facile liar. He passed himself off in Italy as a German noble with excellent connections and in Germany as an insider at the curia with the special confidence of the pope. He flattered Luther mercilessly in formal talks and intimate chats over the dinner table. He was an accomplished gossip, and much of his gossip was duly incorporated into German histories of the Reformation: The pope thought Tetzel was a swine; Cajetan was despised in Rome. From flattery and gossip, he moved unwittingly to one of Luther's secret fears:

"Beware of raising a storm," he said, "which may cause the ruin of Christianity." Religious controversies had never failed to bring turmoil and misery into the world, and Luther would have to take the responsibility not for reforming the church but for destroying it. Luther was not ready for such a terrible prospect; he had thought, even still, that he was engaged in a theological controversy. He faltered, backed down. "I offer," Luther said, "to maintain silence in future on these matters and to allow the affair to die out of itself, provided my opponents are silent on their side. . . . I will do more still. I will write to his Holiness acknowledging that I have been over violent. . . . I consent even to publish a document in which I shall call upon all who read my writings, not to view them as attacking the Roman Church, and urging them to remain subject to that Church."

Miltitz agreed to arrange a hearing for Luther by the Archbishop of Trier, and he spent the early spring trying to keep Cajetan out of the hearing. But he failed in that and in everything. Luther had not agreed to recant; he had agreed to reassure the pope and the people of his loyalty to the church (which he did) and to have a hearing. The vow of silence was useless by now—the printing press had seen to that. His works had spread throughout Europe, and so had the arguments of his opponents. Vows of silence had come too late. If Miltitz did not realize that, Leo did. The pope wrote Luther ("dear son Martin Luther") and expressed his pleasure at hearing of the conversations with Miltitz. Perhaps Cajetan had been too severe; the pope was delighted that Luther had shown a more agreeable attitude with Miltitz, and he was certain that if Luther would come to Rome the matter could be settled in an amicable fashion. The letter was sent to Luther in care of the Elector Frederick, and Frederick did not even bother to pass it along to Luther. Invitations to Rome never sounded like welcome prospects, however cordially phrased. Nothing had changed. Luther had not recanted, and the pope was still trying to get his hands on the rebel. By the time Miltitz got around to delivering the cherished Golden Rose to Frederick, the elector had lost patience and sent word that the pope's emissary could simply drop it off with one of his counselors. If Miltitz achieved anything by his diplomatic mission it was to exasperate Frederick and cause the elector to take a more firmly protective posture toward Luther.

On January 12, Maximilian, Emperor of the Holy Roman Empire, died—an event of importance only to himself. He had long since proven himself an irrelevant whim-wham on the European scene; and the time of his death did not even affect the choice of his successor. Leo had hoped to break the Habsburg power by having Francis I of France installed as emperor, and the pope offered cardinals' hats and benefices right and left to bribe the electors. When it became obvious that Francis had no chance, Leo then turned to Frederick of Saxony with offers of aid. Should Frederick agree to become a candidate, Miltitz told him in Frankfurt, he could even choose any man of his acquaintance to become a cardinal. Luther was not mentioned by name in the offer, but the hint was as broad as it could be. Frederick must have thought Leo mad. The elector knew perfectly well that he hadn't the financial resources to support the office of emperor. And to offer the bribe of a cardinal's hat to Luther—well, the pope simply did not understand the monk. In the end, Leo's last-ditch, desperate attempts to unseat the Habsburgs were futile. Charles V was elected unanimously, although he was not in Germany at the time, and in his reign of forty years he only visited Germany from time to time for a cumulative total of eight years. The election cost him the equivalent of about $30,000,000 in today's currency, of which the Fuggers put up about $18,000,000. Francis I had spent less than $18,000,000 on his candidacy. It was no contest.

It is certainly staggering to see how ineptly Leo handled his political concerns in 1519. Both his slapdash tactics in the imperial election and his carrot-and-stick treatment of Luther and Frederick (a cardinal's hat, or a trip to Rome for the rebel) were crude in the extreme. The old tricks did not seem to work quite as well as they always had, and there are two plausible explanations for Leo's collapse as a politician. First, of course, he neither liked nor understood Germans. Early in the year he and Luther exchanged letters: It was the closest they would ever come in their lives to some personal contact. This unfulfilled correspondence was the moment of the "meeting" between the two men. Their lives were closely related now, and henceforth neither made a move or had a thought or expressed a feeling that did not in some way affect the other. Their histories converge to join completely in 1519; yet, for all the intimacy of their destinies, they were utter aliens to one another. For all the direct influence Leo had on Elector Frederick and his Wittenberg monk, the pope operated at a myopic distance, dependent on the hapless likes of Cajetan and Miltitz for guidance. Secondly, in the midst of election politics, on April 28, Lorenzo de' Medici died, and his death was a catastrophic and paralyzing blow to Leo's dynastic ambitions.

Lorenzo may have died of the *mal Francese*, as the Italians persisted in calling it, which he contracted during his philandering in France. He was preceded to the grave by his wife, who died after delivering Catherine de' Medici. Leo was now reduced to three children to keep the Medici line alive: Catherine, who would be of some marginal use; Alessandro, who was the nine-year-old illegitimate son of Lorenzo and possibly "a Moorish slave" or the illegitimate son of Cardinal Giulio de' Medici; and Ippolito, the eight-year-old illegitimate son of Leo's brother Giuliano and a lady from Urbino. The administration of Florence was taken over by the firm and dexterous Cardinal Giulio, and all the remaining members of the family turned their efforts to raising the three children, with Leo taking the attentive leadership. Alessandro was an ugly but robust boy, and since the Medicis had lost so many of their marriageable secular men through ill health, the healthy Alessandro was raised to assume leadership of Florence. Ippolito was educated under the watchful and delighted eye of Leo at the Vatican for a career in the church (he later became a cardinal). Catherine was briefly considered a good candidate to become Duchess of Urbino but was, of course, finally held in reserve to marry French royalty. Whatever may have been occurring in Germany in the spring and summer of 1519 was of far less urgent concern to Leo X than this reshuffling of his dynastic succession and the question whether Cardinal Giulio would be accepted without too much difficulty as the new leader of Florence.

During the remainder of 1519 there were no "events" whatever. Having "confronted" one another in some fashion, both men retreated into their own worlds. This was, as the saying goes, the calm before the storm. Luther immersed himself in the study of canon law and church history, and he wrote prodigiously. Leo looked after his family and worried over the completion of Raphael's frescoes in the Vatican loggie. Neither man was any longer interested in understanding the other; both returned to their own places of sustenance and gathered strength, and newly self-assured obstinacy, for the struggle ahead.

Raphael's final payment for his frescoes in the loggie was made on June 11, and we can well imagine Leo inspecting the work to see whether Raphael had carried out the assigned subjects well. The frescoes have been known as Raphael's "Bible," though to a large extent they must also be considered Leo's "Bible," for the patron approved the themes. The loggie are made up of thirteen arches, each of which is decorated with four frescoes. Thus, there are fifty-two "chapters" in this Bible, forty-eight from the Old Testament and four from the New Testament. Designed by Raphael, the frescoes were executed by his army of assistants, and the paintings are commonly reckoned one of the most excellent pieces of decorative art of the Renaissance.

A stroll through the loggie reveals most of the expected scenes from the Old Testament: God separates light and darkness, land and water; He creates the sun and moon and the animals. Leo dearly loved animals, both to see their pictures and to see them slaughtered in the hunt, and Raphael and his apprentices turned out a great many menageries for him. Here there are lions and horses and unicorns and peacocks and a fine elephant rubbing against a tree. Next comes the story of Adam and Eve, and the nude Eve is so exquisite that some critics insist Raphael himself stepped in to provide the finishing touches. Next comes Noah and the ark (with some more good animals), Abraham, the flight of

Lot, and the stories of Isaac, Jacob, Joseph, and Moses. In the middle of the frescoes the story of Joshua erupts in vigorous warfare with straining nude soldiers, and the walls come tumbling down with men cascading over the parapets and into the rubble. The coat of arms of Leo X pops up here and there on banners, and then the story of David appears with fine dramatic gestures and spirited white chargers pulling the royal chariot. The Old Testament is thoroughly satisfactory.

Only at the end of the loggie are the frescoes puzzling, for here something is missing. The story of Jesus is told in four panels: the adoration of the shepherds, the adoration of the Magi, the baptism of Christ, and the Last Supper. In his Bible, Raphael gave remarkably short shrift to Christianity, and in his four Christian scenes what is missing is the Crucifixion—the event on which the entire religion is based.

Indeed, we search in vain through the frescoes and paintings and tapestries that Raphael made for Leo X to find a crucifixion. Not that Raphael was uninterested in the subject: He had done a number on the theme earlier in his career. But for Leo he painted the philosophers Aristotle and Plato; he painted animals and pagan gods and goddesses; he painted the coronation of Charlemagne, the event that theoretically established the pope's authority over secular leaders; he painted bits and snatches of a popular history of the church; but he painted no crucifixions. In Raphael's Bible we see Leo's most elaborate expression of his idea of Catholicism. And while Leo's imagination was filled with these esthetic pleasures, Luther's mind was burrowing into a penetrating examination of church history, precedent, and law. Whereas we must search painstakingly even to find the symbol of the cross, the central symbol of Christianity, in Raphael's work for Leo, Luther was basing all his thought on the "theology of the cross." During Leo's pontificate, and reflecting Leo's tastes and desires, Raphael achieved his greatest output of madonnas and holy families, a fitting theme for a man worried about the survival of his own family dynasty.

It might be supposed that Leo intended to have Raphael paint another set of frescoes for the New Testament. In fact, Raphael's next assignment was to decorate the loggetta just above the loggie. In the loggetta, Raphael's apprentices adorned the arches and niches with figures of the four seasons, diaphanously draped female figures in the poses of Classical statues, a giraffe and an elephant, Venus and Cupid, a bullfight, winged divinities, pagan rites, a contest between Apollo and Marsyas, and in one of the larger frescoes just opposite the entrance to the loggetta, seated at his forge is Vulcan, god of volcanoes and of destructive fires.

"The more they rage," Luther wrote to a friend, "the bigger my strides. I give up my first position, they yap at my heels, I move on to the next, and they yap at me there." In the spring and summer of 1519, it was Professor Johann Eck of Ingolstadt who was yapping at Luther. A man with a superb memory for church law, Eck lived to argue, and he thought nothing of a journey to Vienna or Bologna if he got wind of a good theological fight. He was provided an occasion for a scrap in 1519 by one of Luther's colleagues at Wittenberg, Professor Andreas Karlstadt, who had stepped forward to defend Luther. Eck pounced on Karlstadt as a way of drawing Luther out of his vow of silence and into open debate—and Luther leaped at the bait.

Eck issued a set of theses that established the central issue in the controversy as the question of the primacy of the pope. "We deny," his twelfth thesis stated, "that the Roman Church was not raised above other churches previous to the time of pope Sylvester; and we recognize him who has occupied the see of St. Peter, and who has had his faith, as in all times the successor of St. Peter and the vicar of Jesus Christ."

Luther topped Eck with his own thesis in reply: "By the wretched decretals of the Roman pontiffs, composed four hundred years ago, or even later, an attempt is made to prove the primacy of the Church of Rome; but arrayed against that primacy we find the authentic history of eleven hundred years, the plain statements of the Holy Scriptures, and the conclusions of the council of Nice—the holiest of all the councils."

The issue had been clearly joined this time: The question of the pope's primacy did not come up in an ill-considered aside of Luther's, and the theses were firmly, unequivocally stated. Luther's friends were shocked and predicted disaster. The debate promised to be a lively one, and Duke George of Saxony arranged to have it held at his University of Leipzig. Duke George's university had been suffering by comparison to Wittenberg, and he was determined to cut the Wittenbergers down to size. None of his own professors was capable of debating Luther, but the imported Eck seemed ideally suited to the duke's purpose.

The disputants gathered in Leipzig in June. Eck was given a bodyguard of seventy-six to keep him from harm, and the Wittenberg contingent arrived with 200 students armed with battle-axes. Academic debates still aroused strong passions in those days, as soccer matches still do in England, and the atmosphere was both festive and tense. Two wagons carried the Wittenberg celebrities: Karlstadt, by himself, in the lead, followed by the wagon that carried Luther and Philipp Melanchthon. Melanchthon was Reuchlin's great-nephew, a brilliant and frail twenty-two-year-old Classicist who had just joined the Wittenberg faculty and taken his place in the faction of the robust Luther. As they entered town Karlstadt suffered the indignity of having a wheel come off his wagon, and the poor fellow was thrown into the mud, to the intense pleasure of the Leipzig students.

Duke George had originally scheduled the debate for the great hall of the university, but the crowd of counts and abbots and students and other spectators forced him to move the event to the larger auditorium in the castle. Eck's corner was decorated with a picture of Saint George and the dragon and, so that no one might mistake who his real antagonist was, Karlstadt's desk was marked by a picture of Luther's patron Saint Martin. Tapestries adorned the walls of the hall, and the debate was preceded by musical performances, masses, dinners, parades, and other festivities to prolong the delicious feeling of anticipation. The duke sent a stag to Eck, and to make certain no one misapprehended who his favorite was, he gave Karlstadt a mere roebuck.

Debates of this sort had elaborate beginnings to their begin-

nings, and each skirmish over the rules of debate had as much
significance as the shape of the table at an international peace
treaty meeting. Eck insisted that there be no stenographers to
record the debate—he was quick on his feet, but sometimes dis-
torted the niceties of a question. Luther, intent upon having an
exact record so that his opponents could not again misquote him,
argued for stenographers. Eck lost, and aside from the official
transcript of the disputation, at least thirty members of the audience made a verbatim record of the arguments. Next came the
question of judges. Luther argued against any judges—perhaps
simply as a negotiating device; for when it was finally agreed to
have judges, Luther was able to win his case for the universities of
Paris and Erfurt, both of them sympathetic to his case. (Eck had
argued, puckishly, it would seem, to have the pope as judge.)
When the University of Paris agreed to judge the dispute, Luther
then argued to have the entire university, and not only its theological faculty, sit in judgment. "Why then," Eck taunted him,
"don't you refer the case to shoemakers and tailors?" After the
debate began, Karlstadt, nervous and outclassed as a debater, read
passages from his books and notes until more and more members
of the audience dropped off to sleep. Eck demanded that books be
banned from the hall. The audience wanted to be entertained by
sharp repartee, and Eck had no trouble winning his case. Without
his books, Karlstadt had no chance against Eck, and Eck made
short work of him in order to get on with the main event against
Luther.

"Martin Luther," according to one witness of the proceedings,
". . . has become so lean from the intensity of his studies that you
might almost count his bones. He is in the prime of life and has a
clear and sonorous voice . . . he has a vast fund of arguments and
ideas. It is to be desired, perhaps, that he had a little more judgment in putting everything in its proper place. In conversation he
is candid and affable . . . he knows how to accommodate himself
to the peculiarities of everyone; his talk is pleasant and full of
hearty good humor. He displays firmness, and has always the air
of a man who is satisfied, whatever be the threats of his oppo-

nents. . . . He is blamed, nevertheless, for being a little more sarcastic in attacking others than becomes a divine, especially when he has new things to announce in regard to religion."

Eck is described by the same man as tall, "broad-shouldered, and with a strong and thoroughly German voice. He has a hefty chest, so that he could make himself very well heard on the stage, and might even make an excellent public crier. . . . His mouth, eyes, and whole countenance give you the impression of a soldier, or butcher, more than of a divine . . . he is a man of inconceivable impudence. If he finds himself embarrassed, he leaves the point he is treating, pounces on some other, sometimes even lays hold of the opinion of his antagonist, and employing different expressions, attributes to his opponent, with extraordinary address, the very absurdity which he himself had been defending." In all, he was a ferocious debater. He worked up his adrenalin in the mornings by going out for a vigorous horseback ride, and he would enter the hall with riding whip in hand and stride up and down the room, twitting and blasting his opponent, quoting decretals, summarizing vast stretches of church history, the master of extemporaneous debate.

"There is in the Church of God," Eck said, "a primacy proceeding from Christ himself. The Church militant has been settled according to the pattern of the Church triumphant. Now, the latter is a monarchy where all rises hierarchically until we reach the sole chief who is God himself. Therefore is it that Christ has established a like order of things on the earth. What a monster were the Church without a head!"

Luther: "In declaring that the Church universal necessarily has a head, the Doctor does well. If any one here present alleges the contrary let him rise. As for me, I have nothing to do with it."

Eck: "If the Church militant has never been without a monarch, I should very much wish to know who he can be, if not the pontiff of Rome?"

Luther: "The head of the Church militant is Jesus Christ himself and not a man. . . ."

Eck: "The unity of the priesthood, as St. Cyprian said, is to be traced to Rome."

Luther: "As regards the western church I admit . . . I do not deny that should all the faithful throughout the world unite in recognizing as first and sovereign pontiff the bishop of Rome, or of Paris, or of Magdeburg, he ought to be acknowledged as such, because of the respect due to such an accord of the whole church, but this has never been, nor ever will be seen. In our days does not the Greek Church refuse her assent to Rome?"

Eck: ". . . I come to the essential point. The venerable doctor has asked me to prove that the primacy of the Church of Rome is of divine right; I prove it by those words of Christ: 'Thou art Peter, and upon this rock I will build my church.' "

Luther: "Granting even that St. Augustine and all the Fathers should say that the apostle is the stone spoken for by Christ, I would singly oppose them on the authority of Holy Scripture . . . for it is written: 'Other foundation can no man lay than that which is laid, which is Jesus Christ.' Peter himself calls Christ the living corner stone, on which we are built up a spiritual house."

Eck found it impossible to budge Luther from his position. If the pope was not appointed by divine right but merely by human agreement, the whole structure of the church was threatened. The pope became simply one bishop among many with no special rights or powers. The indulgence controversy was now seen as a very minor aspect of Luther's challenge to the church. He opposed the entire structure of authority on which indulgences and all other theological matters rested; he opposed it with Scripture; he opposed it with the individual's right to interpret Scripture. Why not, indeed, have the dispute judged by shoemakers and tailors? If Eck could not prove Luther wrong, he could at least prove him subversive, and he relished his words as he spoke them, deliberately, and without raising his voice.

"It has been acknowledged," Eck said, "from primitive times, by all good Christians, that the Church of Rome holds her primacy from Christ himself, and not of human right." He was a master of timing, and one must imagine the pause, the slow turn away from his desk to face Luther: "I must admit, however, that the Bohemians, in obstinately defending their errors, attacked this doctrine. I beg the venerable Father's pardon. If I am an enemy to the Bohemians because they were the Church's enemies; and if the present disputation reminds me of those heretics; for . . . according to my weak judgment . . . the conclusions at which the doctor has arrived are altogether in favor of those errors. We are even assured that the Hussites openly glory in them."

Eck could not have used a more devastating smear. Bohemia had long been the home of heresy in Europe, and to call a man a Bohemian was to associate him with all dark fears of the disruption of church, politics, society, family life. The Hussites had swept down out of Bohemia to ravage Saxony, and none had forgotten their awful depredations, the rape and bloodshed that had convulsed Saxony until Hus had been condemned and he and his followers burned at the stake at Constance.

"I like not," Luther replied heatedly, "and never shall like any kind of schism. In as much as the Bohemians . . . secede from our unity, they do what is wrong, even though the divine right should be in favor of their doctrines."

Duke George stepped into the proceedings and declared a recess for dinner. The dispute had left the safe ground of theology, and the duke had no taste for the political implications of the discussion. Apparently Luther was more dangerous than anyone had guessed.

Nor did Luther reassure the duke when the debate resumed two hours later. He had spent his intermission time at the university library looking up the records of the Council of Constance that had declared Hus a heretic. To his surprise, Luther discovered that one of the statements for which Hus had been condemned was a close paraphrase of St. Augustine. When the disputants had reassembled, Luther rose and said: "Among the articles held by John Hus and the Bohemians, some are highly Christian. There is no denying this. Such is the following: that there is but one universal church; and this other, that it is not necessary to salvation that we believe the Roman Church to be superior to other churches. Whether it were Wycliff or Hus that said so is of no consequence . . . the statement is true."

The audience erupted with exclamations of surprise. Some of Luther's most faithful supporters were abashed that their hero openly identified himself with the Bohemian heretics and implied that the Council of Constance had erred. Duke George was stunned, and his voice was heard above the others: "The man's a maniac!"

Luther went relentlessly on through the hubbub: "Gregory of Nazianzen, Basil the Great, Epiphanius, Chrysostom, together with an immense number of other Greek bishops, have been saved, and they did not believe the Church of Rome to be superior to other churches. The pontiffs of Rome have no authority to make new articles of faith. Holy Scripture is the sole authority for the faithful Christian. . . ."

But nothing Luther said any longer mattered. Eck had led him to embrace condemned heretics. The debate dragged on for another ten days over such concerns as the human will and divine grace, but, in the estimation of most of the audience, all that was simply nattering. Luther was a "Bohemian heretic, a Hussite," and the label stuck to him firmly and led him, more than anything else he had said or done, to his official trial for heresy. With characteristic perverseness, soon enough Luther stopped denying the charge and said, "We are all Hussites without knowing it. Augustine and Paul were Hussites."

Duke George finally put an end to the debate. He expected noble visitors who were returning from the imperial election, and he needed his hall for entertaining. At the duke's invitation Eck stayed on to meet the celebrities, and the Wittenbergers returned home, disturbed by the evident inconclusiveness of the encounter. The official report of the debate was sent to Erfurt, which refused to judge such distinguished scholars, and to Paris, where the faculty demanded payment for reviewing the records—and that was the end of any notion of a judgment on the case. Disgruntled and disappointed by the outcome of the affair, Luther decided finally to take his case to the shoemakers and tailors, to "all classes," and he commenced a phenomenal outpouring of writings in the vulgar tongue—leaflets, broadsides, pamphlets, treatises, all of them vibrant with the direct, tough, accessible images that made him a master prose stylist and stirring popular leader. For his part, Eck forwarded a report of the debate to Von Hochstraten, the chief inquisitor, and another report of Luther's Bohemian sympathies reached Rome, where the disciplinary wheels continued to turn exceedingly slow, and exceedingly fine.

Christmas, 1519, was an especially notable occasion in Rome. Raphael's finished tapestries were hung in the Sistine Chapel for the first time, and the pope's particular friends and favored diplomats were invited to attend mass amidst the tapestries. "At Christmas," according to the Venetian Marcantonio Michiel, "the pope displayed in his chapel seven pieces of tapestry (the eighth being as yet unfinished) woven in Flanders. They are judged the most beautiful works of this type ever made up to our own day. . . . A great quantity of silk and gold has been used in the tapestries. The weaving has cost fifteen hundred ducats apiece. . . ." Paris de Grassis reported that "the whole chapel was struck dumb by the sight of these hangings; by universal consent there is nothing more beautiful in the world. . . ." At the celebration of mass, Leo sat with his delicate fingertips pressed together, his lips pursed as he hummed along with the choir, his eyes half closed as he gazed happily at his new tapestries.

In all Leo had commissioned ten tapestries, and we need not dwell on Raphael's consummate artistry in the execution of the cartoons from which the weavers worked. Leo had no care for the "working sketches"—they disappeared after they had served their purpose and did not surface again until a century afterward —but was interested only in the silk and gold and, of course, the subjects chosen for illustration. As with Raphael's "Bible," the choice of subjects is interesting, and this time it is not without irony: the conversion of Saint Paul; the blinding of Elymas; the sacrifice at Lystra; Saint Paul in prison; Saint Paul preaching at Athens; Christ's charge to Peter; the healing of the lame man; the death of Ananias; the stoning of Saint Stephen; the miraculous draught of fishes. Around the borders of some of the tapestries were scenes from the life of Leo, as was to be expected. In the border of the "Miraculous Draught of Fishes," Leo can be seen as cardinal, riding to Rome for the conclave at which he was elected pope. Raphael meant no satirical comment, even though it is an amusing irony to see both Leo and Christ making a fine haul in one tapestry.

Indeed, it is because the tapestries are to be considered as personal comments on the reign of Leo that they are especially interesting. In the draught of fishes, we must view the border design more reverently and see Leo as arriving at Rome to become a fisherman for the souls of men. In the "Delivery of the Keys," we see Eck's argument "Thou art Peter and upon this rock" confirmed by Raphael for all to see, and again, it is ironical that when Luther challenged such basic beliefs of the Roman Church, the Vatican was so ill-prepared with counterarguments. They took their theology for granted. It was there in Raphael's paintings and tapestries: Who could doubt it?

The "Healing of the Lame Man" is accompanied by a border design of the liberation of Leo after the Battle of Ravenna—a liberation he wished to have people think was as much the result of divine intervention as the cure of the lame man by Saint Peter and Saint John. If Leo could persuade Luther with tapestries, certainly Luther would have to agree that the pope was pope by some divine right.

In "Elymas Struck with Blindness," it is more difficult to know just what Leo had in mind. Elymas, according to the Biblical account, was turning the Roman proconsul in Asia against the faith, and Saint Paul struck him with blindness for his perfidy. The tapestry was commissioned before Leo had any thought of Luther—perhaps he was harking back to Savonarola, or to heretics in general—but by 1519 the scene reads like a direct comment on the "Luther question."

In the remaining tapestries, the irony begins to turn against the pope. Leo was not hypocritical about the events Raphael has commemorated; he genuinely identified himself with the leading characters of these scenes. Yet what is one to make of the "Death of Ananias"? Here Peter has punished a man who neglected to sell his worldly goods and give the proceeds to the Apostles for distribution. In the border scenes Raphael has shown the restoration of the Medicean rule in Florence, and the connection to Ananias is difficult to make in any way complimentary to the pope. The scene reads, rather, like a Lutheran indictment of the indulgence-collecting, worldly Vatican.

In the "Stoning of St. Stephen," one's mind does not leap instantly to any notion of unjust persecution of Pope Leo; it is, after all, Luther who is about to be stoned. In the "Sacrifice at Lystra" the viewer is asked to remember the miracle of Saint Paul healing a cripple, who in turn wishes to make a sacrifice to this messenger of the gods. Paul prevents the healed man from the idolatrous gesture. Luther, however, had already charged that Leo accepted idolatrous gestures, and this tapestry, too, in hindsight at least, seems to turn against the pope.

But the tapestries that appear most to condemn the pope are the three scenes that explicitly champion Saint Paul: the conversion of Saint Paul, Saint Paul in prison, and the preaching of Saint Paul. Luther had based his theology on the teachings of Saint Paul, and here, on Christmas day of 1519, we have Leo peering contentedly at Luther's inspirer. In the tapestry of Paul preaching at Athens the saint stands with upraised arms in a classically correct square and speaks to an attentive audience. "God that made the world and all things therein, seeing that he is Lord of heaven and earth, dwelleth not in temples made with hands," Paul told the Athenians. "Forasmuch then as we are the offspring of God, we ought not to think that the Godhead is like unto gold, or silver, or stone, graven by art and man's device." Leo had good reason to be pleased with himself and his temple and his new tapestries woven of silk and gold threads. He and his church enjoyed their last moment of peace on Christmas day, 1519.

It was a curious year, a year out of time, packed with non-events, nonconfrontations, noncorrespondence, nondebates, and nondeaths. More curious still, the year 1519 can be seen as a turning point. Whereas in 1518 politics were crucially important in establishing the relationship of Leo and Luther and were full of potential change and dramatic turnabout, by the end of 1519 the political possibilities had become all too predictable. Whereas at the end of 1518 it seemed possible that Luther might subside, by the next year his rebellious course had become set. If it seemed possible in 1518 for Leo to make some accommodation with Luther, by the end of 1519 nothing could have been more unlikely. What had occurred to make all these changes? Nothing but the passage of time that allowed the real nature of the two men to emerge. In the calm before the storm politics and potentialities were held suspended, and for a moment Raphael's art appeared as the lucid, and doomed, expression of the brilliant, contradictory Renaissance church—soon, and now inevitably, to be destroyed by the Bohemian heretic Luther.

XV

1520

UNLIKE the previous year, 1520 has a reassuring purposiveness to it. Where Leo had before hesitated, as though he had some premonition that he was involved in no small contest, now he played out his part like a determinedly fated character in a Greek drama. And Luther, at first fearful of the holocaust he might cause, now welcomed and encouraged it. Johann Eck arrived in Rome in mid-January and buzzed about the curia with reports of the heretic's words. The universities of Louvain and Cologne served the role that Paris and Erfurt had declined and sent to Rome a detailed criticism of Luther's arguments. On February 4, a commission was appointed to draw up a condemnation of Luther. At its head was Cardinal Cajetan, by now a sick man who had to be carried into the meetings of the commission.

Cajetan evidently recognized the seriousness of Luther's challenge at this late date, and he proposed that the commission bring in ten theologians to supplement the panel of theologically illiterate cardinals. At that Eck's modicum of patience was exhausted, and he prevailed on Leo to set up another commission of four members, headed by Eck. For the next three months, while the pope's commission sorted through Luther's statements, other desultory attempts were made to bring the monk to heel. Cardinal Riario wrote to the Elector Frederick ("I exhort you, bring this man to reject his error. . . ."), and the general of the Augustinian Order wrote Staupitz (". . . do your utmost to restrain Luther from speaking against the Church and indulgences. Urge him to stop writing. Let him save our order from infamy"). Staupitz avoided the charge from his superior by resigning as vicar, and the commission ground on in its grim course, with Eck seeking his own justification by making certain that all Luther's challenges to his debating propositions were included in the bill of particulars.

Having set the machinery going, Leo showed his executive mettle by turning his mind freely to other matters. The two men who had done most to shape the Leonine court died in 1520, Raphael and Cardinal Bibbiena. Raphael died in the spring, at the age of thirty-seven, of "a constant and acute fever," which has naturally been assumed to be the result of a venereal disease, though it could just as plausibly have been a virus that seemed to sweep through Rome often in the spring. Bibbiena, being more highly placed among the politicians of Rome, went out with the usual whisperings of poison. "He died before he was really old [at age fifty]," Paolo Giovio wrote, "when he had returned to Rome from an embassy to France, filled with unseasonable ambition to be Pope, if Leo, as was indeed fated, should die: an ambition which was fostered by the general belief that King Francis would be ready to carry out his lavish promises of support. Leo, who was much Bibbiena's junior and much more vigorous, is said to have so resented this aspiration in a weak old man that Bibbiena suspected (though he had no evidence) that the Pope tried to murder him by slow poison contained in fried eggs which he passed him at table." Bibbiena and Leo had been companions and political partners for forty years; for the canny old political manager even to suspect such a plot on Leo's part would seem to indicate that the pope's court was coming apart. Perhaps they were all on edge; perhaps they recognized that the Luther case would not simply be a repetition of the Savonarola case or those other cases in which the pope needed only to turn an excommunicate over to the civil authorities for burning. Don Juan Manuel, an ambassador of the Emperor Charles, was snooping about Rome that spring to see what might be used against the pope to keep him from stirring up allies against the Holy Roman Empire. "If the

Emperor goes to Germany," Don Juan wrote to Charles' advisers, "he ought to show a little favor to a friar who is called Friar Martin, who stays with the Duke of Saxony. The Pope is very much afraid of him because he preaches and publishes great things against his power. They say that he is a great scholar and holds his own against the Pope with much mindfulness. I think that through him the Pope might be driven to make an alliance; but I say this in case he refuses, or, after making it, strives to break it." The emerging nations, the would-be nations, the new emperor— all were determined to diminish the power of the pope, even if they had to diminish the power of all authorities to do so. And the pope was obliged, no matter what the risks or even the foreseeable outcome, to uphold the supremacy of the papacy.

It is unlikely in the extreme that Leo knew that he would preside over a great schism in the Catholic Church. It is probable, since he knew a threat when he saw one, that he anticipated the creation of a small heretical band in Germany. If the appellation "Bohemian heretic" was a terrible one, it was also a common one. Bohemians were expected to be troublesome, and Saxony evidently had been tainted by its neighbors. The church had seen many a small band break off from the church and leave the main body intact. In the long history of the church Leo knew that such things mattered far less than excitable men like Eck thought. Few of the church's followers, Leo knew, had ever had the courage to face God alone, to stand before Him as individuals as Luther urged, without the protection of all the decretals and canon laws and traditions that gave a man the knowledge that he had something real, something legally binding, and someone appointed by God to see him toward salvation. Leo could depend on man's awful anxiety before God. Even so, had Leo foreseen the magnitude of the schism just ahead he would not have behaved differently. He, too, had his beliefs, and, like Luther, he would risk the destruction of Christendom, if need be, to defend them. He tried all the half-measures, all the diplomatic methods, all the means of persuasion he knew; that they were so ineptly carried out on his behalf was—well—a measure of the imperfectness of the world. Now that his course was set, he pursued it with perfect equanimity.

It was not possible for Leo, as it was for Luther, to keep his mind on his business all the time, and he did not let vexing men like Eck distract him from his pleasures. In the year 1520 Leo had his court and friends entertained with a performance of Machiavelli's play *Mandragola*, a masterpiece of the Italian theater that makes Carlo Goldoni look like a struggling college playwright. The plot of *Mandragola* involves a foolish, rich old Florentine named Messer Nicia, his beautiful young wife Lucrezia, a young man just returned from France named Callimaco, and a corrupt, presumably fat, friar named Timoteo. Callimaco burns with desire for Lucrezia. But Machiavelli introduces the novel concept of a completely virtuous wife who would not dream of bedding down with a young lover.

Callimaco and "a local knave" named Ligurio work out a scheme to get Callimaco to bed with Lucrezia. Messer Nicia and Lucrezia have no children, no heirs—an unhappy situation for anyone, an intolerable one for an Italian. Callimaco, posing as a doctor who has treated the ladies of the French court, convinces Messer Nicia to administer to his wife a potion made with the mandragola, or mandrake root, a common narcotic plant.

MESSER NICIA: When would she have to take it?

CALLIMACO: Tonight after supper, because the moon is in its right phase and the time couldn't be more propitious.

MESSER NICIA: That's not such a big thing, by all means prepare it, and I'll make her take it.

CALLIMACO: And now we have to consider this also, that the man who is with her first, after she has taken this potion, dies within a week; and you couldn't save him for the world!

MESSER NICIA: Puke! I don't want any of this slimy business. . . .

CALLIMACO: Pull yourself together; there's a remedy.

MESSER NICIA: What?

CALLIMACO: Get someone else to sleep with her at once, who will draw to himself—being with her the whole night—the full infection of the mandragola. After that you can lie there without danger.

MESSER NICIA: . . . I don't want to turn my wife into a bitch and myself a cuckold!

CALLIMACO: What are you saying. . . . I see you're not the wise sort of man I took you for. So you are going to hesitate to do what the King of France has done, and all the noblemen over there?

Messer Nicia agrees, and then it only remains to convince his wife, Lucrezia. For that purpose, Friar Timoteo is brought in and offered 300 ducats that he may distribute "as alms." "So be it," the friar says, "in God's name. Let it be done as you wish, and all done for God's sake and for charity." Machiavelli's friar is a superb man, a man of business and a man of faith who does not find it at all difficult to hold contradictions in his mind happily, for life, as he knows, is a complicated matter. In brief, the friar agrees to help along a plot that will, so far as he knows, murder a man, betray a faithful wife to adultery, dupe a trusting husband, aggrandize a young rake, and line his own pocket with 300 ducats —and, at the end, bless the entire company in his church. The plot works well. Callimaco sleeps with the girl and reveals who he is; the girl is so offended by the way she has been deceived by her husband and confessor and so taken with Callimaco that she gives him a key to the house so that he may visit her whenever he likes.

This indictment of the corruption of the church—for the friar does stand as the embodiment of the Catholic clergy and its willingness to betray anything for money—was received enthusiastically by the Roman court. Indeed, Leo was so pleased by the play that he forgave Machiavelli all his past political transgressions against the Medicis and told Cardinal Giulio de' Medici to find some employment for the writer. The cardinal commissioned Machiavelli's classic history of Florence. Like Friar Timoteo, Leo was able to hold contradictions in his character and actions easily and cheerfully. To do so was no hypocrisy in his view, it was merely a realistic way of life. The complexities of human existence, Leo believed, could not be reduced to hard and fast absolutes, to consistent positives and negatives. He was too much of a politician to have any other view. Leo was not shocked by Machiavelli's play. Luther, the puritan, would have been, for contradictions had always plagued Luther, and he had spent his life getting rid of them.

On May 2, the men of the Vatican presented the pontiff with a draft of a papal bull *"contra errores Martini Lutheri."* The pope read it with some care and called the cardinals to a consistory on May 21 to examine the document. On May 22, Leo retired to his hunting villa at Magliana. The cardinals met three more times, on May 23, May 26, and June 1. Eck was there, as was Cajetan (who said of the former, "Who let that beast in here?"). The Augustinians, Dominicans, and Franciscans were all represented. In the end the consistory found forty-one articles to condemn, and a draft was sent to the relaxed and jovial pope at Magliana to have him suggest the opening and closing paragraphs. The bull is known as Exsurge Domine, from its first words, "Arise, O Lord." Thinking, perhaps, of the day's activities ahead of him, Leo wrote, "A wild boar has invaded thy vineyard." And then he called on the traditional supporters of the pope: "Arise, O Peter! remember thy Holy Roman Church, mother of all the churches, and mistress of the faith! Arise, O Paul! for behold a new Porphyry who attacks thy doctrines and the holy popes, our predecessors. Arise, in fine, assembly of all the saints! Holy Church of God! and intercede with God Almighty."

The forty-one articles were then enumerated and identified as "heretical, or scandalous, or false, or offensive to pious ears, or seductive of simple minds, or repugnant to Catholic truth, respectively." Dated and sealed on June 15, the bull was not, in fact, a bull of excommunication but only a warning that excommunication would follow within sixty days of receipt if Luther failed to recant. By the time the bull of excommunication came, however, it was a foregone conclusion, and Exsurge Domine is usually regarded as the casting of the die. Eck and a former rector of the University of Paris named Jerome Aleander were given the task of distributing copies of the bull to the proper authorities in

Germany and to Luther. It was several months before Luther received his copy—a delay attributable not to the slowness of communication but to the fact that the civil authorities had to be lined up for action before the heretic would be given an opportunity to respond. On July 8, Leo wrote to Frederick according to the form in such cases: "This Luther favors the Bohemians and the Turks, deplores the punishment of heretics, spurns the writings of the holy doctors, the decrees of ecumenical councils, and the ordinances of the Roman pontiffs, and gives credence to the opinions of none save himself alone, which no heretic before ever presumed to do. We cannot suffer the scabby sheep longer to infect the flock." In the bull, Leo explains, he has selected those teachings of Luther's "in which he perverts the faith, seduces the simple, and relaxes the bonds of obedience, continence, and humility. The abuses which he has vaunted against our Holy See we leave to God. We exhort you to induce him to return to sanity and receive our clemency. If he persists in his madness, take him captive."

While Luther waited for the bull to find him in Wittenberg, he worked up his rage and his arguments for the final battle. He wrote to Spalatin on July 10: "Let them condemn and burn my writings. I, in my turn, if I can find a fire, will condemn and publicly burn all the Papal law, the mask of all heresies. Henceforth there shall be an end of the humility which I have shown in vain. . . ." And again he wrote, "Do not think that this matter can be ended without tumult, scandal, and sedition. Out of a sword you cannot make a feather, nor out of war, peace. The Word of God is a sword, is war, is ruin, is scandal, is destruction, is poison." And when Prierias once more stumbled into the breach, Luther replied with all stops out: "If these opinions and this teaching prevail at Rome, with the knowledge of the Pope and the Cardinals, I pronounce that Antichrist sits in the temple of God, and that the Roman Court is the synagogue of Satan. . . . If we punish thieves by the gallows, and heretics by fire, why not attack Pope, Cardinals, and the brood of the Roman Sodom with arms, and wash our hands in their blood?"

While he practiced his debating posture in occasional private and public sallies, he also published a set of pamphlets that he intended to set the record straight on his teachings. In *Of Good Works* he attempted to answer the charge that his theology would lead to unbridled sinfulness. The Christian, he says, does not do good works to become good, or to be saved; rather he does good works because he is good, because a good tree bears good fruit, "because it is a pleasure to please God thereby. . . ." And he follows this exposition with a set of miniature sermons on the Ten Commandments, setting forth in his disquisition on the first three his doctrine of Christian love and in his comments on the fourth commandment his notion of the virtue of obedience in the home to both temporal and spiritual leaders. In the rest of the pamphlet he expresses dismay over gluttony, licentiousness, and all the other common vices. He thought, no doubt, that such statements would make him appear a perfectly safe, conservative teacher—and they do to those accustomed to Protestantism, although his hatred for luxury and deviousness would only have made the Roman court more suspicious than ever of the puritanical heretic.

In June he published a little work *On the Papacy at Rome*, in which he summarized his belief in what the church actually was: a community of all believers who lived in faith, hope, and charity. Not a physical institution, not a place, not a bureaucratic structure, the church was invisible and existed independently of the ministrations of the clergy, most of the sacraments, and any of the claims for papal supremacy. The pope is a symbol of the unity of Christendom. He stands for the head of the church, who is Christ. Thus, the pope is to be respected as a symbolic figure, but he must "submit himself to be judged by Holy Scripture."

These two works—clear, straightforward, calm—were certainly significant in laying out some of the basic tenets of Luther's theology; in the canon of his writings, however, they stand only as five-finger exercises for the "three primary treatises" of the Reformation: *An Open Letter to the Christian Nobility of the German Nation*, *A Prelude on the Babylonian Captivity of the Church*, and *The Liberty of a Christian Man*.

It must have occurred to Luther in the summer of 1520, as he contemplated the whole weight of the Catholic hierarchy that was about to fall on him, that he had no allies who counted in the politics of Europe, save Frederick, who had still not taken a clear position; he had no large following; he had no program for bringing down the papacy. He had only his ignored or misunderstood theological arguments. They were an excellent and necessary base for his assault on Rome, but evidently Rome was about to crush him in any event. The time had come to relate his theology to a program for which he could enlist allies and followers. And so in his *Open Letter* to the nobility he wrote a preamble that expressed the age-old complaint of the German rulers. They were consistently bullied and harassed and made subservient to Rome. How did Rome manage to do this? It managed, Luther said, by basing its authority on a triple wall. First, the faithful were divided between the temporal and the spiritual estate. But, as Luther had argued on behalf of the priesthood of all believers, "all Christians belong to the same spiritual estate." Any division between estates was sheer invention and sheer nonsense. "For all Christians whatsoever really and truly belong to the religious class, and there is no difference among them except in so far as they do different work. That is St. Paul's meaning in I Corinthians 12, when he says: 'We are all one body, yet each member hath his own work for serving others.' This applies to us all, because we have one baptism, one gospel, one faith, and are all equally Christian . . . there is, at bottom, really no other difference between laymen, priests, princes, bishops, or, in Romanist terminology, between religious and secular, than that of office or occupation, and not that of Christian status."

The second wall protecting papal claims to supremacy was the theory that the pope could not err in interpreting matters of faith and that he alone could interpret Scripture. But that claim could not be supported by Scripture itself; it was another "invention," and a late one at that.

The third wall was the thesis that the pope alone had the authority to convene a council if reform were deemed necessary.

But, Luther said, if a fire started in a town and the mayor alone were empowered to call out the fire brigade, should everyone stand about and watch a house burn down; indeed, should they let the mayor's house itself burn if the mayor were not aware of the fire? Again, using his argument of the priesthood of all believers, Luther maintained anyone might call a council and that temporal rulers by virtue of their authority were obliged to call for a council when necessary.

Luther's arguments in these three instances were drawn principally from his previously stated positions. But the most telling blow he delivered to the church was in his attack on the "Donation of Constantine." The donation was one of the fundamental supports of the papal claim to primacy. According to tradition, the Emperor Constantine, before he retired to reign over the east from Constantinople, bestowed the rule of the west on Pope Sylvester. This donation, confirmed in writing, was the legal basis of the pope's supremacy over temporal rulers. Yet in the previous century the Italian humanist Lorenzo Valla had proven that the donation had been forged in the eighth century. It had been invented for the use of Pope Stephen II to intimidate the illiterate King Pippin. Luther found out about Valla's work from an edition recently published in Germany by Ulrich von Hutten—and impishly dedicated to Leo X. Valla's work was news to Luther, and to the German people, and the rebel made the most of it in exploding Rome's claims to dominance over Germany. In his *Open Letter* Luther brought together theology, history, politics, and the law to convince the nobility of Germany that his cause was also theirs.

But he did not appeal to the nobility alone. He took some pains to arouse a constituency among the German people. Rome, he said, was a city of "buying, selling, changing, exchanging, tippling, lying, deceiving, robbing, stealing, boasting, whoring, knaving." The torrent poured forth now. "It just flows out," Luther said. "I have no need to press or squeeze." He took no money for all his writings and only asked that the printers provide him with a few copies of his works as "payment"—no small request when the printers were working around the clock to satisfy the demand. "I can't supply all the presses that demand their food at my hands," Luther said. "As it is I am feeding something like six hundred printers now."

Luther was and remained politically naïve. He had no idea what elaborate political relationships he was smashing, and he might well have been appalled if he had known. While his pamphlet sold 4,000 copies in Germany in a few weeks—an astonishing sale for that time—and word of it inflamed the German people everywhere, student riots erupted in Wittenberg over some trivial local matter. Luther sided with the authorities and won the contempt of the students by preaching to them on the duties of obedience. What Leo recognized and Luther did not, and what the German leaders had apparently decided to forget in their rivalry with Rome, was that the heretic was undermining all authority in his challenge to Roman authority. We see Luther as one of the first men of the modern age, one of the first anti-authoritarians, and that he was—in ways that delighted him in 1520 and would utterly dismay him later. "I know another little song about Rome and these people," Luther concluded his *Open Letter* lightheartedly. "If their ears are itching I will sing it to them and pitch it as high as I can."

In the fall, with a new hunting season beginning in Rome and the papal bull still wending its way toward the heretic, Luther published his little song, *A Prelude on the Babylonian Captivity of the Church*. In his previous pamphlet Luther had argued that Rome bullied Catholics without right. Still, the church remained as man's only help to salvation. And so in his *Prelude* Luther developed two other essential points: first, that the church was useless in helping men to heaven; and, second, that the church was pernicious in the way it had corrupted the sacraments and misled the faithful. By now it was clear to Luther that if there were any heretics about they resided in the Vatican. "If any are to be called heretics and schismatics," he wrote, "it is neither the Bohemians, nor the Greeks, who take their stand on the gospel; rather, you Romanists are heretics and impious schismatics, who presume on figments of your imagination alone, and fly contrary to plain passages in divine Scripture." In his introduction to the *Prelude* he suggested that everything he had written on indulgences be burned; all that was mere nit-picking and a distraction. Rome's real corruption lay deeper, Luther said. The popes had invented four of the seven sacraments and perverted the other three. These were the essential mistakes to be cleared away. In clearing them away, of course, Luther attempted to clear away the basis of the church's hold on the faithful. If the pope could not use his keys to open the gates to heaven, if the sacraments administered by the priests were useless, then it must follow that the church was all sham.

Only three sacraments were contained in the Bible, Luther declared: baptism, penance, and the Lord's Supper. All the rest were later additions and therefore invalid. He took each sacrament in turn, quoting from Scripture, rebutting arguments of recent scholars, inveighing against the Aristotelians who had tortured theological discussions with notions of "substance" and "accident," and tossing in an occasional bold aside against the "toadies of the pope."

The sacrament of ordination, Luther said, "can nowhere be proved to have been instituted by God." It may be a practice of the church, but it is no sacrament. As a practice it is simply a means of oppressing Christians. "The sacrament of ordination is the prettiest of devices for giving a firm foundation to all the ominous things hitherto done in the church. . . . Now we, who have been baptized, are all uniformly priests by virtue of that very fact. The only addition received by the priests is the office of preaching, and even this with our consent. . . . Thus it says in I Peter 2, 'Ye are an elect race, a royal priesthood, and a priestly kingdom.' It follows that all of us who are Christian are also priests. Those whom we call priests are really ministers of the word and chosen by us; they fulfill their entire office in our name." There may be a priesthood, Luther says, as he said in his *Open Letter*, but priests are not to be set above any other Christian; they perform services as policemen or lawyers or street sweepers do, but that is all.

Of marriage, Luther said, "nowhere in Scripture do we read that anyone would receive the grace of God by getting married. . . . There has been such a thing as marriage itself ever since the beginning of the world, and it also exists among unbelievers to the present day. Therefore no grounds exist on which the Romanists can validly call it a sacrament of the new law, and a function solely of the church."

Confirmation and extreme unction are also taken over the coals of Scripture and found wanting. "Since sermons and prayers for these purposes are not mentioned in Scripture," Luther maintains, "as accompanied by a divine promise, they cannot be called sacraments in which we must have faith; . . . sacraments are instruments which save those who believe the divine promises always attaching to them." Again and again Luther insists that man is saved by faith alone, that these "usages" of the church, which have no sanction in the Bible, cannot help him, and that the pronouncements and threats of priests cannot harm him. Chapter and verse are marshaled to knock down the claims of Rome, until man stands alone before God, his worldly supports cast away. "In this way, you will see how rich a Christian is. . . . Even if he wishes, he could not lose his salvation however often he sinned, save only if he refused to believe. No sins have it in their power to damn him, but only unbelief. If his faith relies on the divine promise made at baptism, all things else are embraced by that same faith, nay by the truth of God; because He cannot deny Himself, if you confess Him and continue to cling to His promise."

Baptism remained intact under Luther's scrutiny, but the sacrament of penance was hugely modified to conform to his theory of *poenitentia.* In discussing the Lord's Supper, he defended the Bohemian heresy that both bread and wine might be given to the faithful and not bread alone. But more than that, he maintained that the sacrament of the Last Supper consisted wholly in the words "Take and eat, this is my body which is given for you. And taking the cup, He gave thanks, and gave to them, saying: All ye drink of it. This cup is the new testament in my blood which is poured out for you and for many for the remission of sins. This do in remembrance of me." Those words, and the communion of the faithful, constituted the entirety of the sacrament. The Catholic mass itself, the central ritual of the Catholic Church, which can be performed only by priests and which gives priests their unique role in Catholicism, is nothing but twaddle, a rigmarole added without any Scriptural foundation.

In the first pamphlet of this trio Luther tried to show why people ought to join him in his battle against the church. In the second he attempted to destroy the church's basis for standing between man and God, to show that men could ignore the church with impunity. In his third pamphlet Luther attempted to build a new and irresistible theology on top of the wreckage. In *The Liberty of a Christian Man* Luther was no longer on the attack, and this little pamphlet, the shortest of the three, has a cheerful, lyric quality about it. He opens with the paradoxical statement, "A Christian man is the most free lord of all, and subject to none; a Christian man is the most dutiful servant of all, and servant to everyone." All of his previous themes, the righteousness of God, *poenitentia*, the promise of God, justification through the sacrifice of Christ, all come together in a panegyric of Christian love. "We are named after Christ not because He is absent from us, but because He dwells in us, that is because we believe in Him and are Christs to one another, and do to our neighbors as Christ does to us." With joyful, free minds, Luther says, we serve our neighbors. "As our Heavenly Father has in Christ freely come to our help, so we ought freely to help our neighbor through the body and its works, and each should become as it were a Christ to the other, that we may be Christs to one another, and Christ may be the same in all, that we may be truly Christians."

At last, with an appropriateness of timing that might persuade one that God looked after both Leo and Luther, the bull Exsurge Domine reached Wittenberg. Alas, poor, sore Eck had not had an easy time of it. Luther's writings had done their work, and Eck had further fouled up the matter by adding, with the pope's permission, the names of a half dozen others to be charged with opinions heretical or scandalous or whatever. Eck added the names of six of his personal enemies, which lent the bull a particularly unhappy odor. In Leipzig, the scene of his recent triumph, he was the subject of satirical songs and had to go into hiding. At Erfurt students had a rollicking time tossing copies of the bull into the river. Even the bishops procrastinated. Aleander, meanwhile, was warned to be on the lookout for Ulrich von Hutten, who wanted to kill the pope's emissary. (In fact, Hutten and the freelance warrior Franz von Sickingen, who had formerly come to the defense of Reuchlin, were urging Luther to declare open war. A hundred knights stood ready to take to the field under Sickingen.) Aleander was called a sodomite in Cologne and was nearly stoned to death in Mainz. When he had a bonfire of Lutheran books at Louvain, the jolly students tossed in some works of scholastic theology, too. On October 10, a courier of Eck's managed to break through to Wittenberg and deliver a copy of the bull to Luther. "This bull condemns Christ himself," Luther said to Spalatin.

Luther's reply was called *Against the Execrable Bull of Antichrist.* "I have heard that a bull against me has gone through the whole earth before it came to me, because being a daughter of darkness it feared the light of my face." Luther maintained that it must be spurious; or if not spurious, then written by "that man of lies, dissimulation, errors, and heresy, that monster Johann Eck"; or if not written by Eck, then "whoever wrote this bull, he is Antichrist." "I protest before God," Luther wrote, ". . . that with my whole heart I dissent from the damnation of this bull, that I curse and execrate it as sacrilege and blasphemy of Christ. . . . This be my recantation, O bull, thou bitch of bulls."

In truth, the bull was a sorry piece of work. It asserted, predictably enough, the principles that the Roman Church was supreme over the other churches, that the pope was the absolute head of the Roman Church, that the pope had the power to use his keys to open and close purgatory, and the other issues that by now Luther had long since abandoned as minor irritants. Incredibly, the commission appeared to have forgotten the papal bull Cum Postquam, issued in 1518, which incorporated many of Luther's statements on indulgences, for the commission indicted Luther for some of his arguments of 1517 that had been proclaimed as official doctrine in Cum Postquam. Luther tore into the bull with zest. "This bull condemns me from its own word without any proof from Scripture, whereas I back up all my assertions from the Bible. I ask thee, ignorant Antichrist, do you think that your naked words can prevail against the armor of Scripture?" And again: "My articles are called 'respectively some heretical, some erroneous, some scandalous,' which is as much as to say, 'We don't know which are which.' O meticulous ignorance! I wish to be instructed, not respectively, but absolutely and certainly. . . . Let them show where I am a heretic, or dry up their spittle. They say that some articles are heretical, some erroneous, some scandalous, some offensive. The implication is that those which are heretical are not erroneous, those which are erroneous are not scandalous, and those which are scandalous are not offensive. What then is this, to say that something is not heretical, not scandalous, not false, but yet is offensive? So then, you impious and insensate papist, write soberly if you want to write."

Enter the indefatigable Miltitz, still wandering hopelessly around Germany, still hoping to bring about single-handedly a reconciliation between Leo and Luther. He spoke to a group of Augustinians that autumn and convinced them to go to Luther and persuade him to write a conciliatory letter to the pope. All was not yet lost, Miltitz said, if Luther would only write the pope and say that he had nothing *personal* against Leo. And so Luther sat down and wrote what Protestant historians have ever since persisted in seeing as a peace offering, the last opportunity for Leo to lay down his arms to a cordial Luther.

"Among the monsters of the age," Luther begins his deferential letter, "with whom I have now waged nearly a three-years war, I am compelled at times to turn my regard toward you, O most holy father Leo." Luther follows his cordial opening by trying to separate the office of the papacy from Leo himself—a task, as anyone who has ever held an office must know, that is impossible and probably disingenuous. "I must . . . most explicitly assure you that, whenever I have had occasion to mention you, I have never done it but in the best and most magnificent terms. . . . I have even endeavored to defend you against your great calumniator Prierias [the pope's appointed spokesman] with a sincerity which any reader will abundantly perceive in my works. . . . I delight not in blazoning the crimes of others, being conscious of the mote which is in my own eye, and not regarding myself as entitled to throw the first stone at an adultress." If calling Leo a whore is a conciliatory remark, then surely we have not yet heard Luther indulge in sarcastic polemics.

Having thus excepted Leo from any negative observations he might offer, Luther continues: "I must, however, acknowledge my total abhorrence of your see, the Roman court, which neither you nor any man can deny is more corrupt than either Babylon or Sodom, and, according to the best of my information, is sunk in the most deplorable and notorious impiety." So much for the court that the virtuous Leo keeps.

"It is, indeed, as clear as daylight to all mankind, that the Roman Church, formerly the most holy of all churches, is become the most licentious den of thieves, the most shameless of whore houses, the kingdom of sin, of death, and of hell; the wickedness of which not Antichrist himself could conceive. . . . The fate of the court of Rome is decreed; the wrath of God is upon it; advice it detests, reformation it dreads; the fury of its impiety cannot be mitigated, and it has now fulfilled that which was said of its mother, 'We have medicined Babylon, and she is not healed; let us therefore leave her.'" Are we to believe that Luther considered this the basis for reconciliation?

Then, to pretend he has not insulted Leo, Luther proceeds: "O most excellent Leo, that you, who are worthy of better times, should have been elected to the pontificate in such days as these. Rome merits you not, nor those who resemble you, but Satan himself, who in fact reigns more than you in that Babylon; would that you could exchange that state which your inveterate enemies represent to you as an honor for some petty living; or would support yourself by your paternal inheritance; for of such honors none are worthy but Iscariots, the sons of perdition."

It is some measure of Miltitz's befuddled mind that he considered Luther's letter conciliatory and forwarded it to the pope along with Luther's essay on Christian liberty, which, as Luther said in concluding his letter, "contains the whole of Christian life in a brief form, provided you grasp its meaning." It may come as no surprise that Leo neglected to reply to Luther's letter, and so in November Luther published both his letter and his reply "against the bull of Antichrist."

The case depended at this juncture on having the civil authorities—that is, Frederick and the emperor—do their duty as defenders of the faith. Rarely had secular rulers declined to carry out their chores in such cases, for they had as little interest as the pope in seeing a popular movement defy constituted authority. But Frederick had already expressed himself in the spring of 1520: "Germany is now full of educated and cultivated men," he said with a measure of German pride, "and the laity have begun to be intelligent, to love the Scriptures, and wish to understand them. The teaching of Luther has a great hold over the minds of many." And he concluded with dispassionate common sense, with a detached understanding of the situation that had never penetrated the Vatican, "if his conditions are refused and he is put down, without legal investigation, only by the censures and ban of the Church, the existing disturbance will be increased and there will be no hope of a peaceful settlement." Hope for a peaceful settlement had vanished that summer, but Frederick stuck phlegmatically by his old condition that Luther be given a trial on German soil.

For his part, the emperor evidently agreed with the pope that Luther had to be put down. The point that the rebel threatened all social order was not lost on Charles. But Luther must be brought under control in a way that would benefit Charles in three ways: so that the pope would be under obligation to him and in some measure dependent upon his goodwill; so that the Germans would see that the new emperor was a man of toughness who held their interests high and to whom they must appeal for satisfaction of their wishes; and so that Luther, though under control, was not altogether annihilated—for he might even still be useful in the future. With those conditions in mind, the emperor announced that he would review "the affairs of the empire," including the Luther case, at a Diet to be held at Worms in January, 1521.

On December 10, after sixty days had expired from the date Luther received the bull, a small bonfire was stoked near the Elster Gate in Wittenberg. Luther had nailed another notice to the door of the Wittenberg church asking "all friends of the evangelical truth" to come and help burn the "godless books of papal law and scholastic theology." No one could locate copies of Aquinas or Duns Scotus that the owners were willing to sacrifice to the flames—Aquinas might be godless, still his books were expensive—but Luther's band of friends was able to come up with volumes of the papal decretals and the canon law, those foundation stones of the papacy, and an odd copy of the *Summa Angelica* of Angelo of Chiavasso. As the doctors stood around somberly watching the thick pages slowly begin to burn, Luther stepped forward and, barely noticed by the others, dropped the bull Exsurge Domine into the fire, quietly mumbling, "May this fire destroy you, because you have obstructed God's truth."

While the students celebrated—much to Luther's disgust that they would turn such a serious occasion into a carnival—the heretic himself went quickly back to his room and wrote a note to Spalatin to tell him what he had done. "This will be news," he said in his only recorded instance of understatement.

XVI

1521

LEO was stunned when he learned that the emperor had invited Luther to appear before the Diet of Worms. Luther, the pope told the ambassador of the Holy Roman Empire, "would not be well received even in hell." Altogether too much fuss was being made over the heretic, Leo thought. He ought to be condemned and arrested and quickly disposed of, before all the attention made a greater popular hero of him. Nor was Leo reassured by the reports he received from Aleander. "Nine-tenths of Gemany," Aleander wrote to the Vatican, "shouts for Luther: the other tenth, if it does not crave for Luther's teaching, at least cries, 'Down with the Roman Court,' and raises the further demand for a Council to be held in Germany." Aleander asked for a package of papal briefs to assuage the grievances of some of the Germans and for money to bribe the emperor's counselors.

The pope sent Aleander both the briefs and the money, along with a letter of advice. Be calm, Leo advised his emissary, and depend upon the emperor and the electors to see that Luther threatened all temporal authority. Remind the electors, Leo said, that Luther would raise the people against their rulers, drive land-owners from their property, and overthrow all lords, clergy, and laymen alike if not firmly suppressed. The issue was by now understood by everyone but Luther: authority versus the individual. And everyone feared the outcome.

Ulrich von Hutten, diminutive, combative, always short of ready money, had enjoyed considerable esteem among the Humanists of Europe by publishing a book meant to teach the art of writing Latin verse. His fame increased when he leaped to the defense of Reuchlin. Now, with his sidekick knight Von Sickingen and their visions of a new, free Germany, he had become a national hero. Everywhere Aleander traveled in his diplomatic missions throughout Germany he found little statuettes of the two "Deliverers of Germany," Luther with an open book and Hutten with a sword. "There are here so many Lutherans," Aleander wrote to Eck, "that not only all men, but even the sticks and stones, cry out Luther." The sticks and stones cried Luther for different reasons: Hutten promoted him as a champion of German nationalism; the peasants rallied around him as a leader for their long-desired uprising; beleaguered nobles, enraged at the taxes of the church, flocked to him as their weapon against Rome. Aleander found that hotel rooms were mysteriously booked up when he tried to get a place to stay, and he wrote again to Rome, "I cannot go out on the streets but the Germans put their hands to their swords and gnash their teeth at me. I hope the pope will give me a plenary indulgence and look after my brothers and sisters if anything happens to me." Pamphlets and broadsides circulated by the hundreds in Luther's defense; the heretic was pictured in some posters with a halo above his head. The rebels had taken the initiative and kept it. Parodies delighted the crowds that assembled for the festivities that accompanied the Diet: "I believe in the Pope," ran a satire of the Apostles' Creed, "binder and looser in heaven, earth, and hell, and in Simony, his only son our Lord, who was conceived by the canon law and born of the Romish church. Under his power truth suffered, was crucified, dead and buried. . . ." The Emperor Charles, for all his attempts to appear bold and purposeful, vacillated, withdrew the invitation to Luther, and extended it again. He hoped, as did the electors, that Luther would refuse to appear. But Luther, still innocent of the challenge he posed to authority, was determined to defend what he thought was the issue. "I must take care," he wrote to Frederick, "that the gospel is not brought into contempt by our fear to attest to it and seal our teaching with our blood."

The Luther question was, or was supposed to be, a relatively minor political matter at the Diet, for the Diet was not so much a German affair as an international diplomatic conference. The English ambassador was present with instructions to arrange an alliance with the new emperor, and he was empowered to offer the twenty-one-year-old bachelor ruler a marriage with a member of the English royal family. The French ambassador carried a declaration of war among his papers. The babel of language added a heady confusion as representatives arrived from Austria, Venice, and Savoy. The Poles were hard put to understand the Spanish, and the Burgundians stood mute before the Hungarians. Emperor Charles, ruler of the Germans, had been raised in the Netherlands and spoke only French. The situation was in that fluid state that politicians both fear and relish. Those sufficiently quick and canny stood to gain something—international alliances for the principals, and for the small fry and hangers-on such crumbs as benefices, pensions, appointments, patents of nobility, errands, commissions, grants, licenses, annuities, gratuities, bribes, boodle, bunce, free drinks, and enough gossip to last a lifetime. When politics palled, the ambassadors and their retinues played with the kings and knaves in decks of cards and pawns and bishops on chessboards. They whored, gambled, tilted, jousted, raced, wrestled, boxed, danced, guzzled, gormandized, and gorged themselves in a four-month nonstop round of saturnalian revels. The racing and jousting went apace, Frederick wrote to his brother, but political questions were decided at a slow and cautious rate and, to be sure, rarely in public. The revelers celebrated they knew not what. They hugged the taverns, drowning their ignorance in drink, and waited for the gossip. There were a gratifyingly large number of rumors. It was said that Luther was prepared to supply the emperor with 100,000 troops if he would invade Italy and reform the church. There was a border war in the Netherlands, a civil war in Denmark, a Turkish threat in the Balkans, riots here and there in Germany, and the nobles whispered in terror of the possibility of a peasant uprising that would consume them all. Not even the emperor himself knew what was happening at his Diet.

If Charles could use Luther to pry concessions from the pope, then the electors could use Luther to pry concessions from the emperor. At first the emperor intended to issue an edict calling for Luther to appear at Worms. Then, fearful of the public commotion Luther's appearance might make, he decided to issue an edict calling simply for Luther's arrest. But the Archbishop of Mainz, who had allowed Luther's books to be burned only a month before, opposed this second edict. Any edict, he insisted, should be issued under the names of the electors and not just the emperor. Frederick argued that the edict must call for a hearing and not a premature condemnation. As Charles was buffeted by arguments from his obstreperous electors, the pope's representative badgered him from the other side. Aleander maintained that the heretic should not be heard but immediately condemned. If he had been officially excommunicated, the electors replied, then that would be their clear duty; but he had not yet been excommunicated and thus the electors still had a right to hear and judge him.

In fact, Luther had been excommunicated, and Aleander had a copy of the bull in his possession, but he did not dare show it. Back in Rome, when it was seen that Hutten supported Luther, the Vatican had added the name of that champion of German nationalism to the bull of excommunication. Aleander knew that if he revealed this latest development, the outcry would be horrendous; so he returned the bull with a request for revision, and argued vainly with the electors. He drafted an edict that called for Luther's arrest and read it to a meeting of the electors, and they erupted in protest. The Elector of Brandenburg supported the edict, and Cardinal Lang had to hold Frederick back from attacking the Brandenburg elector with his fists.

On January 22, a priest named Glapion had preached a sermon in the presence of the emperor in which he turned at one moment and spoke directly to Charles: "If the Pope has done amiss, it is you, the Emperor, who ought to go and correct him." Glapion was one of the emperor's spiritual advisers, and so his remark was rightly interpreted as a tentative statement of imperial policy, meant not for the emperor but for the electors. In effect, Charles asked the electors to recognize him as head of both state and church in Germany; if they would come to him, he would settle their differences with the pope. The Glapion formula, as we shall call it, was perfectly sensible from the German point of view: The Germans would unite against Rome, exact necessary reforms and changes in the relationship between the German clergy and Rome, and achieve a measure of the independence that England and France had already won from the Vatican. It would enhance Charles' power among the electors and free the electors from harassment by the high clergy. Luther, as Glapion's remark in his sermon made clear, was to be the opening wedge in splitting a freer empire from Rome—if the electors would submit to this new arrangement. The overture evoked a response from Frederick's chancellor, and Glapion told him that Luther need only retract his attack on the sacraments in his book on the *Babylonian Captivity* and submit to a German council. It was, considering all that Luther had written against the church, a breathtakingly small concession; it was intentionally made so small in order that Luther would be persuaded, unknowingly, into this new political role.

It was in this context that Aleander pressed to have the emperor issue an edict of condemnation, and the electors fought against it. To be sure, aims and alliances shifted with the breeze, as one elector joined the papal party to reduce Charles' power and another joined the emperor to reduce the power of rival electors. But, to Aleander's frustrated dismay, the Glapion formula prevailed. Duke George carried the electors with him in a speech almost worthy of Luther when he asked them "not to forget [their] grounds of complaint against the court of Rome. . . . All Shame has been laid aside, and people pursue but one object . . . money! more money! . . . so that preachers who ought to be teaching the truth, retail nothing but lies, and these are not only tolerated, but even recompensed, because the more they lie, the more they gain. . . . A universal reform must be effected. A general council must be convened for the accomplishment of such a reform. . . ." Join the emperor, he begged the electors, against their common Roman enemy.

On March 26, Charles sent out an imperial herald to deliver to Luther an invitation to appear before the Diet. The edict reflected the new political structure the Germans were trying to put together on the uncertain foundation of the Luther case. It was issued under the rubric of the estates rather than the emperor himself—the electors had forced that increase in their standing from Charles—and Charles wrote a cordial letter of safe conduct to Luther: The emperor was recognized as guarantor of the law. Wasting no time in cozying up to the useful heretic, Charles styled Luther as "honorable, beloved, and pious." "Zounds!" Aleander is supposed to have exclaimed, "that's no way to address a heretic." From the pope's point of view, the Diet was botching the job terribly, and Glapion, for having promoted the insidious notion of a German council opposed to the pope, was recalled to Rome and assigned a post in the wilderness of America.

For his part, while he awaited the summons to appear at Worms, Luther whiled away some time in writing. Since Luther had never had a personal confrontation with Leo, at about this time he did what no historian would ever have the gall to do. Using the papal bull of excommunication for Leo's side of the conversation, he made one up:

THE POPE: Leo, bishop. . . .

LUTHER: Bishop . . . as a wolf is a shepherd. . . .

THE POPE: . . . Servant of all the servants of God. . . .

LUTHER: In the evening when we are drunk; but in the morning we call ourself Leo, lord of all lords.

THE POPE: . . . According to the duty of the apostolic charge, and for the maintenance of the purity of the Christian faith. . . .

LUTHER: That is to say, of the pope's temporal possessions.

THE POPE: . . . We excommunicate, and we curse, all who falsify our bulls and apostolic letters. . . .

LUTHER: But the Letters of God, the Scriptures of God, all the world may condemn them and burn them.

THE POPE: . . . In like manner we condemn, and we curse all, who in one way or another, do prejudice to the city of Rome, the kingdom of Sicily, the islands of Sardinia and Corsica, the patrimony of St. Peter in Tuscany, the duchy of Spoleto, the marquisate of Ancona, the Campagna, the cities of Ferrara and Benevento, and all the other cities or territories, pertaining to the Church of Rome.

LUTHER: O Peter, poor fisherman! whence have Rome and all these kingdoms come into thy hands? I salute you, Peter! King of Sicily!

On April 16, riding with a few friends in a two-wheeled cart, Luther entered Worms. When word went around town that the monk had arrived, a crowd of 2,000 turned out to escort him to his lodgings in the Augustinian monastery. Aleander looked on morosely at the crowd and recorded his feelings in a letter: "I expect that they will soon say he works miracles." On the following day, at four o'clock in the afternoon, the imperial herald and the imperial marshal called on Luther and, to avoid the crowds, escorted him to the Diet through alleyways and backyards and in a side door of the council chamber in the bishop's palace.

There, in silks and satins and gold chains and silver-handled swords, the assembled authority of the Western world received the gaunt, scruffy monk. The crowd was so great that most of the dignitaries had to stand. Under a canopy at the head of the hall sat Charles V, proud young heir to the fortunes of the House of Habsburg, Augmentor of the Realm of Germany, Lord of Spain, Naples, the Two Sicilies, Jerusalem, Croatia, Hungary, Dalmatia, Duke of Burgundy, Archduke of Austria, Count of Habsburg, of the Flanders and the Tyrol, "by the grace of God elected Roman Emperor," etc., etc. Luther had been advised by Frederick's counselors, by a Wittenberg jurist named Schurff, by Hutten, by Melanchthon, by the imperial herald, and by scores of others, and he could not remember whether he was supposed to kneel in front of the emperor, or genuflect, or whether he was supposed to genuflect and then kneel and then genuflect again. Glancing nervously from side to side, he spotted an old friend in the crowd and hailed him—in too loud a voice. The imperial marshal sharply called out to him that he might not speak until spoken to and then only to answer the questions put to him.

In front of the emperor was a vast pile of books—so vast that the emperor could not believe Luther had written them all. "Martin Luther," the chancellor of the Archbishop of Trier intoned, "his sacred and invincible imperial majesty has summoned you before his throne, in pursuance of the counsel and advice of the states of the Holy Roman Empire, in order that you may be charged to reply to the following two questions: First, do you acknowledge that these books were composed by you? Secondly, do you wish to retract these books and their contents, or do you persist in the things you have therein advanced?"

Luther was about to reply when the cautious lawyer Schurff broke in: "Let the titles be read." When they were, Luther had difficulty in finding his voice, and the assembly had to strain to hear his reply: "With regard to the first, I acknowledge the books enumerated to have been from me; I cannot disown them. As for the second—" At this the electors were particularly attentive. If he were to retract his book on the *Babylonian Captivity*, it would signal that the Glapion formula had been accepted by the heretic. "As for the second, seeing that it is a question that relates to the faith and the salvation of souls, in which the Word of God has an interest . . . I should act imprudently were I to reply inconsiderately. I might affirm less than the case requires or more than truth exacts, and thus make myself offend against that Word of Christ: 'Whosoever will deny me before men, him will I also deny before my Father who is in heaven.' Wherefore I beseech your imperial majesty, with all submission, to allow me time, that I may reply without doing prejudice to the Word of God."

All this was spoken in German, and when the emperor's translator finished rendering it into French for his imperial majesty, Charles was annoyed. He retired to a smaller chamber, however, to consult with the electors, and when they returned the chancellor announced that Luther would be given one day to compose his reply but, to avoid giving him an opportunity to deliver yet another tiresomely long polemic, "on condition that you answer by word of mouth and not in writing."

That evening, as the advisers again bedeviled Luther with their contradictory notions of what he should do and stridently urged him to accept the Glapion formula or some other compromise, Luther sat down to sketch out a few notes on his reply to the Diet. He jotted down the little formal niceties that he must use in addressing the emperor and then worried over whether he would say too much or too little. "And although certain things have slipped into the speech, such as—" The notes break off; perhaps he was interrupted by another adviser. But he knew anyway what he would say.

On the following day he was again escorted to the Diet—and was kept waiting for two hours while other business was conducted to make certain he did not imagine that he was anyone of special importance. It was evening now, and the twilight glowing dully through the stained-glass windows was supplemented by torches.

"Martin Luther, you asked yesterday for a delay which is now expired. It ought not unquestionably to have been granted you, since every man should be sufficiently instructed in the things of the faith, to be ready to render an account to all who may ask it, and especially you who are so great and able a doctor of holy Scriptures. . . . Now then, do you desire to defend your books as a whole, or do you wish to retract any of them?"

Again, the electors waited to hear Luther retract his attack on the sacraments. He opened with a remark that nicely dramatized this confrontation between an individual and the massed authority of the establishment: "Most serene emperor, illustrious princes, gracious lords. . . . If through my ignorance, I shall be found wanting in the usages and proprieties of courts, you will forgive me, seeing I was not brought up in king's palaces, but in the obscurity of a cloister." He then distinguished three categories in the works with which he was presented. First were works on "faith and good works," which no one could ask him to retract, since they were "so pure, so simple, so Christian." Secondly, he had "composed books against the popedom, and therein I have attacked those who by false doctrine, wicked lives, and scandalous examples, desolate the Christian world and ruin souls and bodies." He would not withdraw these either, and murmurings passed through the assembly. If they had been sufficiently distinct, one would no doubt have heard Aleander moan and several of the electors express pleasure at Luther's words. Thirdly, he had written against personal opponents, and "I frankly confess that I have possibly attacked them with more acrimony than became my ecclesiastical profession." Nonetheless, he could not withdraw them either, since "I should thus sanction the impieties of my opponents. . . ."

The chancellor ordered Luther to repeat his statement now in Latin. "I was all in a sweat," Luther later recalled, and one of Frederick's counselors said to him, "If you cannot repeat your discourse, it is enough, Doctor." But Luther took a deep breath and repeated his statement in Latin.

"You have not answered the question addressed to you," the chancellor insisted, hoping still, no doubt, that Luther would retract just the one book. "You are required to give a clear and precise answer."

"Since your most serene Majesty and your high mightinesses require me to give a simple, clear, and precise reply, such I will give: I cannot submit my faith either to the pope, or to councils, inasmuch as it is clear as daylight that these have often fallen into error, and even into gross contradictions with themselves. If, then, I be not convinced by testimonies from Scripture, or by evident reasons, . . . I neither can nor will retract anything, for it is unsafe for the Christian to say anything against his conscience."

Luther's final reply was simple and clear, though it lacked the ring of the individual standing up to all those dignitaries, and so his followers helped him by fixing up his statement with a later addition that became famous: "Here I stand. I cannot do otherwise. God help me. Amen."

The Diet collapsed in confusion. The emperor had heard enough; he rose to go. "If you do not retract," the chancellor shouted, "the emperor and the states of the empire will see what course they ought to adopt towards an obstinate heretic." The emperor was on his way out of the room, with a parting order to stop arguing and take the heretic away. Luther and the chancellor still shouted at one another. Luther was taken from the hall by his claque, and in the tumult some thought that he had been arrested. Arms were brandished; Luther quieted his friends, telling them he had an escort to the monastery. He was hustled from the hall, and, his arms raised triumphantly above his head, his voice rang out with as wrong a remark as he ever made: "It is over! It is over!"

At the monastery that night a servant of the Duke of Brunswick, a member of the pope's party, presented Luther with a silver vase filled with Einbeck beer. "His highness," the servant said, "was pleased to taste it himself before sending it to you." It had reached that point: The papal party was relieved to see Luther oppose the pope as long as he opposed the Glapion formula at the same time. Luther did not understand the gesture; he took it as an act of Christian brotherhood, and he wrote out a prayer to return to the duke: "Whosoever shall give you a cup of cold water in my name, because you belong to Christ, the Savior has said ... he shall have his reward."

On the following day, Charles addressed the electors: "A single monk, led astray by his own folly, rises against the faith of Christendom. I will sacrifice my kingdoms, my power, my friends, my treasures, my body, my blood, my spirit, and my life in putting a stop to this impiety." The crowds in the streets were chanting *"Bundschuh! Bundschuh!"* The threat of a peasant revolt was palpable, and Charles heartily meant that he would sacrifice all in putting a stop to that impiety. "I am about to send back the Augustinian, Martin Luther, forbidding him meanwhile to cause the least tumult among the people; I will then proceed against him and his adherents, as against manifest heretics, by excommunication, by interdict, by all means fitted to ruin them. I call upon the members of the states to conduct themselves like faithful Christians."

But the members of the states had not given up hope on the Glapion formula, and their own fear of a peasant uprising persuaded them that some sort of compromise was essential. Charles agreed to let them hear Luther over the next three days to see whether he would consent to some agreement. At last Luther got a sympathetic treatment from an official commission; but the sympathy was politically motivated, and Luther would have none of it. Luther said he would not condemn all councils, but he could not accept some of them. He preached to the commission, he quoted Scripture, he instructed them—and they asked him whether, as a purely practical matter, he would submit to the judgment of the emperor if not to the judgment of the pope or of councils. No, Luther said, he must abide by the word of God.

Would he agree to the joint judgment of the pope and emperor, or of the emperor and the electors? All the political formulas the electors had been able to imagine were tried out on Luther: Let him accept any one of them; let him determine, not knowing that this was the question he was being asked to resolve, the political structure of the Holy Roman Empire. Would he revoke *something* for the moment (to give the electors and emperor some leverage with the pope and the German people) and submit to a future (German) council? No, he would not. The Elector of Brandenburg: "Then you will not yield unless you are convinced by Scripture?" "No," Luther replied for the hundredth time, "or by clear and evident reasons." Where did authority lie in the world? The discomfited electors and the horrified emperor finally heard Luther's answer distinctly: with the individual.

The electors reported to the emperor that they could not reach any understanding with Luther, and so, on April 25, as Aleander recorded, "the venerable ruffian departed, after drinking many cups of malvoisy, of which he is very fond." An edict calling for his arrest followed Luther—but not immediately. Aleander drafted an edict for the emperor but then had to listen to Charles' complaints about the pope's friendship toward France. Charles and the French were about to go to war, and the emperor grumbled for days about the pope's seeming reluctance to assist the empire. If he had failed with the Glapion formula, Charles could still use Luther to wring something out of Leo. It was no coincidence that the moment Leo signed a treaty with Charles, the edict was signed and promulgated in Germany. In the meantime, Aleander fretted over reports that Luther was being received triumphantly along the road back to Wittenberg. Townspeople turned out to greet the heretic wherever he appeared and risked the emperor's displeasure, or worse, by inviting Luther to preach in their churches. The pope's emissary worried that Luther might escape to Bohemia, and he wrote Leo advising him to have Luther kidnapped before he reached the border.

At Eisenach, where he had sung for his supper in school days and stayed with the Italian family, the Cottas, Luther was again invited to preach the Gospel—over the protests of the parish priest who was in "a great fright" lest he would have to pay for having a heretic in his pulpit. At Eisenach, too, a mysterious pair of horsemen rode into town and closeted themselves with Luther. They told him to avoid the road to Gotha and Erfurt and travel instead on the route to Möhra.

On the next day Luther arrived in Möhra, his father's hometown, where he visited with his grandmother and his other relatives still living there. On the following day, with his brother James and a Wittenberg colleague named Nicholas Amsdorff, Luther set out to Waltershausen, along a road that skirted the dense Thuringian woods. As they approached the deserted church of Glisboch, the travelers heard a commotion in the woods, and a moment later five masked and heavily armed horsemen descended on them. Brother James instantly ran for the woods and did not stop running until he reached Waltershausen that evening. The driver of the cart tried to defend himself and was thrown to the ground. Another of the masked men laid hold of Amsdorff, and the other three seized Luther (who clutched copies of Erasmus'

edition of the Greek New Testament and of a Hebrew Bible),
tossed a cavalry cloak over him, and dragged him into the woods.
It was over in a trice. Luther had disappeared, and no one knew
who had kidnapped him.

At the Diet of Worms, Elector Frederick said he was prepared
to swear that he had no idea of Luther's whereabouts, and it was
true that he did not know where Luther was. In his instructions to
his counselors he had specified that the act be done in great
secrecy so that not even Frederick could know the location of
Luther's hideout. He wanted to be able to swear with a clear
conscience. Indeed, the scheme was pulled off with marvelous
secrecy. Timid brother James did not even know of it, and his
fright was genuine. The planning was so cautious, and so little did
Frederick trust the monk's ability to keep his mouth shut, that the
go-betweens who told Luther of the plan at Eisenach were
unknown to Luther. He would never be able to identify them. If
he embarrassed Frederick by talking, the elector could always
insist that Luther was mistaken.

It sounds like good fun, this charade of horsemen swooping
down and dragging off the protesting heretic, but Frederick had
taken it on himself—without reference to a council, but on his
own individual hook—to defy pope, emperor, electors, and all
those other powers of the world who had assembled at Worms to
condemn Luther. Cautious man that he was, he never let slip a
remark to explain his motive. It could have been pride in his
university: Luther had put it on the map, and Frederick enjoyed
the fame. It could have been pique at the pope: This, surely,
would repay the slights Frederick had suffered at Leo's hands. It
could have been a device to unsettle the arrogant young emperor.
But none of these explanations quite harmonizes with Frederick's
character. He knew, as everyone did by now, that the Luther
controversy threatened to bring down the whole social and political order of Europe. Cautious, phlegmatic man that he was, Frederick would not unleash such monsters of chaos for reasons of
mere vanity or revenge. During the Diet, Frederick had written
his brother, "Were it in my power, I should be ready to support

Luther. You cannot imagine how the partisans of Rome are attacking me. Could I tell you all," he said, in evident reference to the back-room politicking, "you would hear wonders. They are bent on destroying him, and the moment anyone shows any interest in preserving him, he is forthwith cried down as a heretic. May God, who does not abandon the cause of righteousness, bring matters to a good end?" When God neglected to act, Frederick stepped in to do His work. After listening to the arguments in the Diet and in the private chambers where the electors met, Frederick may have become Luther's first convert among men of power. Either that, or the plodding old man may simply have been the only righteous man in Europe. Whatever the motive, the act preserved the reformer—and secured the Reformation.

Luther was confined to two small rooms in the upper reaches of the Wartburg castle, a dank, ugly relic of the Middle Ages, sometime home of Landgrave Hermann of Thuringia, who centuries before had filled its cavernous halls with beautiful women and famous minstrels. Fallen on evil days of peace, the castle now belonged to the electors of Saxony, who never visited there and kept only a skeleton force of watchmen whose sole task in years of service turned out to be guarding Luther. Again, security precautions required that only the captain of the castle know the heretic's identity. Luther was ordered to dress as a knight, cultivate a beard, let his hair grow to disguise his tonsure—and only then would he be allowed to climb down the ladder from his rooms and mix with the castle guard. He was introduced as Junker Jörg.

As the captain of the castle soon learned, Luther was not an easy man to confine. Letters streamed out to his friends headed "From the Isle of Patmos," or "From the Wilderness," or "Above the Birds." His demand for paper and ink was insatiable, and whenever he needed a book he would ride off to Eisenach to borrow one from the Franciscans, each time sending his protectors into a frenzy. When Archbishop Albrecht of Mainz had the audacity to announce a new indulgence and publish a list of the relics he had in his collection (a piece of the dirt from which Adam was created and the bowl Pilate used to wash his hands), Luther attacked stridently and demanded an answer from the archbishop within two weeks. Spalatin remonstrated; Frederick was working at the moment to make an ally of Albrecht. Luther shot back at Spalatin that he would publish what he pleased. The nastiest elements of Luther's character emerged now: He said he would publish his works elsewhere if he could not have them printed in Wittenberg; he would leave Wittenberg and seek his protection from another. He bit the hand that fed him again and again, but there was some excuse for it. The Devil had come back to plague him now that he was alone, and the battle of farting in the Devil's face and throwing ink pots at him raged night after night in the little cell at the Wartburg. He could no longer fight the public demons, Antichrist, and his toadies, and so the fury turned inward again, and Luther lashed out at the Devil with imprecations and with his fists. "I can tell you," he wrote Spalatin, "that it is much easier to fight against the incarnate Devil—that is, against evil men—than against the very spirit of evil borne upon the air and in one's soul."

He was given an opportunity to spend his rage, as Leo did, with the hunt, but the serious-minded Luther could not let himself go. "I stoutly theologized amid the hares and hounds," he said, "and found a mystery of grief and pain in the very heart of this merry pastime. Is not this hunting the very image of the Devil seeking what poor beasts he may devour by the aid of his nets, his traps, and his trained dogs (by which I mean his bishops and his theologians)? . . . I have had enough of such hunting as this. The hunting I shall stick to is for the wolves, bears, foxes—the whole iniquitous horde of Roman beasts that prey upon the world. . . ."

In moments of respite, Luther finished a tract on the *Magnificat*, the song he had loved so passionately when his mother first taught him to sing. "She does not proclaim with a loud voice that she is the Mother of God—but goes about her wonted household duties, milking the cows, cooking the meals, washing pots and kettles, sweeping out the rooms. . . ." As he wrote of the *Magnificat*, Luther was moved to consider the vanity of worldly power and pride, and how, when the arrogance of empires swells to its greatest and seemingly most impregnable force, God reaches out and bursts the "bubble"—or, as it is in Latin, the *bulla*, a word that serves for both "bubble" and "bull."

His commentary on the *Magnificat* shows an appealing side of Luther, and its speculations on tyranny are worthy of some of his finest writing. But his greatest achievement at the Wartburg was his translation into German of the New Testament. There had been previous translations of the Bible into the tongue of Luther's countrymen, but these were expensive editions, and most people had never seen a Bible except in the hands of a priest or teacher or chained to a desk in the inner sanctum of a library. Luther was armed only with the Erasmus Bible and his Hebrew Bible, but that was sufficient. He sat down and produced a translation in his own urgent, lyrical rhythms in a mere ten weeks. It was printed by Hans Luft of Wittenberg, among others, and it is estimated that Luft alone ran off 100,000 copies. Yet, as a contemporary scholar has observed, "Only a very few surviving copies are as undamaged and in such excellent condition as the sumptuous volumes of the previous translations. A contemporary Luther Bible, when it has survived at all, has almost inevitably been read until it is falling to pieces." The year 1521 was the year of Luther's victory; with his appearance at the Diet of Worms, the intercession of Frederick, and the publication of the Bible, the Reformation had become inevitable.

Leo X congratulated himself that at last the Luther affair was satisfactorily concluded. He said that he detected a "second Luther" in the Bishop of Zamora, who was stirring up rebellious peasants in Spain, but it was not worth worrying about. For 1521 was a victorious year for Leo, too. He had finally come to believe that the French posed the greatest threat of any foreign power to Italy, and in his alliance with the emperor he managed to have Parma, Piacenza, and Ferrara promised to him. He was ill; all the old complaints about his fistula, his liver, and his eyes plagued him. But the new hope of a Medici state in Italy buoyed his spirits, and he was still good for a trick or two. In order to keep the French confused and, for a short time, in the mistaken belief that Leo was still cordial to France, he sweet-talked the French envoy and gave him a packet of dispatches to carry back to the papal nuncio in Paris—a packet of blank paper.

In July papal and Spanish forces failed in an effort to drive the French from Milan, and Leo fretted throughout the summer. "His Holiness is almost beside himself with anxiety," Castiglione wrote home, "and would like to hear what is happening in camp every hour, if possible." Castiglione had himself been offered a command in the war against the French but had declined, because "I am no longer a boy." An attempt to surprise Parma only rallied the Duke of Ferrara, and Leo, unable to take the strain of the daily reports he demanded, retired to his hunting lodge at Magliana. Then, the duplicity of the Swiss undermined the French. Swiss mercenaries fought on both sides of the war, and they had been instructed not to fight against one another. The Swiss contingent on the French side withdrew, and the French commander retreated to Milan. Driven out of Milan on November 19, the French were soon forced to surrender Parma and Piacenza. Their defeat was certain now, and when Castiglione brought Leo the news on Sunday, November 24, Leo said exultantly, "This pleases me more than the Papacy."

The pope returned at once to Rome and ordered a three-day celebration. Paris de Grassis quizzed him on his order, reminding the pope that it was not customary to rejoice in the victory of one Christian state over another—unless the church derived some benefit from it. With a smile, Leo replied that he had, indeed, "a great prize in his hands," and plans went forward for the celebration.

Leo had caught a slight chill wandering among the hawks and herons and ferrets in the bitter November weather at Magliana, so he stayed close to the fire that evening to warm himself. And yet, as he thought about how he had secured a big Medici state for his dynasty—and one that seemed destined now to grow even larger from that stable base—he could not stand still. He went to the window to look out on the square and back to the fire and back again to the window, where the harsh November drafts turned his chill to a cold.

By Wednesday he began to flag at the card table and had to retire early. On Saturday night, as he listened to music, his eyes closed, his delicate hand stopped keeping time, and he suddenly slumped. He was carried to bed, where he recovered consciousness in two hours' time, only to fall unconscious again. Unable as usual to commit himself to any definite position, he awoke and dropped off again and awoke and dropped off again through the night. At one moment when he awoke, it is reported that he looked about the room and said to no one in particular, "Pray for me. I want to make you all happy." When Castiglione appeared on Sunday morning, the body was already cold.

The Leonine Age came to an astonished, lurching halt. The pope's debts, it was found, amounted to 850,000 ducats, and the treasury was empty. Creditors roamed through the Vatican and carted off what they could. Banks closed. Businesses failed. Merchants decamped. Construction work on new palaces stopped, and interior decorators left town. Musicians, buffoons, chefs, translators, assistant keepers of antiquities, bibliophiles, printers all left Rome. Bembo went to Padua. Arentino went to Florence. The exodus was so great that an edict was issued forbidding any more to leave the city, and then plague broke out and took hundreds out of Rome in defiance of the edict. There was no money to provide a suitable funeral for Leo, and even the candles used were some that had been left over from the recent funeral of Cardinal Riario.

The age of gold was followed by the age of lead. The newly elected pope was from the Netherlands, a fact that horrified the Italians, who thought they had a permanent claim on the papacy. What was worse, he was, in Castiglione's estimation, "an excellent and holy person." When the barbarian finally arrived in Rome, it was discovered that he spoke Latin with an abominable accent, and he was accordingly mocked by all who were accustomed to the elegant Ciceronian style of Leo's court. Whereas Leo had kept a hundred grooms, the new pope Adrian VI reduced the number to four. He thought at first that he would rent a modest house somewhere in Rome, but the uproar of the Romans ultimately induced him to take up residence in the Vatican. He closed off vast sections of the magnificent quarters and glumly rattled about the frescoed papal apartments with an old Flemish crone who cooked his frugal meals and made his bed. He issued edicts, scornfully ignored, about the proper dress and hair styles for the cardinals; he prayed; he studied; and each evening, in an elaborate display of spendthriftiness, he would reach into his purse and present to his master of ceremonies a single, shiny ducat—to cover all the expenses of the papal household for the following day. In the days of Leo, the Vatican court reached its greatest brilliance. Never before or since did Rome approach the level of witty conversation, *haute cuisine*, artistic and poetic output, excitement of discovery of antiquities and ancient writers, good music and good wine and good theatrical entertainments in the Vatican. And never, it seems, has such an ebullient expression of a civilization so quickly and rudely vanished. For all its excesses and frivolities and, on occasion, its emptiness, the Leonine Age is commonly regarded as the golden age of the Renaissance papacy; it encompassed both the full flowering and the death of the Renaissance.

"You are now devoted to God and the church," Leo's father had written him years before, "on which account you ought to aim at being a good ecclesiastic, and to show that you prefer the honor and state of the church and of the apostolic see to every other consideration. Nor, while you keep this in view, will it be difficult for you to favor your family and your native place." On balance, Leo and his father would have had to conclude that the boy lived up to what was expected of him, and in raising Rome and his family to their most illustrious worldly station, he surpassed all expectations.

At the time of his death, Leo must have been well pleased with himself. He could see a secure Medici dynasty in the future; he could look back on having supported more artists and writers than perhaps any patron ever has; and Luther's "monkish squabble" had been squelched. By the time of Leo's death, the Luther controversy had ceased to disturb his peace of mind. By then, no doubt, he was concerned with more urgent questions—perhaps even that of his own salvation. When at last he lapsed into sleep, he seems to have died untroubled, secure in the knowledge that he had left no really important matters unsettled. He died in triumph and good fortune.

EPILOGUE

THIS book ends abruptly, since that is how Leo's life ended, with no prelude and only a brief and ugly postlude. With our hindsight, we know, as few or none of Leo's and Luther's contemporaries knew, that Luther was the victor in his battle with the church. We know, too, that the great days of the Italian Renaissance, one of the most splendid eras in the history of civilization, had come to an end in 1521. We know, as men only feared or hoped in 1521, that Luther did, in fact, help bring forth some profoundly destructive social forces and a new, dynamic individualism in the Western world. Ultimately, although this may be less interesting to our own secular age, a good many of Luther's ideas were adopted by the Catholic Church—a fact that would have pleased him especially. If Leo and Luther could not resolve their conflict, time has healed many of the wounds. (Indeed, Luther would vehemently protest today, too many. The church persists in blurring theological distinctions. In keeping with the ecumenical movement, Catholics now sing a hymn composed by Martin Luther, "A Mighty Fortress," in which we find the words, "Did we in our own strength confide, Our striving would be losing." Given a proper exegesis, the line contains Luther's central principle of salvation by faith alone and an assault on the concept of good works. Now, on an occasional Sunday one can hear American Catholics sing a line that is heretical according to the church's current teachings.)

To trace the development of all these vast generalizations would certainly require, as others have said, other books. But we can look briefly at some of the immediate events that Leo escaped by death. In March, 1522, Luther returned to Wittenberg to find that the Reformation had proceeded without him and had

291

exceeded a good many of his teachings. The clergy were marrying; laity were being given both bread and wine at the celebration of the Lord's Supper; holy images were smashed and trampled; monks were abandoning their monasteries; apprentices rebelled against their masters; students, for lack of ecclesiastical scholarships, were leaving the universities; fast days were no longer observed; priests dressed in ordinary street clothes to conduct their ceremonies; violence broke out. Luther wrote his *Sincere Exhortation to Beware Revolt and Insurrection*, taking up his position as conservative defender of social order and earning such epithets from the revolutionary students as "Doctor Sit-on-Fence" and "Doctor Slime."

After a brief reign by Pope Adrian VI, Cardinal Giulio de' Medici was elected pontiff and took the name Clement VII. The Italians rejoiced at this restoration of the Medicis and anticipated a return to the good days of Leo. The Vatican conducted business as usual, still operating in the belief that the Lutheran revolt would go away if properly ignored.

The German knights rose up in bloody civil war, and then the peasants emulated them. Luther called on the nobility to "stab, smite, throttle, slay these rabid mad dogs without mercy . . . for nothing can be more poisonous, hurtful, or devilish than a rebel. He that shall be slain on the side of law and order is a true martyr before God. . . . He that perishes on the side of rebellion is doomed eternally to hell. . . ." Having triumphed, Luther did not fancy himself a rebel; he had always said that the heresy was on the other foot, that Rome had rebelled against the teachings of Christ. With Luther's sanction, indeed with his battle cry goading them on, the nobles slaughtered the peasants by the thousands.

In 1525 Luther married a nun named Katherina von Bora, who came from a modestly noble family and whose strong will would have been a match for any but Luther's own. "I would not exchange Katie for all France or Venice, because God has given her to me," Luther said, adding, "and other women have worse faults." She bore him six children who survived infancy, and the children gave Luther the most intense pleasure. "Hans is cutting his teeth and beginning to make a joyous nuisance of himself," Luther reported. The master of the house was hospitable, inviting in hordes of students and poor relatives, tossing his clothes carelessly about the house, and leaving messes of papers here and there about the rooms. And he sat at the dinner table talking, and talking, and talking—telling jokes, bringing up old barnyard images to spice up his parables, lashing out at the pope. His "table talk," recorded by his young disciples, fills volumes. Once, to cut the flow short, Katherina pretended to faint—but it stopped Luther's outpouring of words only briefly. Katherina bore up well, and evidently happily, as the wife of the rambunctious reformer, and Luther adjusted to married life with his customary zest. "In truth there is a lot to get used to in marriage. One wakes up in the morning and finds a pair of pigtails on the pillow which were not there before."

In July, 1526, as papal forces marched north toward the Alps, the emperor called a Diet at Speyer, and his regent signed a decree that the states were free to choose whatever religion they wished. With the Edict of Speyer, the Reformation was officially established, and a Protestant party came into existence in the Holy Roman Empire.

Then, in 1527, Clement VII lived to see what his cousin Leo could never have imagined. The troops of the Holy Roman Emperor descended on Italy and marched straight to Rome. Clement offered them a feeble resistance and, with that, the army stormed the Vatican and battered down the doors of private palaces; the awful sack of Rome, which wreaked more damage than the barbarian invasions had, was on. Murder, rape, fire, plundering—it was all a standard part of warfare. Ordinarily a commanding officer would let his troops indulge in the spoils in this way for a few days or a week. But the sack of Rome went on for six months, with Clement watching helplessly from the impregnable Castel Sant' Angelo. And when the bodies filled the streets and the water supply gave out and diseases of all sorts raged through the city, the conquering troops retired to the countryside and plundered all the towns around Rome for another six months.

Drunken German knights dressed as cardinals paraded through the streets and ended up in front of Clement's fortress, shouting up to the pontiff: "Luther for Pope! Luther for Pope!"

Luther raged against such displays of license, against those who deviated from his own teachings about Scripture, against peasants, and, ferociously, against Jews. Given unaccustomed liberty, it was true that individualism could run amok, with the great Luther himself as well as with drunken *landsknechts*. It is also true, however, that Luther inspirited many followers, who, perhaps because it was not such an intoxicating new idea, were able to shape his inspiration to the ideal of disciplined individual liberty to which he himself aspired.

We grieve that Luther was not able to understand the manifest virtues of the Italian Renaissance ideal; we lament the destructive result of his influence; and yet we rejoice still in the figure who stood up before the Diet of Worms and asserted the sovereign rights of the individual. And if we grieve to see how the world of Leo X was destroyed, we know, too, that in this archetypal struggle between the establishment and a revolutionary, the establishment fostered, nourished, and helped to shape the destructive forces that brought it down.

Today we see all about us the old controversy of the individual asserting his rights of sovereignty against authority—in Luther's own town in East Germany, in radical movements throughout Europe, in movements among the young, the black, and other disgruntled citizens in America. None of these movements has yet found its Luther, and perhaps none will. But the establishment, unhappily, maintains the breeding ground for him, nourishing the forces of its own ruin, clinging desperately and indiscriminately to its virtues and its corruptions, its liberties and its tyrannies, its ideals and its injustices—secure, like Leo X, in the knowledge that the powerful will prevail.

NOTES

The number of books on Luther's life is so great, and the same stories and quotations appear in so many of them in substantially the same form, that these notes do not attempt to identify more than the sources most frequently consulted for each chapter and the sources of those very particular bits of information that are not commonly found in biographies of Luther. Books for further reading about Leo are difficult to find outside—or, for that matter, even inside—libraries, although copies of William Roscoe and Herbert M. Vaughan can occasionally be found in second hand bookstalls. Paolo Giovio and Paris de Grassis, the other two most useful chroniclers of Leo's life, are not available in English but can be found in Latin or Italian editions in some libraries. These and other useful volumes on Leo's Rome are noted in the List of Principal Sources below.

Chapter I

William Roscoe's biography is the one essential book on Leo's life, and the documents in the appendix to his biography are helpful, too. He also wrote a biography of Leo's father, though it is surpassed by the more recent work of Ferdinand Schevill and Cecilia M. Ady, among others. For general background on Medici Florence Vincent Cronin's *The Florentine Renaissance* is superb reading. The source for much of the information about Medici finances comes from Raymond de Roover. Quotations from letters are taken from Janet Ross' edition of the Medici correspondence. *Daily Life in Florence*, by J. Lucas-Dubreton, is a readable and largely accurate account of mores of the time. For the Medici palace, see R. A. B. Hatfield.

Chapter II

The statistic on Little Hans' record of convictions can be found in Edith Simon, page 38. Luther's mother's relationship with demons figures in V. H. H. Green, page 28. Roland H. Bainton, Edith Simon, Preserved Smith, and especially Erik Erikson were relied on for much of the rest of the information in this chapter. And oddly enough, the nineteenth-century English journalist Henry Mayhew wrote a quasi-fictional biography of Luther that has a fine, imaginative sense for the house in which Luther grew up.

Chapter III

Frederick Baron Corvo wrote a slightly mad defense of the Borgias that makes good reading; for facts, however, I have relied on Michael Mallett. The information on Savonarola is taken mainly from Johann Burchard, pages 144 ff., 194, and 221. The reaction of the Italian traveler to Germany is in Vincent Cronin, *The Flowering of the Renaissance*, page 76.

Chapter IV

Both Gordon Rupp and Erik Erikson are good on this period of Luther's life.

Chapter V

The Costabili quotation is in Vincent Cronin's *The Flowering of the Renaissance*, page 53, as is Julius' remark about his testicles (page 35). The Guicciardini quotations come from pages 295 and 296 of his history. The council's opinion of Julius is in Orville Prescott's *Princes of the Renaissance*, page 360. I used the John Wilson edition of Erasmus' *The Praise of Folly* for the passage at the end of the chapter.

Chapter VI

Erik Erikson and Roland H. Bainton are the best guides to this period of Luther's life.

Chapter VII

D. S. Chambers is good on the Roman court at this time, and Herbert M. Vaughan provides the best description of the Sacro Processo.

Notes

Chapter VIII

The principal general sources for this chapter are Gordon Rupp, Heinrich Boehmer, Robert H. Fife, Charles Beard, and especially, Uuras Saarnivaara. The quotation *"In justitia . . ."* can be found in Erik Erikson, page 202. The description of Luther as lecturer is in V. H. H. Green, page 48. The battle with the Devil is in Laurance Teeter's unpublished thesis.

The primary question in this chapter is precisely when Luther had his so-called tower experience, and it is a question that has engaged a great many scholars. A discussion of the arguments over the dating can be found in Kenneth G. Hagen. A full bibliography of the controversy would run to more than 100 titles, but, in broad terms, one group argues that the revelation came to Luther before his lectures on the Psalms—that is, between 1508 and 1512; this group includes Heinrich Boehmer, Otto Ritschl, Karl Holl, and Reinhold Seeberg. Another group argues that Luther made his discovery during the preparation of his lectures; this group includes J. Mackinnon, the later editions of Boehmer's work, Joseph Lortz, and a host of others. Preserved Smith (in "A Decade of Luther Study," *Harvard Theological Review*, 1921, page 112) and a few others argue for a date just after the lectures on the Psalms. And, finally, Paul Reiter, Uuras Saarnivaara, J. Dillenberger, and a great many others insist on a date between 1517 and 1519. In all this I have followed Saarnivaara's superb textual analysis of the lectures but, on the basis of his own analysis, I have concluded that Luther's changing language indicates the date given in the chapter and not the later date Saarnivaara gives. Obviously Luther's ideas developed over a period of time, and it is possible to see the beginnings of his revelation in 1508 and to see his ideas fully articulated only some years later. While, as many scholars have said, Luther may have been mistaken in his recollection of the date of the moment of full insight, a crucial change in his manner of expression occurs in 1513 that I believe could not have been accidental. However, for another view, Saarnivaara gives the best rebuttal to my choice of date.

Chapter IX

Most of the quotations in this chapter can be traced easily to the bibliography. Giorgio Vasari, John Pope-Hennessy, D. Redig de

Campos, and Ettore Camesasca provided the bulk of the information included here on Raphael. For an excellent description of Leo's court see Vincent Cronin. For Castiglione and Isabella d'Este's visit see Ralph Roeder. For Erasmus see J. Huizinga. Leo's remark about the "fable of Christ" is in John Bale, *The Pageant of Popes*, published in 1574. Leo's talent for poetry is displayed on page 495 of William Roscoe, Vol. II. The translation of Paris de Grassis is my own, I hope accurate, rendering of the original Latin that can be found in a footnote in Roscoe, Vol. II, page 477.

Chapter X

Luther's comment on the Reuchlin case is in Edith Simon, page 112. The quotation from *Letters of Obscure Men* comes from *Original Sources of European History*, Vol. II, published by the University of Pennsylvania. Luther's "complaint" about his heavy work load is quoted in Gordon Rupp, page 45; his cheerfulness over the triumph of "our theology" is on page 46 of Rupp. For more on Reuchlin see Mandell Creighton. For a theological interpretation of the meaning of Luther's actions one must go to very old, unfashionable histories; but my own interpretation differs from these in any case.

Chapter XI

For the politics see James Bryce. For politics and a very good explanation of the history of indulgences see Richard Friedenthal. The extended quotation of Tetzel comes from J. H. Merle d'Aubigné.

Chapter XII

These theses are quoted from Bertram Lee Woolf. Vincent Cronin notes, incidentally, that the key words in these theses are "tribulations," "fear," "punishment," "despair," "horror"—all of which would have been bewildering to an Italian. The conspiracy of the cardinals is described in Herbert M. Vaughan.

Chapter XIII

The most useful and illuminating sources for this and the following several chapters are Richard Friedenthal, Edith Simon, Roland H. Bainton, Gordon Rupp, and William Roscoe. The quotations from

Notes

Luther can be found in the first four books as well as elsewhere. Simon seems to me to have the best knack for rendering Luther in English, and I have used her translations for the most part. Some exceptions: For Luther's remark about doing penance by walking, Bainton, page 66; for Luther's remark on his sermon after his return from Heidelberg, Friedenthal, page 166; for the passage about "these sons of Nimrod," Bainton, page 69; the dialogue with Cajetan is quoted extensively in J. H. Merle d'Aubigné.

Chapter XIV

The confrontation with Eck is quoted in J. H. Merle d'Aubigné; the politics are best described, once again, by Richard Friedenthal.

Chapter XV

Richard Friedenthal and Edith Simon were again used for this chapter. The translation used for *Mandragola* is noted in the bibliography. Gordon Rupp, pages 72–90, discusses the treatises of the year. Leo's letter to Frederick is quoted in Roland H. Bainton, pages 114–15. Luther's remark at the end of the chapter is in Mandell Creighton, page 143.

Chapter XVI

The bedeviling of Aleander is in Gordon Rupp, pages 92–93. The Diet is discussed at length in both Edith Simon and Richard Friedenthal. The observation about the poor state of surviving Luther Bibles is Friedenthal's. The death of Leo and its aftermath are described in William Roscoe and Ralph Roeder (pages 413–19).

Epilogue

The quotations on Luther's family life are taken from Edith Simon.

A Note on Currencies

I have translated all currencies into ducats, the Roman *ducato di camera*. When I have quoted, for example, Tetzel's income in ducats,

he was, of course, paid in gulden. When I have noted what Botticelli was paid for a painting, I have quoted ducats, though Botticelli
was paid by his Florentine patrons in florins. I have, in short, tried to
make these mundane matters easier for the contemporary reader than
they were for the Fuggers, who had to deal with 500 different currencies.

A LIST OF PRINCIPAL SOURCES

Allen, Percy Stafford, *The Age of Erasmus*. Oxford, 1916.

Ariosto, *Orlando Furioso*, trans. by William Stewart Rose. London, 1902.

Bainton, Roland H., *Here I Stand*. New York, 1955.

Beard, Charles. *Martin Luther and the Reformation*. London, 1896.

Berenson, Bernard, *The Italian Painters of the Renaissance*. New York, 1956.

Bibbiena, Bernardo da, *Calandria*, in *The Genius of the Italian Theatre*, Eric Bentley, ed., trans. by Oliver Evans. New York, 1964.

Boccaccio, Giovanni, *The Fates of Illustrious Men*, trans. and abridged by Louis Brewer Hall. New York, 1965.

Boehmer, Heinrich, *Road to Reformation*. Philadelphia, 1946.

Bornkamm, Heinrich, *Luther's World of Thought*, trans. by Martin H. Bertram. St. Louis, 1950.

Bryce, James, *The Holy Roman Empire*. New York, 1961.

Burchard, Johann, *At the Court of the Borgia*, ed. and trans. by Geoffrey Parker. London, 1963.

Camesasca, Ettore, ed., *All the Frescoes of Raphael*. New York, 1963.

Campos, D. Redig de, *The Stanze of Raphael*. Rome, 1957.

Castiglione, Baldassare, *The Book of the Courtier*, trans. by Charles S. Singleton. Garden City, New York, 1959.

Chambers, D. S., *Cardinal Bainbridge in the Court of Rome, 1509 to 1514*. London, 1965.

Clark, William Robinson, *Savonarola, His Life and Times*. London, 1890.

Corvo, Frederick Baron, *A History of the Borgias*. New York, 1931.

Creighton, Mandell, *A History of the Papacy During the Period of the Reformation*, 4 vols. Boston, 1887.

Cronin, Vincent, *The Flowering of the Renaissance*. New York, 1969.

D'Aubigné, J. H. Merle, *History of the Reformation in the Sixteenth Century*. Glasgow, 1843.

De Roover, Raymond, *The Rise and Decline of the Medici Bank, 1397–1494*. New York, 1966.

Dillenberger, J., ed., *Selections from Luther's Writings*. New York, 1961.

Erasmus, Desiderius, *The Epistles of Erasmus*. New York, 1901–18.

———, *The Praise of Folly*, trans. by John Wilson. Ann Arbor, 1958.

Erikson, Erik, *Young Man Luther*. New York, 1958.

Fife, Robert Herndon, *Young Luther*. New York, 1928.

Friedenthal, Richard, *Luther, His Life and Times*, trans. by John Nowell. New York, 1967.

Giovio, Paolo, *An Italian Portrait Gallery*, trans. by Florence Alden Gragg. Boston, 1935.

———, *Libro di Mons*. Venice, 1560.

Gobineau, Count, *The Golden Flower*. New York, 1924.

Grassis, Paris de, *Il Diaro de Leone X*. Rome, 1884.

Green, V. H. H., *Luther and the Reformation*. New York, 1964.

Grimm, Harold J., *The Reformation Era*. New York, 1954.

Guicciardini, Francesco, *History of Italy*, trans. by Sidney Alexander. New York, 1968.

———, *Maxims and Reflections of a Renaissance Statesman*, trans. by Mario Domandi. New York, 1965.

Hagen, Kenneth G., "Changes in the Understanding of Luther," *Theological Studies*, Vol. 29, 1968.

Hatfield, R. A. B., "Some Unknown Descriptions of the Medici Palace in 1459," in *The Art Bulletin*, The College Art Assoc. of America, September, 1970.

Hillerbrand, H. J., *The Reformation in its Own Words*. London, 1964.

Holmes, George, *The Florentine Enlightenment 1400 to 1450*. London, 1969.

Huizinga, J., *Erasmus and the Age of Reformation*. New York, 1957.

Huizinga, M., *The Waning of the Middle Ages*. New York, 1949.

Jacob, E. F., ed., *Italian Renaissance Studies*. London, 1960.

Jones, Rosemary D., *Erasmus and Luther*. Oxford, 1968.

Klaczko, Julian, *Rome and the Renaissance*, trans. by J. Bennie. New York, 1903.

La Bedoyere, Michael de, *The Meddlesome Friar*. London, 1957.

Landucci, Luca, *A Florentine Diary*, trans. by Alice de Rosen Jervis. London, 1927.

Lucas-Dubreton, J., *Daily Life in Florence*, trans. by A. Lytton Sells. New York, 1961.

Luther, Martin, *Early Theological Works*, J. Atkinson, ed. London, 1962.

———, *Treatises*, Vol. 44, Helmut T. Lehmann, ed. Philadelphia, 1966.

Machiavelli, Niccolo, *Mandragola*, trans. by Ann and Henry Paolucci. New York, 1957.

Mackinnon, J., *Luther and the Reformation*. New York, 1925.

Maddison, Carol, *Marcantonio Flaminio*. Chapel Hill, 1965.

Mallett, Michael, *The Borgias*. New York, 1969.

A List of Principal Sources

Pastor, Ludwig, *History of the Popes from the Close of the Middle Ages.* London, 1891.

Pauck, Wilhelm, *The Heritage of the Reformation.* Glencoe, Illinois, 1960.

Plaidy, Jean, *A Triptych of Poisoners.* London, 1958.

Pope-Hennessy, John, "Introduction" in *The Raphael Cartoons.* London, Her Majesty's Stationery Office, 1966.

Portigliotti, Giuseppe, *The Borgais.* London, 1928.

Prat, F., *The Theology of St. Paul.* London, 1957.

Prescott, Orville, *Princes of the Renaissance.* New York, Random House, 1969.

Ranke, Leopold von, *The Popes of Rome.* London, 1941.

Roeder, Ralph, *The Man of the Renaissance.* New York, 1966.

Roscoe, William, *The Life and Pontificate of Leo the Tenth.* 2 vols., London, 1846.

Ross, Janet, *Lives of the Early Medicis as Told in Their Correspondence.* Boston, 1911.

Rupp, Gordon, *Luther's Progress to the Diet of Worms.* Chicago, 1951.

———, *The Righteousness of God.* London, 1953.

Saarnivaara, Uuras, *Luther Discovers the Gospel.* New York, 1951.

Schevill, Ferdinand, *The Medici.* New York, 1968.

Simon, Edith, *Luther Alive,* Garden City, New York, 1968.

Smith, Preserved, *Erasmus.* New York, 1923.

———, *The Life and Letters of Martin Luther.* New York, 1911.

Spinka, M., *John Hus and the Czech Reform.* Chicago, 1941.

Teeter, Laurance Philip, *Identity and Young Man Luther: A Reinterpretation,* Unpublished thesis, General Theological Seminary, New York, 1965.

Thomas, William, *The History of Italy.* Ithaca, 1963.

Tillmans, Walter G., *The World and Men Around Luther.* Minneapolis, 1959.

University of St. Thomas Art Department, *The Popes as Builders and Humanists.* University of St. Thomas, Houston, Texas, March-May, 1966.

Vasari, Giorgio, *Lives of the Artists,* trans. by E. L. Seeley. New York, 1957.

Vaughan, Herbert M., *The Medici Popes.* New York, 1908.

Woodward, W. H., *Cesare Borgia.* London, 1913.

Woolf, Bertram Lee, trans. and ed., *The Reformation Writings of Martin Luther,* Vol. I, in *The Basis of the Protestant Reformation.* London, 1953.

INDEX

INDEX

Index

Foix, Gaston de, 81
Fonte Dolce abbey, 26
Ford, Ford Maddox, 127
Fornarina, La, 132
Fossanova abbey, 47
France and the French, 65, 109, 169, 170, 171, 287
Francis I, King of France, 145, 169, 236
Franciscans, 256
Franco, Matteo, 21
Frederick the Great, 11
Frederick the Wise, Elector of Saxony, 92, 174–75, 181, 188, 214, 215, 217, 229, 230, 231, 233, 235–36, 237, 251, 257, 259, 268, 272, 276, 283–84, 285, 286
Fregoso, Federico, 124, 125, 126
Fugger, Jakob, 173
Fugger banking family, 150, 173–74, 178, 236

Gabbionetta, Archdeacon, 141
Gennazzano, Mariano de, 58–60
George of Savoy, Duke, 204, 241, 245, 246, 274
Germany and the Germans, 65, 173, 174–75, 178, 200, 214, 216, 237, 253, 260, 268, 271, 274, 292
Ghiberti, Lorenzo, 95
Giovio, Paolo, 252
Giustinian, Antonio, 75
Glapion, Father, 273–74, 275, 277
Gli Asolani (Bembo), 130
Golden Bull (1356), 174
Goldoni, Carlo, 254

Gonzaga, Elizabetta, 123, 131
Gozzoli, Benozzo, 21
Grapaldo of Parma, 149
Grassis, Paris de, 102, 103, 120, 121, 146, 184, 287
Gratius, Ortwin, 156, 158–59
Grossi, Cardinal, 130
Grünenberg, Johann, 187
Grünewald, Mathias, 175
Guicciardini, Francesco, 46–47, 79–80
Guidobaldo of Montefeltro, Duke, 123

Habsburg family, 172, 173, 174, 214, 216, 231, 236
Henry II, King of France, 167
Henry VIII, King of England, 108, 169, 186
Heresy, 22, 212, 292
Hochstraten, Jakob von, 155, 156, 158, 160, 247
Hohenzollern family, 174, 175
Holy Roman Empire, 155, 169, 170, 171–75, 252, 270, 277, 281, 293
Huizinga, Johan, 137
Humanists, 45, 61, 128, 271
Hus, John, 152, 245–46
Hutten, Ulrich von, 158, 175, 260, 265, 271, 273, 276

Indulgences, 161–65, 218, 228, 284; politics of, 166–81; selling of, 177–81, 186–89, 203
Innocent VIII, Pope, 27, 28, 29, 41, 43, 146

Index

James IV, King of Scotland, 108
John XXII, Pope, 42, 99, 103
John of Vendosme, Duke, 204
Judenspiegel (Pfefferkorn), 154
Julius II (Giuliano della Rovere), as Cardinal, 43, 44, 45–46, 48, 57, 59, 64, 65–66, 67; as Pope, 67, 68, 75–78, 82–83, 85, 100, 103, 128, 137, 146, 150, 167, 169
Julius Exclusus (Erasmus), 137
Juterbog, Germany, 181, 187

Karlstadt, Andreas, 240, 241, 242
Knowledge, human and divine, 71
Köln University, 156, 158

Landucci, Luca, 103
Lang, Cardinal, 273
Lanzol, Juan Borgia, 48
La Tour, Madeleine de, 204
Lateran Church, Rome, 96
Leibnitz, Gottfried Wilhelm von, 11
Leo IV, Pope, 133, 162
Leo X (Giovanni de' Medici), Pope, birth, 17; childhood, 20–33; coronation, 102–7; corruption of the church and, 154; court, 120–50; created a cardinal, 28; creation of new cardinals, 185–87; death, 287–90; education, 23, 28–29, 41–60; election, 98–101; experience of religion, 121–22; family background, 18–21, 166–67; holy orders, admission to, 26; Luther and, 201, 202, 204, 209–10, 231–33, 234, 235, 238, 248, 249, 251–54, 257, 266–68, 270, 286, 290, 291; obsession for the hunt, 22, 78, 121, 122, 147–49; ordination, 102; parents, 20–33; patron of the arts, 122, 129–39, 238–40, 247–49; plot to assassinate, 182–86; politics, national and international, 168–74, 175–77, 210–11, 231, 236–38, 286–87
Leo the Great, Pope, 101
Leonine Age, 103, 288, 289
Leonine Rome, 123, 131
Letter to Silvio Savelli (Marciani), 61
Letters from Illustrious Men (Reuchlin), 157
Letters of Obscure Men, 158
Liberty of a Christian Man, The (Luther), 258, 264
Lollards, 152
Lombard, Peter, 94
Lombardy, 170
Longolius, 204
Lotto, Lorenzo, 76
Louis XI, King of France, 26
Louis XII, King of France, 65, 66, 82, 83, 108, 145, 169
Louis of Bourbon, Cardinal, 186
Luft, Hans, 286
Luther (Lytter or Luder), Hans, 34–35, 36, 40, 70, 71–72, 73, 88–90
Luther, Heinz, 34
Luther, James, 282, 283
Luther, Little Hans, 34
Luther, Margarete Ziegler, 34, 35–36

Index